ANIMATION
TECHNIQUES
IN WIN32®

NIGEL THOMPSON
With a Foreword by Charles Petzold

PUBLISHED BY

Microsoft Press
A Division of Microsoft Corporation
One Microsoft Way
Redmond, Washington 98052-6399

Copyright © 1995 by Microsoft Press

Library of Congress Cataloging-in-Publication Data
Thompson, Nigel, 1955–
    Animation techniques in Win32: a C++ programmer's guide to DIBs,
  palettes, and sprites / by Nigel Thompson.
        p.   cm.
    Includes index.
    ISBN 1-55615-669-3
    1. Computer animation.   2. Computer graphics.   3. Microsoft
  Win32.   4. C++ (Computer program language)   I. Title.
  TR897.7.T56   1994
  006.6--dc20   94-41216
                                                           CIP

Printed and bound in the United States of America.

1 2 3 4 5 6 7 8 9   QMQM   0 9 8 7 6 5

Distributed to the book trade in Canada by Macmillan of Canada, a division of Canada
Publishing Corporation.

A CIP catalogue record for this book is available from the British Library.

Microsoft Press books are available through booksellers and distributors worldwide. For further information
about international editions, contact your local Microsoft Corporation office. Or contact Microsoft Press
International directly at fax (206) 936-7329.

Electronic Arts is a registered trademark and TuneLand is a trademark of Electronic Arts. Microsoft,
MS-DOS, and Win32 are registered trademarks and Visual C++, Win32s, Windows, and Windows NT are
trademarks of Microsoft Corporation. MIPS is a registered trademark of MIPS Computer Systems, Inc.
Sound Blaster is a trademark of Creative Labs, Inc.

Acquisitions Editor: Dean Holmes
Project Editor: Erin O'Connor
Technical Editor: Jim Fuchs

To my young son Mark, who is as lively, noisy,
and animated as any father could wish.

The Miami Herald

A Knight-Ridder Newspaper

October 14, 1994

Nigel Thompson
Microsoft Corporation
One Microsoft Way
Redmond Wa 98052-6399

Dear Nigel Thompson --

      I'm afraid I can't write a blurb for your book; I'm
already swamped with blurb requests. (Also I have no idea
what "DIB's" are, and am pretty hazy on "Sprites.") But I
wish you luck.

Sincerely,

Dave Barry

DB/js

One Herald Plaza, Miami, Florida 33132-1693 (305) 350-2111

CONTENTS AT A GLANCE

TABLE OF CONTENTS

TABLE OF CONTENTS

FOREWORD

In the nine years since the release of Microsoft Windows 1.0, the world of computer graphics has slowly shifted in emphasis. Look at any of the older "classic" books on computer graphics, and you'll find them devoted almost entirely to "vector" graphics—the drawing of lines and filled areas based on principles derived from analytical geometry and more advanced mathematics.

In more recent years, "raster" graphics has moved to the forefront. Raster graphics mostly involves the storage, manipulation, and rendering of bitmaps, the subject of Nigel Thompson's exciting new book. While the disciplines of vector graphics are still important, of course, no programmer for Windows can afford to be ignorant of the techniques described in these pages.

Bitmaps can originate from a variety of sources. In many cases, bitmaps represent real-world images, usually captured through a scanner or—more frequently these days—a video capture board. Bitmaps can also be created "manually" within a paint program, or algorithmically from program code. Wherever it originates, a bitmap usually encodes an image that is simply too complex to be described or rendered efficiently using the lines and filled areas of vector graphics.

What is the impetus for this change in focus from vector graphics to raster graphics? Part of it is better hardware, specifically, huge gobs of memory and processors fast enough to manipulate bitmaps and shovel them to the display. Yes, bitmaps require lots of memory, particularly when they describe real world images with accurate color. Working with such bitmaps under Windows 1.0 was simply inconceivable given the 640K memory limit and the monochrome displays then in common use. (Only the elite ran Windows 1.0 on a 16-color EGA.)

The other impetus for this change has come from the ever-expanding personal computer user base. In the early days, the engineering and scientific communities were satisfied with their CAD programs, and the business community saw graphics only as a means to transform spreadsheet data into bars and pies. These are traditional jobs for vector graphics.

As more varied types of users began to flex their mental muscles in front of PCs, vector graphics lost its dominance. For example, graphics artists and desktop publishers needed to integrate real world images into their documents. Even traditional users found real world images to be useful. And now, at long last, we are finally seeing more and more users from that group destined to change personal computing forever—the family.

Family computing and multimedia computing go hand in hand. No kid I know would consider a PC to be complete unless it had a CD-ROM drive and a pair of stereo speakers. Besides introducing sound, including music, into the PC, multimedia involves real world images, animations, and full-motion video. These are all jobs for raster graphics.

As Nigel Thompson points out, Windows has always supported bitmaps, but in the early days these were closely tied to the hardware of display devices. Use of bitmaps as an interchange medium was severely limited. It wasn't until the introduction of the Device-Independent Bitmap (DIB) and the Palette Manager in Windows 3.0 that programmers had adequate tools for dealing with complex visual data.

Unfortunately, the number of DIB-specific functions in Windows 3.1 can be counted on one six-finger hand. Programmers attempting to do anything interesting (or even just versatile) with DIBs inevitably find themselves building a whole library of functions to deal with them.

Nigel Thompson takes some of the sting out of this job by writing such a library for you. Throughout this book, he discloses the rationale for structuring the library as he has, and shows you how to use it to display bitmapped images and animations under Windows.

It's a fun and fascinating ride, and one that I hope will persuade many more programmers to integrate images and animations within their applications.

Charles Petzold

ACKNOWLEDGMENTS

This book is the end product of many hours of discussions, e-mail, white board sessions, and head banging. The list of people who have contributed in some way is huge. I've tried to mention most of them here. I hope that those I've forgotten to mention will accept my apologies. My thanks to:

Todd Laney for his willingness to instruct me in the ways of the DIB and the palette and his enthusiasm for getting my code working.

Ron Gery for his knowledge of the Windows Palette Manager. Much of Chapter 3 was taken directly from Ron's article "The Palette Manager: How and Why," published in the Microsoft Developer Network Development Library.

Mike Abrash, Patrick Haluptzok, Wendy Wu, and Eric Kutter of the Windows NT GDI group for help with understanding the Windows NT GDI implementation and *CreateDIBSection* in particular.

My colleagues in the Developer Network group for their review efforts, encouragement, and criticism and especially Dale Rogerson for his help with C++ issues, prompt reviews, occasional silly comments, and not letting me fall off the rock when he was belaying me.

Scott Randall and Dean McCrory of Microsoft's AFX group for help with MFC issues.

My Development Library editor, Diane Stielstra, for editing the draft copies of the chapters, changing my English to American, and especially for asking, "To what does *it* refer?" 43,000 times.

Richard Noren for his very thorough and thoughtful reviews of both the text and the code samples.

Herman Rodent, from whose articles much of the work in the book was shamelessly stolen.

Jason Smith for his help with the help file for the class library.

David Holter for his artwork. Mary Chi for the Snow picture and Tareh Kruger for the BeyondTi picture.

Jim Fuchs of Microsoft Press for getting all the code samples straightened out and presentable. Erin O'Connor of Microsoft Press for standing up for my writer's rights while editing the text. The other staff of Microsoft Press for their contributions.

Many other folks inside and outside Microsoft for their comments.

And finally, my wife, Tammy, and my children, Mark, Nell, and Ron, for putting up with me through the "obsessive" phase of the writing.

INTRODUCTION

This is a book about bits—pixels, actually—those tiny colored dots that make up what you see on the screen when Microsoft Windows is running on your PC. All programmers for Windows use at least some of the graphics capabilities of Windows when they are learning to create a Windows-based application. They learn to draw lines, ellipses, rectangles, and so on. Some go on to explore regions, fonts, and printing. A few explore bitmaps, and a handful play with palettes.

During the early days of learning how to write programs for Windows, we try to accept what we are told, learn as much as we can from the sample code, and hope that we will be able to apply this new knowledge to the creation of a compelling Windows-based application of our own design.

Unfortunately, the road from the first line of code to the final application is full of forks. There are a very large number of functions to learn about and seemingly endless ways to achieve the same end result. How should we choose which way to go?

Until the last year or two, the amount of information published on how Windows works and on how to write great applications for Windows was rather limited. Some will remember the awful days of the Windows version 1.0 Software Development Kit (SDK) samples—code that barely compiled, let alone ran—and the documentation with its oddly grouped list of application programming interface (API) functions and hardly a word about how it all fit together.

In more recent times, Microsoft has tried to do a better job of educating the community of developers who program for Windows. The SDKs have had better samples, the documentation has been more thorough, and various groups have published articles on how their parts of the system work. In addition, Microsoft has started up the Developer Network to publish and distribute information about the workings of each of the variants of Windows and about ways to deal efficiently with Windows when creating applications.

Today the Developer Network Development Library is a CD-ROM packed with hundreds of megabytes of data. It is distributed directly to thousands of developers and borrowed by even more. Yet with all this information available to developers, commercial applications are still coming out with windows that flicker when they are updated, with horribly long intervals during which the user gets to watch the hourglass cursor and wonder what's happening, with an almost complete absence of color beyond the dreadful Day-Glo colors the system provides, or simply with bad performance. Why is this?

The simple answer is that it's quite unreasonable to expect every developer to learn every aspect of Windows and to code down to the bone to make applications work the way users expect them to. The great requirement today is to have more of the essential stuff packaged so that programmers can use it without necessarily knowing a whole lot about how it works inside.

The introduction of Visual C++ changed the way many programmers viewed development under Windows. No longer did they need to register window classes—they could simply create a window. No longer did they need to devise long-winded switch statements to handle window messages—the tools would create mappings directly from menu events to function calls. Obviously, this was the way to go. With C++ classes to take care of the tasks all Windows applications have in common, the programmer is released to build other classes that implement great applications for Windows.

I was greatly inspired by this idea and decided to challenge the approach with the most daunting task I could think of—creating a set of C++ classes, based on classes in the Microsoft Foundation Class Library (MFC), that would implement an animation engine.

This book is an examination of what is required to create sprite-based animations in Windows. It starts with the basics of bitmaps and ends with a fully animated scene that even includes sounds. The samples were all developed using Visual C++ and the Microsoft Foundation classes on Microsoft Windows NT. As the book progresses from chapter to chapter, we'll develop a set of C++ classes to deal with device-independent bitmaps (DIBs), palettes, sprites, and sounds. We'll package the final code into a static-link library usable in a wide variety of applications.

The Sample Code

I wrote the sample code in this book for you to use in your own work. You may use it any way you want to. You can copy the library as is or modify individual modules to suit your needs. You don't need to pay a license fee or royalty. You may not sell these code samples, of course.

All the samples that accompany this book were written using Visual C++ version 1.1 on Microsoft Windows NT version 3.1 and the Microsoft Windows NT version 3.5 prerelease. They were tested on Windows version 3.1 under the Win32s extensions and on internal build 179 of Windows 95 (code-named Chicago). All of the programs work correctly on the Win32 platforms. A bug (under investigation) in Win32s prevents some of the programs from working correctly; programs that do not use the low-level sound services do work correctly. This bug should be fixed in Win32s version 1.3. In the meantime, see the next section, "Building Applications for Win32s."

The code is written to the Win32 API set, and I have made no attempt to make it capable of compiling in the older, 16-bit, Windows environment. The 32-bit executables will run on Windows 3.1 under the Win32s add-on with much the same performance as they do on Windows NT.

Using 32-bit code has enabled me to get away from peculiar Windows variable types such as *LONG* and *DWORD* and to return for the most part to simple types such as *int* and *char*. Pointers are pointers—not near pointers or far pointers, but simply pointers. If you are new to programming for Windows,

32 bits is the way to go. You'll never need to deal with the nightmare of far pointers that wrap unexpectedly when they meet a 64K segment boundary or with any of the other oddities caused by the fascinating intricacies of 16-bit Windows architecture.

I wrote the sample code to demonstrate the possibilities for high performance in a C++/MFC application, but the code is not designed to cover all situations. The class I developed to handle device-independent bitmaps works only with 8-bit-per-pixel DIBs (256 colors), for instance. I did this deliberately to simplify the code and support the most common display format: 256-color super-VGA cards.

Building Applications for Win32s

Despite the claim that all 32-bit Windows applications are created equal, that is not exactly the case. In just a few cases, the idiosyncrasies of Win32s require you to alter your code slightly. And like all systems, Win32s has its bugs, so we need to be aware of how those bugs will affect applications we create.

Let's begin with the bugs. There is only one bug that affects the samples I created for this book. Under Win32s version 1.2, the version that was shipping when this book was published and that we include on the book's CD, it was not possible to have the *sndPlaySound* function play a sound based in memory. This means that the *CSound* class won't work on that version of Win32s. The bug has been fixed, and future shipping versions of Win32s won't have this restriction. So that the majority of the samples that use sounds wouldn't be compromised by this bug, I altered the samples to use the *CWave* class instead of the *CSound* class and added a *LoadResource* function to the *CWave* class. This brings us to the next feature of Win32s that we need to be aware of—memory allocation.

I have tried to keep my sample code as simple as possible by using common C functions such as *malloc* instead of Windows-specific functions such as *GlobalAlloc*. In almost every case, *malloc* can be used instead of *GlobalAlloc* with no side effects. The one case in which this is not true is the case in which the application is to run under Win32s. If large blocks of memory (such as the blocks of memory we need for the bits of a DIB or the samples of a .WAV file) are to be allocated, then because of the way the runtime memory allocation works under Win32s we must always use *GlobalAlloc*.

I have made the code in the library sample use macros for memory allocation and freeing in the *CWave* and *CDIB* classes. The macros are defined in MEM.H and allow you to configure them to use either *malloc* or *GlobalAlloc* according to your needs. The default is to use *GlobalAlloc*, which ensures Win32s compatibility. As Win32s improves (or goes away with the advent of Windows 95 on desktops everywhere), we can switch back to using *malloc* and forget the nasty days of *GlobalAlloc* for good. The Author, Bee, Farm, RunDog, and Wizard samples all use the library, so they should all work correctly under Win32s. For the other samples you will need to manually alter the *CDIB* and *CWave* classes to call *GlobalAlloc* or use the macros in the library MEM.H file.

Those Other Samples

As a programmer, my ability as an artist is limited. Although moving a few blobs of color or some nice rectangles around can illustrate what the code does, it isn't quite what the marketing people would call "a totally killer demo." I thought it would be nice to show off what can be done by producing a few scenes similar to those you might find in a real world application. So I got together with artist David Holter and created the Farm, Wizard, and Bee samples you'll find on the CD.

My favorite multimedia games are the ones created for small children. The best are lively and fun and also have a good educational core. The Farm sample is loosely based on that kind of game. It shows a bright colorful scene with several animated animals. Clicking on an animal brings it to life. The animal noises are extremely realistic, as I'm sure you'll agree, and were done in my office at great expense by me (with the exception of one of the pigs, the one with the midwestern American accent, which was done by David).

Older children need a bit more of a challenge, and we intended the Wizard sample to be an example of the many puzzle games that are becoming available. Unfortunately, time didn't allow us to create anything more than a simple scene for this sample. A number of hot spots in the scene cause the wizard to move about doing various wizardy things when they're clicked.

The Bee sample was created by means of the same code technology, but the artwork was done with a 3D rendering package. David rendered shots of the bee from various angles and used those shots to create the sprite frames. The choreography of the bee and the buzzy noises are courtesy of my colleague Dale Rogerson, who thinks that bees should behave much the same way that helicopters do.

Before You Begin

I make some assumptions about your programming knowledge. I assume that you are familiar with C++, but you don't need a tremendously advanced knowledge of C++ to read this book. A few hours with Visual C++ and its SCRIBBLE tutorial will give you all the experience you need to follow the text and play with the sample code.

Even if you are a C programmer with no C++ experience at all, you should still be able to follow the text and understand the code. I'm not much of a C++ expert myself, so my code uses only the simplest C++ concepts.

I also assume that you know a little about programming for the Windows environment. Again, you don't need a lot of experience here, only some understanding of the terminology and which bits of Windows do what. There are plenty of other books—Charles Petzold's *Programming Windows 3.1* (Microsoft Press, 1992), for example—that cover this material to whatever depth you feel the need to go.

CHAPTER

Bitmaps

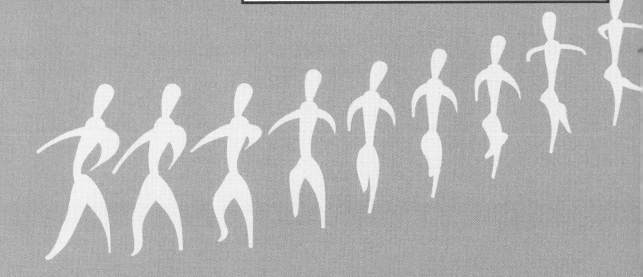

ur first step in creating a stunning multicolored animation will be to take a look at the most primitive component for holding an image in the Microsoft Windows operating system: the bitmap.

Bit Basics

A bitmap is a data structure used to hold information that describes a rectangular image. We consider an image to be constructed as a number of lines, and each line is a series of pixels (picture elements) as shown in *Figure 1-1*.

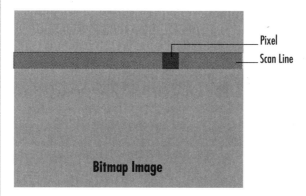

Pixel

Scan Line

Bitmap Image

Figure 1-1   *The elements of an image.*

In the simplest case, the rectangular bitmap image is monochrome (actually, two colors), and each pixel of the image needs only 1 bit of storage in the bitmap. The convention for monochrome bitmaps in Windows is that a 0-bit value represents the current foreground color and a 1-bit value represents the current background color in the device context (DC) into which the bitmap will be drawn. So if the foreground color of the DC is set to black and the background color is set to white, the image comes out black and white. Change the foreground color to red, and the image will come out red and white.

In the early days of Windows, it wasn't uncommon to see a 640-by-480 monochrome screen, and in that context monochrome bitmaps were very useful. As the graphics world has progressed to more colorful displays, the humble monochrome bitmap remains useful only for some printing applications and for creating masks for its more colorful successors.

By using more than 1 bit per pixel (bpp), we can represent more colors. For example, by using 4 bits per pixel, we can represent 16 colors. This became the standard for VGA displays running Microsoft Windows version 2.0. The screen resolution was 640 by 480, which provides 307,200 pixels. Using 4 bits of storage for each pixel, we require 1,228,800 bits, or 153,600 bytes, of storage, which fits nicely into the typical 256K of video RAM (262,144 bytes) commonly found on the VGA cards of the Windows 2.0 era. The big question was, *which* 16 colors should we have? The answer to that question was resolved by assigning 1 bit each for red, green, and blue primaries and the last bit to control intensity—low or high. So the standard 16 VGA colors came out as shown in **Table 1-1**.

A 4-bit-per-pixel bitmap could display these wonderful subtle colors on a suitable monitor. They might not have been the best colors in the world, but they were a fixed set available on every Windows/VGA combination, so a bitmap that had the value 1101 binary for one of its pixels was going to come out magenta when it was displayed. This guarantee that a fixed set of colors

Table 1-1
The 16 VGA Colors

Bit Value (IGBR)	Color
0000	Black
0001	Dark Red
0010	Dark Green
0011	Light Brown (Dark Yellow)
0100	Dark Blue
0101	Dark Magenta
0110	Foul Green
0111	Dark Gray
1000	Light Gray
1001	Bright Red
1010	Bright Green
1011	Yellow
1100	Bright Blue
1101	Magenta
1110	Bright Cyan
1111	White

NOTE

Describing these colors is an interesting business. For example, the value 0011 is "Dark Yellow" to some but "Light Brown" to others. This relativity is, of course, indicative of the whole problem of color matching, which we will stay well away from— at least for now.

was always available was very convenient—for displaying icons, for example. Each icon had a 4-bpp bitmap, which defined the pixel colors from the 16-color set, and a 1-bpp (monochrome) bitmap, which defined which bits were transparent.

These bitmaps I've been talking about are more correctly called device-dependent bitmaps (DDBs) because their actual organization and location in memory are determined by the device driver that manages them. Thus, they depend on the device driver to manipulate them. Why do we care? For two reasons. First, because if an application doesn't know how the bits of data are organized in the bitmap memory, it can't manipulate them directly. Second, because the device driver can choose to use any memory it can access (including spare video memory on the video adapter card) to create a bitmap, and that memory might not be accessible in the address space of the application. So even if the application did understand the organization of the bits of data, it might not be able to get a pointer to the memory anyway.

In order to alter the contents of a bitmap, an application must fill a table in memory with the new pixel values and then call *SetBitmapBits* to request the owner of the bitmap to take the data from the application's table and insert it into the correct places in the bitmap memory as shown in **Figure 1-2**. This process is rather indirect and can be extremely wasteful of memory for large images.

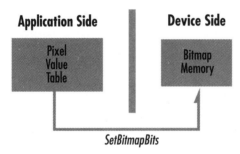

Figure 1-2   *Transferring image data from the application to a device-dependent bitmap (DDB).*

The reason for letting the device driver choose the memory and organization for the bitmap is simply to help the device driver be as efficient as possible. If the video hardware is organized in a particular way, organizing the bitmaps in the same way makes copying data from a bitmap to the screen faster. So the bottom line for these old-style DDBs is that they are fast and efficient for the device driver to use and can be useful in a variety of applications even though they don't allow as much flexibility as we might like.

An Example Application: Bitmaps

Let's create an application to display some 1-bpp and 4-bpp bitmaps. See the box for a list of the steps we'll take to create the application in Visual C++.

Procedure

1. Use AppWizard to create a basic single-document interface (SDI) application.

2. Add a *CBitmap* m_pbm* variable to the document class header file as a private member.

3. Add a *GetBmp* function to return *m_pbm* in the header file.

4. Initialize *m_pbm* to NULL in the constructor for the document class, and add code to delete the object in the destructor.

5. Add reinitialization code to the document class for a new document.

6. In the view class, add draw code if *m_pbm* is not NULL.

7. Use App Studio to create a monochrome bitmap (IDB_MONO) and a 16-color bitmap (IDB_COLOR).

8. In App Studio, add two menu items to the View menu to show the bitmaps: ID_VIEW_MONO and ID_VIEW_COLOR.

9. Use ClassWizard from within App Studio to add handler functions for the menu items to the document class.

10. Add code to the document class to load the appropriate bitmap in response to a menu selection and update the views. (Define a helper function to do the common work.)

We'll go through these steps, one at a time, looking at the bits of code you need to add to the framework that AppWizard generates.

Preparing the Application (Steps 1–5)

This example application doesn't really need a document-view architecture, but that architecture comes for free with the code that AppWizard generates, and it's easiest to simply add to the code rather than alter it too radically.

\anim32\bitmaps

We are going to use an object of the *CBitmap* class, so the first thing to do is add a private member variable to the definition of the document class in the header file BMPDOC.H.

```
class CBitmapsDoc : public CDocument
{
    :
    :

private:
    CBitmap* m_pbm;
    :
    :

}
```

Note that I chose to use a pointer to the object rather than an instance of the object itself. This is simply because it's generally awkward to take an existing object (say, a bitmap image of your cat) and turn it into a different object of the same class (say, a bitmap image of your foot). This is really a result of the way the classes in the Microsoft Foundation Class Library (MFC) wrap around Windows graphics device interface (GDI) objects. It's much easier to create a new object when we need one and delete it when we are finished with it than to try to convert an object for one use to another use. The pointer is NULL if no object is currently present; otherwise, it points to a valid object.

Since this member is private to the document class and we will need to get access to it later—when we want to draw it—we'll now add a member function to the document class header (BMPDOC.H) to return the pointer to the bitmap:

```
class CBitmapsDoc : public CDocument
{
    :
    :
public:
    CBitmap* GetBmp() {return m_pbm;}
    :
    :

}
```

Having added the member variable *CBitmap* m_pbm* to the document class, we'll now add some housekeeping code to the constructor and destructor in BMPDOC.CPP to manage the variable:

```
CBitmapsDoc::CBitmapsDoc()
{
    m_pbm = NULL;
}

CBitmapsDoc::~CBitmapsDoc()
{
    if (m_pbm != NULL) {
        delete m_pbm;
    }
}
```

In the constructor, the pointer is set to NULL to indicate that there is currently no bitmap present in the document. In the destructor, a test is made to see if a bitmap is present, and if it is, it is deleted. Note that if we were to leave out the destructor code, the pointer object would be deleted as the document class was destroyed, but the bitmap object addressed by the pointer would be left to clog up the system memory.

Applications that use the single-document interface (SDI) under MFC also need to be able to reinitialize a document to handle the File New command. This means resetting the document data structures to the state they would be in if a new document object had just been created and its constructor had been called. AppWizard creates a function called *OnNewDocument* to which we add code to reinitialize our document variables:

```
BOOL CBitmapsDoc::OnNewDocument()
{
    if (!CDocument::OnNewDocument())
        return FALSE;
    if (m_pbm != NULL) {
        delete m_pbm;
        m_pbm = NULL;
    }
    return TRUE;
}
```

This is very much the same thing as calling the destructor and then the constructor for the document object. Any existing bitmap is deleted, and the pointer is set back to NULL.

Drawing the Image (Step 6)

So much for the easy stuff. Now let's move on to add some code to the view class to draw the bitmap. AppWizard creates a skeleton of the *OnDraw* function to which we will add our code. Here's the final version of *OnDraw* from BMPVW.CPP:

```
void CBitmapsView::OnDraw(CDC* pDC)
{
    CBitmapsDoc* pDoc = GetDocument();

    // See if a bitmap is present in the doc.
    CBitmap* pbm = pDoc->GetBmp();
    if (pbm == NULL) return; // No BMP to draw

    // Get the size of the bitmap.
    BITMAP bm;
    pbm->GetObject(sizeof(bm), &bm);
```

(continued)

```
// Create a memory DC for the bitmap.
CDC dcMem;
dcMem.CreateCompatibleDC(pDC);

// Select the bitmap into the memory DC.
CBitmap* pbmOld = dcMem.SelectObject(pbm);

// Blt the bitmap to the screen DC.
pDC->BitBlt(0, 0,        // Destination
         bm.bmWidth,  // Width
         bm.bmHeight,// Height
         &dcMem,      // Source DC
         0, 0,        // Source
         SRCCOPY);    // Operation

// Done with memory DC now, so clean up.
dcMem.SelectObject(pbmOld);
}
```

Although the code for *OnDraw* above contains only a few function calls, it does contain quite a lot of interesting stuff. Let's go through this code in detail since understanding some of the fundamentals of drawing will stand us in good stead later on.

First the code must obtain a pointer to the document associated with this view by calling *GetDocument*. The document is then asked to return a pointer to the bitmap by a call to the *GetBmp* function we created a little earlier. If the return value is NULL, there is nothing to draw, and the *OnDraw* function simply returns.

If a bitmap is present, the next step is to get its dimensions. The *CBitmap* class contains a *GetBitmapDimension* member, but this doesn't do what we want. *GetBitmapDimension* works only if a call has previously been made to *SetBitmapDimension* to set the values, which isn't done automatically. The way to obtain the size of the bitmap is to call the base class function *GetObject*, which (for a bitmap object) retrieves a BITMAP data structure containing the information we want in the *bmWidth* and *bmHeight* fields.

Device Contexts: An Aside

Now that we have a pointer to the bitmap object and we have its size, we can draw the object to the view's client area. There is no function in Windows to directly copy a bitmap to the screen. All drawing is done through the use of device contexts, and GDI provides many functions to manipulate DCs and the other objects it manages, such as bitmaps. In order to draw a bitmap to the screen, we must deal with DCs.

A *device context* is a data structure owned by GDI and attached to a device driver (a screen driver or a printer driver, for example). The data structure contains data that describes how drawing is to be performed on the physical device. At any one time, the DC has a pen, a brush, a font, or a bitmap (or other type of drawing surface), and several other properties defined for it. When the DC is first created, it is fitted out with a set of default objects. Generally, the DC has only one of each type of object at any given time. It begins life with a black pen, for example. So if we want to draw a red line, we must select a red pen into the DC before calling the line drawing function. As we select new objects into the DC, we need to keep track of each object we replace so that it doesn't get lost in memory. Right before we finish with a DC, we are responsible for restoring it to the state it was in when we first started using it. Windows is very fussy about this; failing to keep track of objects in this way is a common source of memory leaks in applications.

As far as drawing images is concerned, the most interesting aspect of a memory DC is the bitmap that it currently has selected. The default is a 1-by-1 monochrome bitmap, which is not really very useful. If we select a bitmap into a DC and perform drawing operations to the DC using a GDI operation such as *Ellipse* or *Rectangle*, the image is actually drawn onto the bitmap. The screen and other device DCs, such as printers, are a kind of special case in which the device hardware is like a large bitmap selected into a memory DC, so drawing to the DC draws directly to the device memory. If you think about this a bit, you can see why it is that device-dependent bitmaps are often tailored by the device driver to be similar in structure to the hardware the driver supports.

We can create more than one DC at a time. To create other DCs in memory with the same format as a device DC, we call *CreateCompatibleDC* and pass it a pointer to the DC we want to clone. There are two common reasons for creating a memory DC. One is so that drawing can be performed to a bitmap selected into the DC. (The bitmap is then perhaps saved to a file to be reused as an image later.) The second is so that a bitmap can be drawn to another DC—typically the screen DC.

Copying bitmaps between DCs is usually done by calling the *BitBlt* (bit block transfer) function. *BitBlt* copies a rectangular area from one DC to another. If the source DC contains a bitmap and the destination DC belongs to the screen, the result is that the bitmap is transferred to the screen. The reverse situation works too. You can use *BitBlt* to copy a chunk of the screen DC to a bitmap selected into a memory DC.

An important point to remember is that *BitBlt* can move data only between DCs that belong to a common device driver. This simple rule is often forgotten when a programmer first tries to copy an image from the screen to a printer. Both devices have DCs, but the DCs belong to different drivers. There is no way for one driver to understand the bitmap format of the other, so an attempt to use *BitBlt* to copy data from the screen to a printer DC usually results in garbage because the call to *BitBlt* will fail if the DCs don't match, leaving the destination bitmap in what is often an uninitialized state. There is an exception to this rule: the *BitBlt* function *can* copy a monochrome bitmap from one DC to another—because the format of monochrome bitmaps is fixed and therefore the same for every driver.

Let's get back to the problem of drawing our bitmap to the screen. We can see that the *OnDraw* function has a device context pointer (a pointer to the screen DC) as a parameter, and we can conveniently create a memory DC directly from this pointer by creating a new *CDC* object and then calling the *CreateCompatibleDC* member function. (*CDC* is an MFC class for a device context.)

Having created a memory DC compatible with the screen DC, we call *SelectObject* to select the bitmap into the memory DC. Remember that a DC can contain only one bitmap at any one time and that it is our responsibility to take care of the old one that is returned by the *SelectObject* call until we are finished with the DC. That's what the *pbmOld* variable is used for.

Having selected the bitmap into the memory DC, we can ask the owner of the DC (the video display device driver) to copy the bits from the memory DC to the screen DC by calling the *BitBlt* function.

Once the drawing is done, the original bitmap is returned to the memory DC by means of another call to *SelectObject*, again with *pbmOld* as an argument. The memory DC is deleted automatically as we exit from the *OnDraw* function.

Creating the Bitmaps (Step 7)

Now that we have a draw function, all we need are some bitmaps to draw and we are finished. We use App Studio to create and add a number of bitmaps to the application as resources. I created two—a monochrome bitmap and a 16-color bitmap, the only two choices App Studio allows.

Modifying the Menu (Steps 8–10)

NOTE

Note that when it adds menu item handler functions, ClassWizard adds the functions to the view class by default, so you must manually select the document class as the class you want them to be added to.

We use App Studio next to add some items to the View menu—one for each bitmap—and use ClassWizard to attach a handler function to each menu item in the document class. Now all that remains to be done is to look at the code that handles the menu selection. Because there is a lot of code common to the menu handler function, I implemented a helper function to do a lot of the work in BMPDOC.CPP. (Don't forget that each new function in the class also needs a definition in the header file.)

```
void CBitmapsDoc::LoadBmp(UINT uiRes)
{
    // Delete any current bitmap.
    if (m_pbm) delete m_pbm;

    // Load the new bitmap.
    m_pbm = new CBitmap;
    m_pbm->LoadBitmap(uiRes);

    // Show the change.
    UpdateAllViews(NULL);
}
```

The *LoadBmp* function takes a resource ID for the bitmap we want to select. It deletes any current bitmap and replaces it with a new one loaded from the bitmap resource. The last thing it does is notify all the views (only one in this case since it is an SDI application) that the document has changed so that the views will redraw themselves. (The framework will call *OnDraw* for each of them.)

The code in the BMPDOC.CPP file to handle the menu choices then becomes trivial:

```
void CBitmapsDoc::OnViewMono()
{
    LoadBmp(IDB_MONO);
}

void CBitmapsDoc::OnViewColor()
{
    LoadBmp(IDB_COLOR);
}
```

Compile and Test

Now the application is complete and can be compiled and tested. Note that it has a few redundant buttons—File Open, for example. The only menu items of interest are the ones we added to the View menu for selecting the bitmap you want to show. *Figure 1-3* shows the application with a simple monochrome bitmap selected.

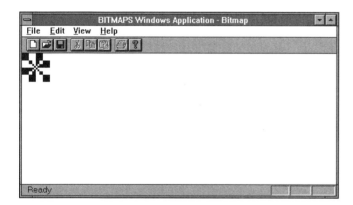

Figure 1-3   *The application showing a monochrome bitmap.*

As we have seen, a simple bitmap can be displayed in a window without too much trouble. A lot is missing, though. We have no idea how to load such a bitmap from a file, for example. We cheated here, using App Studio to build the bitmap directly into the application. And what if we want more than 16 colors? We'll look at bitmaps with more than 16 colors in the next chapter.

Confused About GDI?

In describing the humble bitmap, I've tried to give you a little background on GDI, device contexts, and so on. If you haven't followed all of this, don't worry. We'll get along without needing to understand it all fully. The details of how it works will simply become part of the C++ classes we'll develop. After all, the whole idea of creating C++ classes is to hide the mechanism below and get on with the business of creating the application. If you're still worried that you don't understand enough, trot off to the book store and buy one of the many Windows primers—Charles Petzold's excellent book *Programming Windows 3.1* (Microsoft Press, 1992), for example.

2

CHAPTER

Device-Independent Bitmaps (DIBs)

evice-dependent bitmaps (DDBs) provide a simple way to create monochrome or 16-color images, but what if we want more colors? How can we generate a bitmap with 100 colors, 1000 colors, or even 1,000,000 colors? How do we pick the colors that make up the color set? Let's look at these problems in order—first at how we can add more colors to a bitmap and second at how colors will be chosen.

Defining DIB Colors

Defining storage for more colors in our bitmap is relatively simple: we just use more bits per pixel to define the color of a given pixel. If we use 8 bits per pixel, we can define 256 colors. With 16 bits per pixel, we can define 65,536 colors; with 24 bits per pixel, we can have 16,777,216 colors; and with 32 bits per pixel, we can have even more. For the moment, let's look at using 8 bits per pixel. That will give us 256 colors to choose from—a lot more than the 16 VGA colors we have considered so far—and will allow us to consider all the problems that might be involved without going crazy.

How do we decide which 256 colors will be available? When there were only 16 colors, it was relatively easy. We used one bit each for red, green, and blue and the remaining bit for high or low intensity. Perhaps with 8 bits we could have 3 bits each for red and green, and 2 bits for blue. That arrangement would give us better shades of the primary colors and quite a few more mixed colors but would provide nothing very useful for rendering flesh tones. The answer to the 256-color question is that, no matter how you try to decide on the set of fixed colors, for drawing lifelike images the result will be only marginally better than with the 16 VGA colors. The effective solution is to allow for a variable set of colors so that each bitmap can choose its own set of 256 colors.

Wow, what a terrific solution! I can have a picture of my mother right next to a perfect (well, close anyway) rendering of a Salvador Dalí painting, and some computer art in there too, with its own set of colors. Unfortunately, graphics life is not quite that simple. The idea of defining the color set in the bitmap itself is a good one, but most PCs out there today can display only 256 colors *total*. So we have to find some way to share the 256 colors that the machine can make available among all the images. We'll come back and look at how that's done later, when we look at the Microsoft Windows Palette Manager. For now, let's hang out in the ideal world and see what we have to do to allow bitmaps to define their own color sets.

Unfortunately, the device-dependent bitmap format that was designed for Microsoft Windows version 1.0 doesn't have any place for storing a color table. That doesn't stop us from having 256-color, device-dependent bitmaps; it just means that the color table will have to exist in a separate data structure, and someone (guess who?) is going to have to keep track of which color set goes with which bitmap. The problem with this approach is that, when we save one of our device-dependent bitmaps to a file (as COLOR256.BMP, for example), no color table will be saved with it. Consequently, the bitmap can't be drawn again later on another machine with the correct colors unless the color table is somehow sent along with it in a separate file. There is no specification for such a color table file, and even if there were, having to keep track of pairs of files would be a nightmare.

Defining the DIB Format

The advent of 256-color super-VGA cards happened to coincide roughly with the development of Windows version 3.0, and since many MS-DOS applications were starting to use 256-color images, it was obvious that a way had to be found to support storing these images in Windows. Probably even more important, whatever new method was chosen had to support more than only 256-color images. The method needed to support other than 8-bit-per-pixel formats—16-bpp or 24-bpp formats, for instance—and maybe even one of several compression techniques to help keep down the size of these potentially massive images.

Those of you who have followed the development of Windows from flat, low-resolution, tiled windows all the way to its present state will be aware that, no matter what the problem, the developers of Windows always managed to find a solution by simply adding more data structures and functions to the system. The problem of adding color information to bitmaps was solved in the same way: a new set of data structures was designed, and some new function calls appeared in the system software. Curiously, though, not quite enough functions were added, but we'll come back to that problem later.

And so the device-independent bitmap (DIB) file format was born. The organization of a Windows DIB file is shown in *Figure 2-1*. A Windows DIB file contains two parts: in the first, a BITMAPFILEHEADER with information about the file itself, also a BITMAPINFOHEADER with information about the DIB, and an optional color table that consists of an array of RGBQUAD structures; in the second, the DIB image bits.

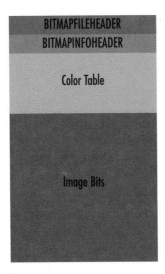

Figure 2-1 *Format of a Windows DIB file.*

There are actually two file formats. (You just knew I was going to say that, didn't you?) One format is called the Windows DIB file format and the other isn't—it's called the Presentation Manager DIB file format. The difference between the two is that the Presentation Manager (PM) DIB files have a BITMAPCOREHEADER instead of a BITMAPINFOHEADER, and Presentation Manager DIBs use an RGBTRIPLE (24-bit) structure to define a color table entry instead of the RGBQUAD (32-bit) structure used to define a Windows DIB color table entry. We will ignore the Presentation Manager format until we look at the code for loading a DIB file. At that time we'll add a bit of extra code to convert a Presentation Manager DIB file to its Windows-equivalent form in memory. In that way, we'll be able to read either format but will have to deal with only the Windows format in the code.

Simply defining a new file format wasn't quite enough, though. Some way of dealing with this new organization of bitmap data in memory was needed too. One of the goals for DIBs was that the application would be able to manipulate the pixels directly. That meant having a defined organization. It was decided that it would be simplest if the file image bits could be read directly into memory and used without modification. So a DIB's bits in memory, as shown in *Figure 2-2*, look exactly like the DIB's bits in a file. The DIB header in the file is also used "as is" in memory. Note that each DIB in memory still consists of two separate parts: a header (with its color table) and the bits. You still have to keep track of which header belongs to which set of bits, but at least now they can both be written into one file for transport to another machine. Note that DIB files use the same .BMP extension that the older bitmap files used.

Figure 2-2 *A DIB in memory with its header and color table.*

A DIB—device-*independent* bitmap—is so named because it can be moved from one Windows environment to another and still retain its correct appearance. There are a few "gotchas" here, though. It is obviously rather difficult to do justice to a 24-bit-per-pixel image on a 256-color display. The image will have to be mapped to the current color set, with some consequent loss of color information. The good news, though, is that the user of the 256-color machine can upgrade his or her video adapter to provide the needed color depth, and out the images will come—just as anticipated by their creator. The image data is all there, ready to be seen if the hardware can do it.

One curious feature of DIBs is that the lines of the image are organized the opposite way up from the way they are organized in the older DDB files. This difference came about because, although OS/2 and Windows were both to use the new DIB format, OS/2 used a different origin for its graphics device interface (GDI) coordinate system. Instead of being the top-left corner of the window, as it is in the default mode for Windows, the origin in an OS/2 Presentation Manager window is the bottom-left corner. Microsoft and IBM decided that a bottom-left origin was the way of things to come and (to make it simple to draw these new DIBs on Presentation Manager windows) that the DIBs should be organized with the scan lines the other way up. Windows-based applications, it was decided, would just have to deal with it. More recently, in Win32, the DIB specification has been modified so that, if the height of the DIB is specified as a negative value, the scan lines are ordered the same way as for a DDB. So the world today (please, don't put this book in a time capsule!) has two varieties of Windows DIBs: bottom scan line first and top scan line first. We will confine our discussion to the normal, "inverted," DIBs, shown in relation to the screen's ordering of scan lines in *Figure 2-3* on the next page, since these are predominant today.

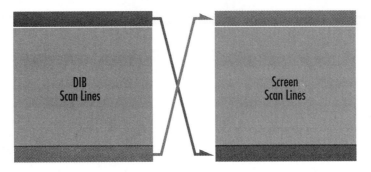

Figure 2-3 *The normal DIB scan lines order inverted from the screen scan lines order.*

As we've noted, DIBs are capable of supporting 1-, 4-, 8-, 16-, 24- or 32-bpp images with a variety of compression techniques. Our use of DIBs will confine itself to the 8-bpp uncompressed variety both because these will give us the images we need in order to draw to the most popular display adapters on the market today and because they will provide an excellent compromise between color depth and storage space. Sticking to one variety will also simplify the code a great deal, which I hope will help you see how things work without your getting lost in dealing with all the possible variants.

DDBs haven't gone away just because we now have DIBs. Device drivers are still free to organize data in a DDB any way they wish. In practice, many modern video adapters have memory organizations that are similar to the way data is organized in a DIB, so the device driver's DDB comes out to be a DIB anyway. Don't get too excited—you still can't have direct access to the DDB. Besides, I'm going to show you that if you have DIBs, you don't need DDBs at all.

The 8-Bit-per-Pixel DIB

Let's look at the 8-bpp DIB a little more closely. I mentioned earlier that it has a color table to define the set of colors it uses. This table can have up to 256 entries—one for each color used in the image. There is no restriction at all on what those colors are, so it is quite possible to create a DIB with 256 shades of blue in it. Now that I've given you the gun and the bullets, I'd better make sure you don't shoot your eye out with them. On a Windows system, you can't use all 256 colors and expect to see the image drawn perfectly. You are limited in practice to 236 colors of your own choice and a set of 20 fixed system colors.

Why is that, Dad? Well, Son, I'll tell you. When DIBs were invented to fix all the known image problems in the universe, someone decided that it might be nice if all the zillions of DDB files (bitmaps, icons, and cursors) out there in Windows-land still came out in the same awful VGA colors when they were used on one of those newfangled 256-color systems. Since the older DDB files have no color tables in them, some way had to be found to provide them with the sets of colors they had before. Furthermore, some way had to be provided to allow Windows to draw icons, cursors, window borders, and plain text in a visible way even if an application had set all the colors in the machine to pink. In any case, not all applications would need or want to use lots of colors, and they needed to still be programmable in the same way regardless of whether a set of colors had been chosen to work with. So the original set of 16 VGA colors was made part of a fixed system set that would always be available to all applications and that the system could use to draw old-style 16-color DDBs.

The 16 VGA colors needed to be set in the system color tables so that, if an image using these colors were color-inverted, it would come out the same way it did on a 16-color system. To achieve this adaptability, half of the VGA colors were placed at the low end of the system color table and the other half at the top end. In this way, a pixel set to the value 0x00 would index to the color black, and when inverted so that its value became 0xFF, it would index to the color white. All very clever.

Then the big nasty man who lived next door came round to spoil the fun we were having. Being of a corporate disposition, he said that we had to have "money green" in our standard color set, and that it would be wise also to include a nice shade of light blue for the corporate desktop. That meant adding two more colors to the bottom end of the table, for a total of 18 reserved colors. Because there was also the possibility that "money green" or "corporate desktop blue" could be inverted, another two locations were assigned at the top of the table and filled with colors so memorable that I forget their names at the moment. The net result was 20 reserved system colors.

Take time out here to run the SysPal application, which displays the current state of the color table in the display-driver hardware. On a VGA or other nonpalettized display, you will see the standard 16 VGA colors displayed 16 times. On a 256-color display, you will see 10 reserved colors at the beginning of the table and the other 10 at the end, the remaining 236 colors having been set initially by the graphics device interface (GDI) and later by whatever applications have used them. On a display with more than 256 colors, you'll see 256 shades of red, from black to bright red.

\anim32\syspal

What all this means to you as an application author is that you can define up to 236 colors in a DIB and it will (generally) be drawn as you authored it. If you use more than 236 colors, the colors in your DIB may not all come out as expected since 20 of the available 256 colors have already been chosen for you. Of course you can choose to use the 20 system colors in your image *as well as* 236 of your own choosing. However, when the image is drawn, you still may not get exactly what you expected because the system colors actually vary slightly from machine to machine depending on the display driver. So in order to get reasonably accurate color rendering, you can rely only on having 236 colors to work with.

I've omitted a few provisos from the discussion here, and we'll get to those later, when we look at the Palette Manager.

Working with DIBs

The file format for a DIB provides for all the data needed to draw the bitmap correctly, but how do we get the DIB file data into some form we can copy to a device context (DC) the way we did DDB data? We could perhaps read the entire file into memory, call *CreateBitmap* to create a DDB, and then use the *SetBitmapBits* function to copy the DIB bits to the bitmap. Then we would have a DDB to select into a DC, and we could call *BitBlt* to draw it. Well, there are a few things wrong with that approach. First, the process I've just described would use a huge chunk of memory to temporarily hold the image while we created the bitmap. This process could be very expensive for a big image. (A 640-by-480 image contains 307,200 pixels.) Second, the format of the data required for a call to *SetBitmapBits* isn't quite the same as the format of the DIB image in its file. And third, we will have lost the color information along the way, so who knows what will get drawn?

When the DIB was defined, the rules for using some of the existing functions changed, and some new functions were added to the system to support the DIB. The *CreateBitmap* function, for instance, is now used only to create monochrome bitmaps. For all color bitmaps, applications should call the new *CreateDIBitmap*. The bits in the bitmap created with *CreateDIBitmap* can be set by using the new *SetDIBitmapBits*, which deals correctly with the way bits are organized in a DIB in memory. Even with these new functions, though, we don't seem to have any color data; in fact, we are still required to deal with color data separately by creating a palette from the DIB color table data and using this palette in a DC when we draw a DIB. *Figure 2-4* shows what would be involved in drawing a DIB using *BitBlt* by creating a DDB and a palette from the DIB.

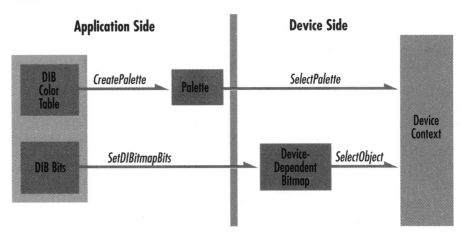

Figure 2-4 *From DIB to image using a device-dependent bitmap.*

We can avoid creating DDBs altogether and use the DIB as is once it has been copied from the file to memory. The image in memory can be drawn to a DC by means of another of the new DIB functions, *StretchDIBits*. A new function named *SetDIBitsToDevice* performs the same sort of job but without stretching. Don't use this function in new work: always use *StretchDIBits* because it is the function best optimized in the device driver. Use *StretchDIBits* even in the case in which the image will not be stretched at all. This, at least, is how the party line goes. In practice, the *SetDIBitsToDevice* and *StretchDIBits* calls can both end up in the same place in the device driver under appropriate circumstances, so you are not likely to see a performance difference. However, since *StretchDIBits* provides both 1-to-1 and stretched blts, it will be most convenient to use only this one function in all your code. *StretchDIBits* is the core function for high-performance screen updates on Windows version 3.1 and Windows NT version 3.1. We'll be looking at how *StretchDIBits* works (and at how the brand-new *CreateDIBSection* in Windows 95 and Windows NT 3.5 works) in more detail in Chapter 6.

I briefly mentioned that an application can directly manipulate the bits of a DIB. This is fairly obvious since the DIB exists in a piece of memory allocated by the application. The less obvious significance of this capability is that an application can, for example, create a 24-bpp DIB image in memory, perform some complex color operation on the image, and then draw the image to a 256-color display, reducing the image colors to a simpler set. The important point here is that the image in memory contains the full color information even though the display device can't use it all. If we were to rely solely on bitmaps that matched the display resolution, a paint program running on a 256-color machine would be severely limited since the subtle changes possible for a 24-bpp image cannot be performed if the image has been reduced to an 8-bpp 256-color image.

A C++ Class for DIBs

Windows provides very little support for manipulating DIBs directly, which is a shame because DIBs offer a lot to a programmer who wants to use images in an application. So why not define a new C++ class to encapsulate a DIB and provide all the member functions we commonly need to manipulate these structures? From this point on, we'll begin to evolve a class for DIBs (called *CDIB*) and later a class to handle the color palettes (called *CDIBPal*) we need to draw DIBs. To keep things simple for the moment, we'll begin by ignoring the issue of palettes and lay the groundwork for the *CDIB* class.

You might have noticed that I intend to create a palette separate from the DIB itself. It is a tempting idea to design a class to hold both the DIB bits and the DIB color palette, but in practice this would prove to be wasteful because the common case is to share one palette among many DIBs. The *CDIB* class does include the color table for the DIB, so we can construct a palette for the DIB at any time. We'll be looking at palettes in more detail later.

Since the Microsoft Foundation Class Library (MFC) provides the *CBitmap* class already, you might be tempted to derive the new *CDIB* class from *CBitmap*. This wouldn't help, though, because *CBitmap* has no way to deal with DIBs directly. We need to back up a bit and derive *CDIB* from a more fundamental class, *CObject*.

The *CDIB* object will be a wrapper around a BITMAPINFO structure and a chunk of memory containing the image bits. The normal object-oriented approach would require us to create a set of member functions to manipulate the encapsulated data, but totally encapsulating the data involves us in two problems. The first problem is that the Windows system functions that deal with DIBs require pointers to the header and bits, so our *CDIB* object must be able to furnish these pointers to its internal structures. The second problem is that, if we were to create functions to manipulate the image bits, performance would be very poor compared to performance from manipulating the bits directly. This is exactly the problem we already face with device-dependent bitmaps. So in the eyes of the purists the object model will be broken. The performance will be stunning, though, so you can smile all the way to the bank. *Figure 2-5* shows the modified object model we'll use.

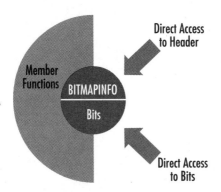

Figure 2-5   *The data access model for* CDIB *objects.*

Our first goal in developing the *CDIB* class will be to create a simple application that can open a DIB file and display its image. We will follow the technique MFC uses for wrapping Windows GDI objects: we'll have a very simple object constructor and other member functions that actually initialize the object. This division of labor will make it much easier to handle errors involved with initially setting up a new object. The constructor for the *CDIB* class will create a very small, simple DIB as a way of initializing the object and setting the member variables to a known state. The actual creation of a real *CDIB* object will be done with other member functions, and we will create several of these objects as the *CDIB* class evolves.

CDIB Data and Function Declarations

We'll begin to create the *CDIB* class by looking at its member variables. Here's an extract from DIB.H showing the member variables:

```
class CDIB : public CObject
{
    :
    :
protected:
    BITMAPINFO* m_pBMI;          // Pointer to BITMAPINFO struct
```

```
    BYTE* m_pBits;                  // Pointer to the bits
    :
    :
};
```

The object has two protected member variables. The first member is *m_pBMI*, which is a pointer to a BITMAPINFO structure containing a BITMAPINFO-HEADER and a color table consisting of as many as 256 RGBQUAD structures. The second member is *m_pBits*, a pointer to the image bits.

We are going to allow direct access to the image bits, and we are going to also need access to the header information. So a number of functions are provided in the header file to return the address of the bits and various pieces of information from the header.

The header file also contains declarations for the various public member functions used to control the object. A few more private functions are included to provide width and height information extracted from the header, which will be used later when we draw the image. Here's the complete *CDIB* class declaration from the header file DIB.H:

```
class CDIB : public CObject
{
    DECLARE_SERIAL(CDIB)
public:
    CDIB();
    ~CDIB();

    BITMAPINFO* GetBitmapInfoAddress()
        {return m_pBMI;}                        // Pointer to bitmap info
    BYTE* GetBitsAddress()
        {return m_pBits;}                       // Pointer to the bits
    RGBQUAD* GetClrTabAddress()
        {return (LPRGBQUAD)(((BYTE*)(m_pBMI)) +
                sizeof(BITMAPINFOHEADER));}     // Pointer to color table

    virtual BOOL Create(int width, int height); // Create a new DIB
    virtual BOOL Load(CFile* fp);               // Load from file
    virtual void Serialize(CArchive& ar);
    virtual void Draw(CDC* pDC, int x, int y);

protected:
    BITMAPINFO* m_pBMI;         // Pointer to BITMAPINFO struct
    BYTE* m_pBits;              // Pointer to the bits

private:
    int DibWidth()
        {return m_pBMI->bmiHeader.biWidth;}
    int DibHeight()
        {return m_pBMI->bmiHeader.biHeight;}
};
```

In my initial design for the *CDIB* class, I set the *m_pBMI* and *m_pBits* members to NULL in the constructor. This seemed sensible because they would be set later when one of the "real" creation member functions was called. However, this measure proved awkward in the code because I had to constantly check that these pointers were not NULL before using them in all the internal functions. I decided, therefore, that it would be much simpler if the constructor created a small DIB right from the start, and any other creation functions would simply replace the original data structures. This design improved things in two ways: first, the code need not constantly check that the pointers are non-NULL; and second, the other creation functions can be called multiple times on the same *CDIB* object with no ill effects. To implement this scheme, I added a member function called *Create*, which is used in the constructor to set the initial state of the object.

Here are the constructor and the destructor for the *CDIB* class:

```
CDIB::CDIB()
{
    m_pBMI = NULL;
    m_pBits = NULL;
    Create(16, 16);
}


CDIB::~CDIB()
{
    // Free the memory.
    if (m_pBMI != NULL) free(m_pBMI);
    if (m_pBits != NULL) free(m_pBits);
}
```

The constructor sets the two pointers to NULL and then calls the *CDIB* member function *Create* to create a small DIB. The destructor frees any memory attached to the *CDIB* object through its pointers.

Let's look at the *Create* function, which actually creates a DIB of a given size. I've simplified the code here a bit by removing some of the error handling to improve readability:

```
BOOL CDIB::Create(int iWidth, int iHeight)
{
    // Delete any existing stuff.
    if (m_pBMI != NULL) free(m_pBMI);
    if (m_pBits != NULL) free(m_pBits);

    // Allocate memory for the header.
    m_pBMI = (BITMAPINFO*) malloc(sizeof(BITMAPINFOHEADER) +
                                256 * sizeof(RGBQUAD));

    // Allocate memory for the bits (DWORD aligned).
    int iBitsSize = ((iWidth + 3) & ~3) * iHeight;
    m_pBits = (BYTE*)malloc(iBitsSize);
```

```
    // Fill in the header info.
    BITMAPINFOHEADER* pBI = (BITMAPINFOHEADER*) m_pBMI;
    pBI->biSize = sizeof(BITMAPINFOHEADER);
    pBI->biWidth = iWidth;
    pBI->biHeight = iHeight;
    pBI->biPlanes = 1;
    pBI->biBitCount = 8;
    pBI->biCompression = BI_RGB;
    pBI->biSizeImage = 0;
    pBI->biXPelsPerMeter = 0;
    pBI->biYPelsPerMeter = 0;
    pBI->biClrUsed = 0;
    pBI->biClrImportant = 0;

    // Create a gray scale color table.
    RGBQUAD* prgb = GetClrTabAddress();
    for (int i = 0; i < 256; i++) {
        prgb->rgbBlue = prgb->rgbGreen = prgb->rgbRed = (BYTE) i;
        prgb->rgbReserved = 0;
        prgb++;
    }

    // Set all the bits to a known state (black).
    memset(m_pBits, iBitsSize, 0);

    return TRUE;
}
```

Any existing header or bits memory is freed, and new memory is allocated. Note that the memory for the DIB bits must always be *DWORD* aligned (32-bit), so the width value is rounded up to the next *DWORD* boundary. Note also that I am using *malloc* for the memory allocation, not the C++ *new* operator, because the memory blocks are not of a fixed size. I've also been rather bad, as I warned you I would be, in that I haven't handled the case in which the memory allocation fails. Beware: *malloc* is a C rather than a C++ function, so it won't throw an exception to report the failure.

The header information is filled out with a description of an 8-bpp DIB, and the color table is filled with a gray scale. The bits are set to a defined state—in this case, to all black. It isn't really necessary to initialize the color table or the bits at all. Most likely the table and the bits will be set later from values in a DIB file or in some other source, but setting them to a defined state here helps with debugging the code and gives us something to look at if we draw a *CDIB* object immediately after it has been constructed.

The next thing to look at is loading the DIB image and attributes from a file. The function we'll create will read the DIB data from an open *CFile* object. I mentioned that DIB files come in two flavors—Windows format and Presentation Manager (PM) format. In the *CDIB::Load* code, we'll convert a Presentation Manager format DIB to Windows format as we read the file.

See the box for the basic order of events in reading the file and creating the
CDIB object.

Procedure for Loading a DIB Image

1. Read the file header and validate it.

2. Read the BITMAPINFOHEADER and validate it. If this
   fails, back up and try to read a BITMAPCOREHEADER
   for a PM-format DIB.

3. Compute the size of the memory blocks required for
   the DIB header and bits.

4. Allocate the memory for the header.

5. Copy the header information and the color table data.
   If the file is in PM format, convert the data to Windows
   format as it's copied.

6. Allocate the memory for the bits.

7. Seek to the start of the bits in the file and copy the bits.

Here's the code that creates a *CDIB* object from an open *CFile* object. I've
removed some of the comments and error handling for clarity.

```
BOOL CDIB::Load(CFile* fp)
{
    BOOL bIsPM = FALSE;
    BITMAPINFO* pBmpInfo = NULL;
    BYTE* pBits = NULL;

    // Get the current file position.
    DWORD dwFileStart = fp->GetPosition();

    // Read the file header to get the file size and to
    // find out where the bits start in the file.
    BITMAPFILEHEADER BmpFileHdr;
    int iBytes;
    iBytes = fp->Read(&BmpFileHdr, sizeof(BmpFileHdr));

    // Check that we have the magic 'BM' at the start.
    if (BmpFileHdr.bfType != 0x4D42) {
        TRACE("Not a bitmap file");
        goto $abort;
    }
```

```
// Make a wild guess that the file is in Windows DIB
// format and read the BITMAPINFOHEADER. If the file turns
// out to be a PM DIB file, we'll convert it later.
BITMAPINFOHEADER BmpInfoHdr;
iBytes = fp->Read(&BmpInfoHdr, sizeof(BmpInfoHdr));

// Check that we got a real Windows DIB file.
if (BmpInfoHdr.biSize != sizeof(BITMAPINFOHEADER)) {
    // Set a flag to convert PM file to Win format later.
    bIsPM = TRUE;

    // Back up the file pointer and read the BITMAPCOREHEADER
    // and create the BITMAPINFOHEADER from it.
    fp->Seek(dwFileStart + sizeof(BITMAPFILEHEADER), CFile::begin);
    BITMAPCOREHEADER BmpCoreHdr;
    iBytes = fp->Read(&BmpCoreHdr, sizeof(BmpCoreHdr));

    BmpInfoHdr.biSize = sizeof(BITMAPINFOHEADER);
    BmpInfoHdr.biWidth = (int) BmpCoreHdr.bcWidth;
    BmpInfoHdr.biHeight = (int) BmpCoreHdr.bcHeight;
    BmpInfoHdr.biPlanes = BmpCoreHdr.bcPlanes;
    BmpInfoHdr.biBitCount = BmpCoreHdr.bcBitCount;
    BmpInfoHdr.biCompression = BI_RGB;
    BmpInfoHdr.biSizeImage = 0;
    BmpInfoHdr.biXPelsPerMeter = 0;
    BmpInfoHdr.biYPelsPerMeter = 0;
    BmpInfoHdr.biClrUsed = 0;
    BmpInfoHdr.biClrImportant = 0;
}

// Allocate the memory blocks.
// Copy the BmpInfoHdr we have so far,
// and then read in the color table from the file.
int iColors;
int iColorTableSize;
iColors = NumDIBColorEntries((LPBITMAPINFO) &BmpInfoHdr);
iColorTableSize = 256 * sizeof(RGBQUAD);
int iBitsSize;
int iBISize;
iBISize = sizeof(BITMAPINFOHEADER) +
        iColorTableSize;
iBitsSize = BmpFileHdr.bfSize -
        BmpFileHdr.bfOffBits;

// Allocate the memory for the header.
pBmpInfo = (LPBITMAPINFO) malloc(iBISize);
```

(continued)

```
        // Copy the header we already have.
        memcpy(pBmpInfo, &BmpInfoHdr, sizeof(BITMAPINFOHEADER));

        // Now read the color table in from the file.
        if (bIsPM == FALSE) {
            // Read the color table from the file.
            iBytes = fp->Read(((LPBYTE) pBmpInfo) +
                        sizeof(BITMAPINFOHEADER), iColorTableSize);
    } else {
            // Read each PM color table entry in turn and convert it
            // to Win DIB format as we go.
            LPRGBQUAD lpRGB;
            lpRGB = (LPRGBQUAD) ((LPBYTE) pBmpInfo +
                                    sizeof(BITMAPINFOHEADER));

            int i;
            RGBTRIPLE rgbt;
            for (i=0; i<iColors; i++) {
                iBytes = fp->Read(&rgbt, sizeof(RGBTRIPLE));
                lpRGB->rgbBlue = rgbt.rgbtBlue;
                lpRGB->rgbGreen = rgbt.rgbtGreen;
                lpRGB->rgbRed = rgbt.rgbtRed;
                lpRGB->rgbReserved = 0;
                lpRGB++;
            }
        }

        // Allocate the memory for the bits
        // and read the bits from the file.
        pBits = (BYTE*) malloc(iBitsSize);
        if (!pBits) {
            TRACE("Out of memory for DIB bits");
            goto $abort;
        }

        // Seek to the bits in the file.
        fp->Seek(dwFileStart + BmpFileHdr.bfOffBits, CFile::begin);

        // Read the bits.
        iBytes = fp->Read(pBits, iBitsSize);

        // Everything went OK.
        if (m_pBMI != NULL) free(m_pBMI);
        m_pBMI = pBmpInfo;
        if (m_pBits != NULL) free(m_pBits);
        m_pBits = pBits;
        return TRUE;

$abort: // Something went wrong.
```

```
    if (pBmpInfo) free(pBmpInfo);
    if (pBits) free(pBits);
    return FALSE;
}
```

The *dwFileStart* variable is used to find the current file position when the function is first called. This variable was added to make the function a bit more general and will allow the function to be used when we add serialization to the *CDIB* class. When a document is serialized, we can store *CDIB* objects in their Windows DIB file format and conveniently use the *Load* function above to extract the objects from the archive again later.

Note that the color table we create for the DIB always has 256 entries even if the source DIB doesn't. This makes it much easier to manipulate the DIB colors later if we need to without having to worry about the size of the color table.

The *NumDIBColorEntries* helper function is used to compute the number of colors in the color table based on data in the header. This function is private to the module. It uses another helper function, *IsWinDIB*, to determine whether the DIB is in Windows format or Presentation Manager format. Here are the two helper functions:

```
static BOOL IsWinDIB(BITMAPINFOHEADER* pBIH)
{
    ASSERT(pBIH);
    if (((BITMAPCOREHEADER*)pBIH)->bcSize ==
        sizeof(BITMAPCOREHEADER)) {
        return FALSE;
    }
    return TRUE;
}


static int NumDIBColorEntries(LPBITMAPINFO pBmpInfo)
{
    BITMAPINFOHEADER* pBIH;
    BITMAPCOREHEADER* pBCH;
    int iColors, iBitCount;

    ASSERT(pBmpInfo);

    pBIH = &(pBmpInfo->bmiHeader);
    pBCH = (BITMAPCOREHEADER*) pBIH;

    // Start off by assuming the color table size from
    // the bit-per-pixel field.
    if (IsWinDIB(pBIH)) {
        iBitCount = pBIH->biBitCount;
    } else {
        iBitCount = pBCH->bcBitCount;
    }                                                   (continued)
```

```
        switch (iBitCount) {
        case 1:
            iColors = 2;
            break;
        case 4:
            iColors = 16;
            break;
        case 8:
            iColors = 256;
            break;
        default:
            iColors = 0;
            break;
        }

        // If this is a Windows DIB, then the color table length
        // is determined by the biClrUsed field if the value in
        // the field is nonzero.
        if (IsWinDIB(pBIH) && (pBIH->biClrUsed != 0)) {
            iColors = pBIH->biClrUsed;
        }

        return iColors;
}
```

The *IsWinDIB* function uses the *bcSize* field of the header to determine whether the DIB is in Windows format or Presentation Manager format. Note that the test is performed against the size of the BITMAPCOREHEADER structure, which will never change. The BITMAPINFOHEADER structure could possibly change size in a future version of Windows.

NumDIBColorEntries uses the number of bits per pixel to determine the probable number of colors for 1-, 4-, or 8-bpp DIBs. The switch statement covers all the Presentation Manager DIB cases. For Windows format DIBs, the *biClrUsed* field is tested, and if nonzero, this value is used for the number of entries in the color table. This allows an 8-bpp DIB, for example, to have only 25 colors, say, in its color table—its color table doesn't have to have all 256 entries present in the file if it doesn't use them all.

Let's add a function to draw the DIB to a DC so that we can see whether what we have done so far works:

```
void CDIB::Draw(CDC* pDC, int x, int y)
{
    ::StretchDIBits(pDC->GetSafeHdc(),
                    x,                      // Destination x
                    y,                      // Destination y
                    DibWidth(),             // Destination width
                    DibHeight(),            // Destination height
                    0,                      // Source x
```

```
          0,                        // Source y
          DibWidth(),               // Source width
          DibHeight(),              // Source height
          GetBitsAddress(),         // Pointer to bits
          GetBitmapInfoAddress(),   // BITMAPINFO
          DIB_RGB_COLORS,           // Options
          SRCCOPY);                 // Raster operation code (ROP)
}
```

As you can see, drawing the image to a DC is simply a case of calling *StretchDIBits*. The *Draw* function allows the DIB to be drawn with its top-left corner at an arbitrary point in the destination DC. The *CDC* class doesn't have *StretchDIBits* as a member function, so we are calling the Windows GDI function directly here. (Note that I used the *::* scoping operator to make that more obvious in the code despite the fact that it wasn't necessary.) *StretchDIBits* takes an *HDC* object as its first parameter, so we have to extract the object from the *CDC* object by calling the *GetSafeHdc* function. The *DibWidth*, *DibHeight*, *GetBitsAddress*, and *GetBitmapInfoAddress* functions are those defined in DIB.H (pages 10–11).

The only remaining parameters are *DIB_RGB_COLORS* and *SRCCOPY*. The *DIB_RGB_COLORS* parameter tells *StretchDIBits* that the color table parameter we are passing contains a set of RGB colors, and these should be mapped to the current system color set. The *SRCCOPY* flag means to simply copy the source rectangle over the destination rectangle, replacing it.

An Example Application: BasicDIB

Now we have built just enough functionality into the *CDIB* class to build a simple application that can create a DIB and draw it to the screen. We'll create a simple application that can load a DIB from a file and display it. For the example, I chose to give the application a single-document interface (SDI) rather than a multiple-document interface (MDI). It doesn't really matter. I chose an SDI because it will make for less code in the example. That should better show off the code we are developing. See the box on the next page for a list of the steps we'll take to build the application.

\anim32\basicdib

Let's take a look at the code that was added to the document and view files. We'll begin with the document header file BASICDOC.H:

```
class CBasicDibDoc : public CDocument
{
    :
    :
// Attributes
public:
    CDIB* GetDib() {return &m_dib;}
    :
    :
```

(continued)

```
// Implementation
private:
    CDIB m_dib;
       .
       .
       .
};
```

The *m_dib* variable will contain the current *CDIB* object. Notice that in this case I chose to use an instance of the object and not a pointer to it. This simplifies the code in the document class but does rely on the *CDIB* object's being capable of being initialized multiple times. If the *CDIB* object weren't capable of multiple initializations, we would have to use a pointer to the object here, and the current object would have to be deleted and replaced by a new one every time we loaded a new DIB file.

The *GetDib* function returns a pointer to the *CDIB* object. This pointer is used by the view code when it draws the DIB.

Procedure

1. Use AppWizard to create a basic SDI application. I called mine BasicDIB.

2. Create DIB.H and DIB.CPP files, or copy the ones from the example.

3. Add DIB.CPP to the project. Add a statement to include DIB.H in all the .CPP files that include the document header file, and scan all dependencies.

4. Use ClassWizard to add handler functions to the view class for File Save and File Save As. The handlers do nothing—they simply prevent the default File Save code from being called. If you don't do this, the save action will erase any files you open.

5. In the document header file, add a *CDIB m_dib* member variable and a function to return a pointer to the variable for access from the view class.

6. In the document *Serialize* function, add code to load a DIB from the file.

7. In the view code file, add code to the *OnDraw* function to draw the DIB.

The document code file just needs to have a small piece of code added to load the current DIB from a file in response to a call to the *Serialize* function (BASICDOC.CPP):

```
void CBasicDibDoc::Serialize(CArchive& ar)
{
    if (ar.IsStoring()) {
        ASSERT(1); // We don't do this.
    } else {
        // Get the file from the archive.
        CFile* fp = ar.GetFile();
        ASSERT(fp);
        ar.Flush();
        // Load the DIB from the file.
        if (!m_dib.Load(fp)) {
            AfxMessageBox("Failed to load image");
        }
    }
}
```

The function supports loading only, not saving. We use an ASSERT statement to be sure we don't save by accident, which would destroy the DIB file. Loading the DIB is achieved by first asking the archive object for its *CFile* object. Then the archive is flushed as suggested in the class library reference documentation before the *CFile* pointer is used to access the file. Actually, loading the DIB is simply a case of calling the DIB's *Load* member function, passing the file pointer as a parameter. A message box alerts the user if the load operation fails.

That's all we need to add to the document class. Let's look at what we need to add to the view class code in order to display the DIB. The only change is to add a small piece of code to the *OnDraw* function in BASICVW.CPP:

```
void CBasicDibView::OnDraw(CDC* pDC)
{
    CBasicDibDoc* pDoc = GetDocument();

    // Get a pointer to the DIB.
    CDIB* pdib = pDoc->GetDib();

    // Tell the DIB to draw itself.
    pdib->Draw(pDC, 0, 0);
}
```

The *GetDib* function is used to get a pointer to the current DIB from the document, and then the DIB is asked to draw itself to the top-left corner of the DC.

As you can see, writing an application to load and display a DIB isn't very hard at all. So where's the catch? Compile and run the application, or just run the BasicDIB sample, and we'll have a look at its limitations.

When you first run BasicDIB, you should see a small black rectangle in the top-left corner of the client area. This is the default DIB created when the *CDIB* object was constructed for the document. Use the File Open menu selection or the toolbar button to open a DIB. Try a 1-bpp (monochrome) DIB first. Then try some 4-bpp images and finally a few of the 8-bpp images. There are several images in the \anim32_images directory on the CD that comes with this book.

You should see that 1-bpp and 4-bpp images work just fine. The colors come out as you would expect. You can get a second opinion on the colors by loading the files into another application such as Paintbrush. The 8-bpp images don't come out too well, though. Their colors seem to be all messed up. What's actually happening is that Windows is mapping the colors in the DIB (which we supplied through the call to *StretchDIBits* when the DIB was drawn) to the current palette in the DC, and the default palette has only the 20 system reserved colors. It's a miracle that some 8-bpp images are recognizable at all!

So, although we can open and draw a DIB, not all the cases work correctly, and to fix those problems, we need to take a look at palettes and the Windows Palette Manager. We'll do that next.

CHAPTER

Palettes and the Palette Manager

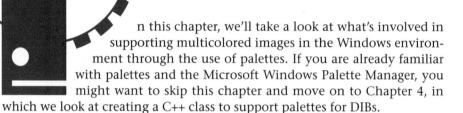

n this chapter, we'll take a look at what's involved in supporting multicolored images in the Windows environment through the use of palettes. If you are already familiar with palettes and the Microsoft Windows Palette Manager, you might want to skip this chapter and move on to Chapter 4, in which we look at creating a C++ class to support palettes for DIBs.

Palettes: The What and the Why

What is a palette? Why do I need to use a palette? These are the two most common questions about them. The short answers are that a palette is the set of colors that a given image uses and that you need to use a palette if you want to display images containing more than the 16 VGA colors on a machine that has an 8-bit-per-pixel (bpp) display.

This is the bit in the movie where the actor starts to look all dreamy and the screen dissolves into wavy lines as we go back into the past—what a friend of mine refers to as "mental throwups." A few years back, two facts determined the destiny of the universe: applications developers wanted to use more than 16 colors, and video memory was expensive. These circumstances led to the so-called super-VGA cards, which contained 512K of video memory and were capable of running a 640-by-480 display with 8 bits per pixel. These super cards could display 256 colors. The set of colors was determined by loading appropriate RGB (red-green-blue) values into the hardware palette registers. What has memory price got to do with this? Well, consider memory as half the price. The same card could have had enough memory for a 640-by-480 display with 16 bits per pixel, giving us a display capable of 65K worth of colors and no palette to worry about. If the memory had been even cheaper, we might have had a 640-by-480 display with 24 bits per pixel, which would have given us amazing color resolution.

A few more factors were involved (and I have rather distorted history to suit my own needs here), but the end result was that a large number of super-VGA cards were manufactured with the capability of displaying 256 colors.

Many MS-DOS–based games took immediate advantage of these new cards, and the results were stunning in comparison to the older, 16-color, games. The addition of the hardware palette also enabled the memory-cheap animation technique of palette cycling, in which movement can be simulated by altering an image's coloration over time. The new MS-DOS–based applications had the great advantage of having only themselves to consider when they were running on the machine. The applications developer could set whatever colors he or she wanted by writing directly to the hardware in the video adapter, giving the application total control and excellent performance. Applications such as these set the standard for animation on the PC.

Then, during development, it seemed clear that the upcoming Microsoft Windows version 3.0 should support the new super-VGA cards so that Windows-based applications could take advantage of the increased color capability. Windows would run more than one application at the same time, though, so it wouldn't be acceptable to simply let any application alter the palette in the display adapter to whatever color set it needed. This would have affected the displays of other applications, as well as the display of the system itself. The Windows team had to find some way to allow an application to make use of the increased color range without doing too much damage to the appearance of the other applications that might be running at the same time. And of course it was important that the system always be capable of showing a dialog box, for example, without having to worry about setting the colors it would need into the display adapter hardware first.

The solution underwent several iterations before it was considered acceptable. The key word here is *acceptable*—as opposed to *right*. An application creates and uses a *logical palette,* which contains a description of the color set the application would *like* to use. The system reserves the set of 20 colors we noted in Chapter 2, the set that all applications and the system itself can use at any time without regard to the current hardware palette state. The application currently in the foreground gets first choice in choosing the set of colors in the actual physical hardware palette. By giving the foreground application first choice of the palette colors, the system keeps the user happy most of the time because the application that is getting most of the user's attention is the one that gets to select the color set. Applications in the background have to make do with the colors they're given, but Windows helps the background applications out a bit by trying to accommodate their color needs too. If the foreground application hasn't used all the free hardware palette color entries, the background applications get to use the remaining entries on a first-come-first-served basis. When all the free slots are used up, Windows tries to map the colors requested by the background applications to those currently set in the hardware. This accommodation results in a recognizable, if not wonderful, rendition of the background application's images.

A lot of details are involved in palette management for Windows. Some are more relevant to the design of an application, some less so. We'll look at the ones that affect us as we encounter them.

Logical Palettes

An application creates and uses a logical palette to request a set of colors it would *like* to work with. A logical palette can have from 1 through 256 entries. Each entry in the logical palette describes the red, green, and blue levels of the color as a value from *0* through *255*. Each entry also contains some optional flags that modify the ways in which the color is used. Creating a logical palette involves filling in the data in a LOGPALETTE structure and calling the Windows *CreatePalette* function. Here is the LOGPALETTE structure from WINGDI.H:

```
typedef struct tagLOGPALETTE {
    WORD         palVersion;
    WORD         palNumEntries;
    PALETTEENTRY palPalEntry[1];
} LOGPALETTE, *PLOGPALETTE, NEAR *NPLOGPALETTE, FAR *LPLOGPALETTE;
```

The key fields are *palNumEntries*, which determines the number of colors in the palette, and the *palPalEntry* array, which holds the color and flag entries. Each entry consists of a PALETTEENTRY structure, which is shown below:

```
typedef struct tagPALETTEENTRY {
    BYTE         peRed;
    BYTE         peGreen;
    BYTE         peBlue;
    BYTE         peFlags;
} PALETTEENTRY, *PPALETTEENTRY, FAR *LPPALETTEENTRY;
```

Note that each of the red, green, and blue entries is a *BYTE* value from *0* through *255*. The *peFlags* field is normally set to *0* but can be set to one of the values shown in **Table 3-1**.

Table 3-1
PALETTEENTRY flags

Name	Value	Meaning
PC_EXPLICIT	0x02	If this flag is set, the entry is considered to be a single *DWORD* value whose low-order *WORD* is an index into the hardware palette. This enables an application to request a specific hardware palette entry that can be used to show the current palette color.
PC_NOCOLLAPSE	0x04	If this flag is set, the color can't be mapped to an existing color in the hardware palette; it must have an entry of its own.
PC_RESERVED	0x01	If this flag is set, the color will be used for palette animation, so don't map another application's color to this entry.

Once the entries in the LOGPALETTE structure are complete, you can create a palette this way:

```
LOGPALETTE lp;
CPalette pal;
    ⋮
pal.CreatePalette(&lp);
```

When the application wants to use the colors defined in the logical palette, it selects the palette into a device context (DC) in a way similar to selecting a pen or a brush. Then the application asks the system to set the colors in the logical palette:

```
CDC* pDC;
CPalette* pOldPal;
    ⋮
pOldPal = pDC->SelectPalette(&pal, FALSE);
pDC->RealizePalette;
```

Note that we don't use the *SelectObject* function and that simply selecting the palette into the DC is not enough—we must also make a call to *RealizePalette* to get the colors actually mapped into place. From then on, the application can use colors that are in the palette for drawing to the DC, and the result should come out as expected. When the drawing is complete, the DC is restored to its original state:

```
pDC->SelectPalette(pOldPal);
```

What do I mean by "should come out as expected"? Well, the results of requesting a given logical palette are not always exactly what you might like.

If your application is not currently the foreground application, it's quite possible that the application in the foreground has set the current color set to one of its own choosing, and your application's request for a color set must somehow be made to fit in with the color set that has already been chosen. The chances of your getting what you expected are therefore slim.

Let's say your application *is* the foreground application. What are the limits now? The system reserves 20 colors for its own use. If your palette consists of 256 colors, none of which are the same as any of the 20 reserved system colors, you obviously can't have all the colors in your palette active—you'd be trying to fit 256 colors into 236 free slots. Some of them would have to go.

To understand this better, let's look at the system hardware palette and at how colors are mapped to it.

The Hardware Palette

The organization of colors in the hardware (physical) palette might at first seem irrelevant to an applications programmer's color concerns, and for application colors other than the 20 system reserved colors, it is. The 20 reserved system colors are often inverted by means of the XOR operator and then restored by use of the same operator again. On a VGA display, the color red, for example, always inverts to cyan, and cyan inverts to red. In order for this to work on a palettized display, the index value for red must become the index value for cyan when it's inverted. So if the index value for red is *1* (0x01) and it's given that we have 8 bits or 1 byte for each pixel, the index value for cyan has to be *254* (0xFE). That accounts for the reason the system colors have to be placed, as we noted in Chapter 2, half at one end of the hardware palette and half at the other end. *Figure 3-1* shows the arrangement.

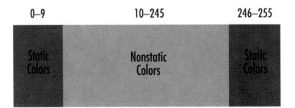

Figure 3-1   *The layout of the hardware palette.*

Table 3-2 on the facing page lists the static colors, their positions in the hardware palette, and their color values.

Close scrutiny of the table reveals some weirdness: entry 247 is 160, 160, 164, for instance. Why? Who knows—I guess it just looked better that way on someone's monitor in those bygone days. Since our eyes don't perceive different colors that have the same intensity as having the same brightness, it is reasonable to alter the physical intensity levels in order to compensate for the nonlinearity of our optical systems.

Mapping Logical Colors to the Physical Palette

On to more important stuff—the way your colors get mapped to the hardware palette. When you make the call to *RealizePalette*, each color in your logical palette is mapped to a color in the system palette. The process starts with the first color in your logical palette and ends with the last one. Because of this mapping order, the colors at the beginning of your logical palette have a higher probability of being realized exactly than those at the end. If some colors are more important to you than others, put them at the beginning of the logical palette.

To map a color from the logical palette to a physical palette entry, the Palette Manager first looks for an existing entry in the physical palette with an exact match of the red, green, and blue values. It looks first at entry 0 and walks up through entry 255. If it finds an exact match, it maps your color to that physical palette entry.

If it doesn't find an exact match, the Palette Manager searches the physical palette, starting again from index 0, for an unused entry. If it finds

Table 3-2
The 20 Static Colors

Index	Color	Red	Green	Blue
0	Black	0	0	0
1	Dark Red	128	0	0
2	Dark Green	0	128	0
3	Dark Yellow	128	128	0
4	Dark Blue	0	0	128
5	Dark Magenta	128	0	128
6	Dark Cyan	0	128	128
7	Light Gray	192	192	192
8	Money Green	192	220	192
9	Sky Blue	166	202	240
246	Cream	255	251	240
247	Medium Gray	160	160	164
248	Dark Gray	128	128	128
249	Red	255	0	0
250	Green	0	255	0
251	Yellow	255	255	0
252	Blue	0	0	255
253	Magenta	255	0	255
254	Cyan	0	255	255
255	White	255	255	255

an unused entry, it copies the RGB values of your color to the physical palette, and your logical color is thus mapped to that physical palette entry. If there are no free entries in the physical palette, the Palette Manager searches the palette, starting at index 0 again, for the color that most closely matches the color your logical palette requested and maps your palette entry to that physical palette entry.

The closeness of the colors to one another is determined by considering the red, green, and blue components of a color as orthogonal vectors in a three-dimensional space. The distance between one color and another is the square root of the sum of the squares of the differences among the colors' individual red, green, and blue vectors. This algorithm provides an acceptable result in a reasonable computation time. I wouldn't say it's a wonderful algorithm. It's just the one that's in there, so it's the one we need to understand and deal with.

Several factors modify the color-mapping process. The most important is whether your application is the foreground application or one of the background applications. If it's the foreground application, there is a good chance that none of the nonstatic colors is in use; therefore, there are 236 unused entries in the hardware palette for your colors to be mapped into. If your application is currently not the foreground application, there may be no free entries at all in the hardware palette, and all of your colors will have to be mapped to whatever colors are currently defined.

The mapping process is further modified by the optional flags we saw in Table 3-1 that are used to define the colors in the logical palette. If a color in the hardware palette has the PC_RESERVED flag set, no other colors will be mapped to it. This flag is set by an application that will animate the palette entry. Obviously, there is little point in the Palette Manager's mapping your color request to a hardware palette entry that is going to change with time. If you set the PC_NOCOLLAPSE flag in one of your logical palette entries, the Palette Manager will not try to map that color to any existing entry. Instead, the Palette Manager will begin by searching for a free entry in the hardware palette. The PC_NOCOLLAPSE flag is often used in paint programs, in which the palette may contain several entries that are the same color at the time the palette is realized but that may change later at the user's discretion.

Figure 3-2 shows in general terms how entries in a logical palette are mapped to the physical palette for the foreground application. In this case, the logical palette does not contain any of the 20 reserved system colors.

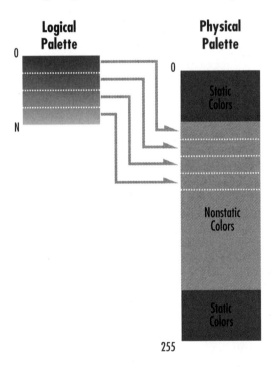

Figure 3-2 *Mapping a foreground application's colors to the physical palette.*

If the same application were not the foreground application, the mapping would look something like that shown in **Figure 3-3**.

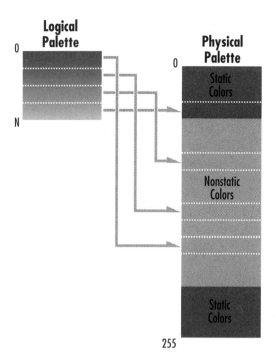

Figure 3-3 *Mapping a background application's colors to the physical palette.*

Figures 3-2 and 3-3 don't quite do justice to the way GDI actually maps logical to physical palette indices. The process is a little more complex than I've indicated here, but trust me, seeing more detail doesn't make the picture any easier to understand!

As you can see, the foreground application typically gets the majority of the colors it requests and a background application has to make do with what has already been defined.

Using the COLORREF Macros to Specify the Color You Want

Having created a palette, selected it into a DC, and realized it, how do we use the colors we've defined in it? Windows functions that use color take a COLORREF structure as an argument. A COLORREF is a 32-bit value that is used to hold either an RGB value or a palette index. Three variants of the COLORREF structure are shown in **Figures 3-4**, **3-5**, and **3-6**.

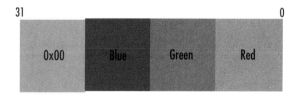

Figure 3-4 *The component parts of a COLORREF structure holding an RGB value.*

Figure 3-5 *The component parts of a COLORREF structure holding a palette index value.*

Note that the 32 bits are used here in a way totally different from the way they are used to hold an RGB value, for example.

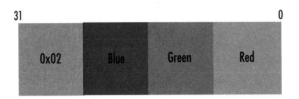

Figure 3-6 *The component parts of a COLORREF structure holding a palette RGB value.*

The simplest of these three variants is the one shown in Figure 3-4, in which the color is simply defined as the amounts of red, green, and blue it contains. The RGB macro can be used to create a COLORREF structure this way. For example, we could create a solid red brush:

```
brRed.CreateSolidBrush(RGB(255,0,0));
```

<table>
<tr><td>

NOTE

Dithering (in case you don't know) is using patterns of dots in a number of fixed colors (typically two colors) to simulate a different color. For example, if we alternate between black and white pixels and stand far enough away that we can't distinguish the individual pixels, we see gray. The eye integrates the individual elements, giving us the impression of a single solid color.

</td></tr>
</table>

On a palettized display device, RGB colors are always matched to a simple VGA color or dithered from the VGA colors, so even if you have a current palette with the same RGB values as you use in the RGB macro, you won't get the color in your palette. (More about this in a minute.)

If you know the palette has the color you want at a specific index position, you can construct a COLORREF structure using the PALETTEINDEX macro, supplying the index value:

```
brRed.CreateSolidBrush(PALETTEINDEX(23));
```

On the palettized display device, you will always get the color in the currently selected palette that corresponds to the index value you supply.

It is often convenient to create a "general" palette containing a wash of various RGB combinations that will provide acceptable results for a range of images. It is unfortunate that using the RGB macro to select a color won't result in one of the palette colors being picked. As I mentioned above, the RGB macro will result in a dithered color on a palettized device. We can avoid this problem by using the PALETTERGB macro, which specifies that the RGB values provided should be matched against the nearest color in the current palette and that the index for that color should be used just as if we had used the PALETTEINDEX macro. So knowing that we have a palette with a variety of colors in it, we can specify RGB combinations and be sure to get a solid color, not one dithered from the VGA color set, this way:

```
brRed.CreateSolidBrush(PALETTERGB(29,37,5));
```

If an exact match isn't made, the nearest palette color is used. To summarize, you can specify colors in three ways: as an arbitrary RGB value, as an RGB value to be matched against colors in the current palette, or as an index into the current palette.

Palette Messages

Applications that use palettes need to handle two palette-specific messages: WM_QUERYNEWPALETTE and WM_PALETTECHANGED. For purists, there is another message, WM_PALETTEISCHANGING, but this is a Friday-afternoon feature of the system and should be ignored for all new development work.

NOTE

A Friday-afternoon feature is one that was added without too much thought in order to get something to work before the weekend.

The WM_QUERYNEWPALETTE message is sent to your application as a part of the activation process in which your application receives the focus and gives you an opportunity to select and realize the palette you want the application to work with. Remember that Windows shares the physical palette among all applications, so as the user clicks from application to application the physical palette needs to be remapped from whichever application is currently in the foreground. The WM_QUERYNEWPALETTE message is the start of the remapping process.

After the foreground application calls *RealizePalette* and the hardware palette changes, Windows sends a WM_PALETTECHANGED message to all applications to let them know that the hardware palette has changed and to give each of them an opportunity to realize their own palettes and remap their colors to the current hardware palette. Background applications can also redraw themselves at this time to maintain the best possible image. The foreground application that caused the palette to change should not respond to the WM_PALETTECHANGED message. If it does, a loop may occur within Windows. (I know—you'd think this would be detected automatically, but it isn't, so we have to deal with it.) The WM_PALETTECHANGED message *wParam* value contains the window handle of the window that caused the system palette to change.

A typical C-code application with only one palette to manage might have a window message procedure something like this to handle its palette messages:

```
case WM_PALETTECHANGED:
    if (wParam == hWnd) {
        break;
    }
    // Else fall through
case WM_QUERYNEWPALETTE:
    hDC = GetDC(hWnd);
    hOldPal = SelectPalette(hDC, hpalCurrent, FALSE);
```

(continued)

```
    i = RealizePalette(hDC);
    if (i != 0) {
        InvalidateRect(hWnd, NULL, TRUE);
    }

    SelectPalette(hDC, hOldPal, TRUE);
    RealizePalette(hDC);
    ReleaseDC(hWnd, hDC);
    return i;
```

Note that if *RealizePalette* returns a nonzero value (actually the number of colors that were changed) then we need to perform a paint operation to ensure that we repaint the entire window with the correct colors. We'll look at handling palette messages in a Microsoft Foundation Class Library (MFC) application in the next chapter, where we'll also look at handling multiple palettes in one application.

Will My Code Run on a Nonpalette Device?

Yes. Next question. If you use the RGB or PALETTERGB macro to define a color, the actual red, green, and blue values are used as the color. If you use the PALETTEINDEX macro to define a color, the index value is dereferenced in the current logical palette color array to find the actual red, green, and blue values. No palette messages are sent if the display device doesn't have a palette. So your application runs exactly the same way even when no palette is present. **Table 3-3** shows the behavior of the three COLORREF-generating macros on palettized and nonpalettized devices.

Table 3-3
Color Macros and Their Behavior on Different Display Devices

Macro	Behavior on Palettized Device	Behavior on Nonpalettized Device
RGB	Matches to solid VGA color or dithers from VGA colors.	Matches to a device color or dithers from device colors.
PALETTEINDEX	Uses the color at the index location in the current palette. This is always a solid color.	The index value is dereferenced in the logical palette to obtain the RGB values of the color. Same behavior as for the RGB macro.
PALETTERGB	*GetNearestPaletteIndex* is used to find the closest color in the current palette. This is always a solid color.	Same behavior as for the RGB macro.

When dealing with nonpalettized devices, you should bear a few points in mind. On a 24- or 32-bpp display, an RGB value will be used "as is" to set the color, but on a 16-bpp display this is not possible. Consider a 16-bpp display that uses 5 bits for red, 5 bits for green, and 5 bits for blue. Because you can specify RGB values as 8 bits each for red, green, and blue, you can obviously specify colors that can't be stored exactly on a 16-bpp display. If the color can't be stored exactly, it is constructed by means of dithering from some of the "device" colors—that is, the set of colors that *can* be stored directly on the 16-bpp display.

This dithering on 16-bpp displays can sometimes result in a worse-looking image than is possible on an 8-bpp palettized display. How can a 65,000-color display look worse than a 256-color display? Consider a color wash that fades from bright blue (RGB—0,0,255) to black. On an 8-bpp palettized display, we can use 236 colors for the wash (ignoring the 20 reserved system colors). That means that on a 640-by-480 display a wash from top to bottom (480 lines) will have a different physical color for approximately every two lines, which will result in a very nice looking wash. The same wash done on a 16-bpp 5-5-5 display won't look as good. If the display doesn't dither, there are only 2^5 (32) possible shades of blue, so a 480-line wash will have a physical color change only about every 17 lines, which is nowhere near as good as we had for the 8-bpp device. If the 16-bpp display uses dithering, it can smooth out the transitions between the physical colors, but the result will be somewhat grainy and still not as good as in the 8-bpp palettized case.

Looking at the Current Hardware Palette

Since it can be rather hard to tell whether your palette was realized in the manner you expected, it's useful to have a way to view the current state of the hardware palette. The SysPal sample application draws the current state of the system palette in its window and allows the mouse to be used to test the RGB values of any point on the screen. You can look at the actual RGB values of the system palette entries by clicking a color in the SysPal window, or you can click in the SysPal window to capture the mouse, move over the entire screen, and observe the RGB values of any pixel.

\anim32\syspal

SysPal was initially created with AppWizard as a basic single-document interface (SDI) application. I then ripped out all the code for the document-view architecture and implemented what I wanted in two source modules: SYSPAL.CPP and MAINFRM.CPP. Because SysPal is such a trivial application, we'll look at only the salient points here. I'll leave you to browse through the rest of the code some other time.

Since I removed all the document-view code that indirectly created the main window, I had to create the main window myself. The initialization code from SYSPAL.CPP is shown on the next page.

```
BOOL CSyspalApp::InitInstance()
{
    CFrameWnd* pWnd = new CMainFrame;
    RECT rcWnd;
    rcWnd.top = 0;
    rcWnd.left = ::GetSystemMetrics(SM_CXSCREEN) * 4 / 5;
    rcWnd.bottom = ::GetSystemMetrics(SM_CYSCREEN) / 5;
    rcWnd.right = ::GetSystemMetrics(SM_CXSCREEN);
    pWnd->Create(NULL,
                 "SysPal",
                 WS_OVERLAPPEDWINDOW,
                 rcWnd);
    pWnd->ShowWindow(SW_SHOW);
    m_pMainWnd = pWnd;
    HCURSOR hCur = LoadCursor(IDR_MAINFRAME);
    SetClassLong(pWnd->GetSafeHwnd(), GCL_HCURSOR, (LONG)hCur);
    return TRUE;
}
```

As you can see, this is quite simple. A frame window is created in a fixed position, and the cursor is changed to be a more useful shape for selecting a single pixel. The rest of the code is in MAINFRM.CPP. Here's the constructor code that creates the palette we'll be using:

```
CMainFrame::CMainFrame()
{
    // Create a palette.
    // Allocate a logical color palette and fill it with the
    // color table information.
    LOGPALETTE* pPal = (LOGPALETTE*) malloc(sizeof(LOGPALETTE) +
                                     256 * sizeof(PALETTEENTRY));
    if (pPal) {
        pPal->palVersion = 0x300;   // Windows 3.0
        pPal->palNumEntries = 256; // table size
        for (int i=0; i<256; i++) {
            pPal->palPalEntry[i].peRed = i;
            pPal->palPalEntry[i].peGreen = 0;
            pPal->palPalEntry[i].peBlue = 0;
            pPal->palPalEntry[i].peFlags = PC_EXPLICIT;
        }
        m_pal.CreatePalette(pPal);
        free (pPal);
    }
    m_bCaptured = FALSE;
}
```

A LOGPALETTE structure is set up with 256 color entries. Each entry is set up to be an explicit index into the system palette by means of the PC_EXPLICIT flag. Note that we are not creating a red color here. The "red" byte is simply the low-order byte of the palette index word. See Figure 3-6 back on page 48 if you still don't follow this. A *CPalette* object is created and kept as a member of the *CMainFrame* object so that we can use it later.

Here's the paint routine that shows the current system palette state:

```
void CMainFrame::OnPaint()
{
    CPaintDC dc(this); // Device context for painting
    dc.SelectPalette(&m_pal, FALSE);
    dc.RealizePalette();
    CRect rc;
    GetClientRect(&rc);
    int i, j, top, left, bottom, right;
    for (j=0, top=0; j<m_iYCells; j++, top=bottom) {
        bottom = (j+1) * rc.bottom / m_iYCells + 1;
        for (i=0, left=0; i<m_iXCells; i++, left=right) {
            right = (i+1) * rc.right / m_iXCells + 1;
            CBrush br (PALETTEINDEX(j * m_iXCells + i));
            CBrush* brold = dc.SelectObject(&br);
            dc.Rectangle(left-1, top-1, right, bottom);
            dc.SelectObject(brold);
        }
    }
}
```

The palette is selected and realized in the window DC, and a series of rectangles is drawn, each one with a different brush that is created by means of the PALETTEINDEX macro, which specifies its color. The organization of the cells is chosen in an attempt to keep the aspect ratio approximately square as the shape of the window changes.

If the mouse is clicked in the window area, the mouse is captured and the current pixel RGB value is displayed in the window caption area:

```
void CMainFrame::OnLButtonDown(UINT nFlags, CPoint point)
{
    SetCapture();
    m_bCaptured = TRUE;
    ShowRGB(point);
}

void CMainFrame::OnLButtonUp(UINT nFlags, CPoint point)
{
    if (m_bCaptured) {
        ReleaseCapture();
        m_bCaptured = FALSE;
        SetWindowText("SysPal"); // Restore title.
    }
}
```

(continued)

```
void CMainFrame::OnMouseMove(UINT nFlags, CPoint point)
{
    if (m_bCaptured) {
        ShowRGB(point);
    }
}

void CMainFrame::ShowRGB(CPoint point)
{
    HDC hDC = ::GetDC(NULL);
    ClientToScreen(&point);
    COLORREF rgb = ::GetPixel(hDC, point.x, point.y);
    char buf[64];
    sprintf(buf, "RGB(%d,%d,%d)",
            GetRValue(rgb),
            GetGValue(rgb),
            GetBValue(rgb));
    SetWindowText(buf);
    ::ReleaseDC(NULL, hDC);
}
```

Not much rocket science here—which is as it should be. The mouse coordinates in the window are converted to screen coordinates. A DC for the screen is obtained, and *GetPixel* is used to retrieve the RGB value of the pixel. The red, green, and blue values are then shown in the application's title bar area.

Oh No, I've Burst My Brain!

Don't panic. The fear you are feeling is a perfectly natural reaction to dealing with palettes in Windows. I recommend a brief lie-down followed by a good practical experiment.

Run SysPal and see what happens as other applications that use palettes are run on the system. Experiment with making different applications the foreground application, and see what happens. If you don't have any applications that use 256-color images, try running the ViewDIB sample. You can run two instances of ViewDIB or just open two different images in a single instance of ViewDIB. As you change the currently active image, you'll see the system palette change. Play with this for a while and then review the chapter. You'll find it's not as hard to follow as you might at first think.

Now that we understand a bit about palettes, we can move on to create a C++ class to handle palettes in a way that will be useful to us in drawing 256-color DIBs.

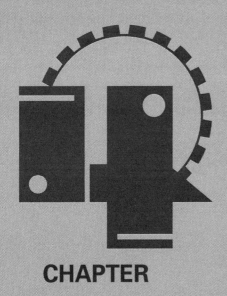

CHAPTER

A Palette
Class for DIBs

The *CDIBPal* Class

An Application for Viewing Palettes

An Application for Viewing DIBs

Confused?

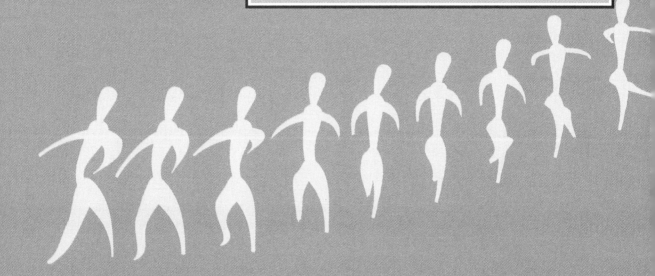

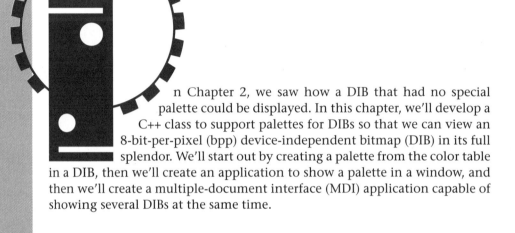

n Chapter 2, we saw how a DIB that had no special palette could be displayed. In this chapter, we'll develop a C++ class to support palettes for DIBs so that we can view an 8-bit-per-pixel (bpp) device-independent bitmap (DIB) in its full splendor. We'll start out by creating a palette from the color table in a DIB, then we'll create an application to show a palette in a window, and then we'll create a multiple-document interface (MDI) application capable of showing several DIBs at the same time.

The *CDIBPal* Class

The examples in this chapter use and enhance the *CDIB* class from Chapter 2. *CDIBPal* is a very simple class derived from *CPalette*. The *CPalette* class is provided by the Microsoft Foundation Class Library (MFC) as a wrapper around a Microsoft Windows palette object. *CDIBPal* provides a few functions that *CPalette* doesn't have and in particular allows you to create a *CDIBPal* object from the color table in a *CDIB* object.

To support creating a *CDIBPal* object from a *CDIB* object, we first have to add to the *CDIB* class a function that returns the number of entries in the DIB color table. DIB.CPP already has a private function to calculate the number of color table entries given a pointer to a BITMAPINFO structure, so adding a public function to return the number of color table entries in the DIB becomes trivial:

```
int CDIB::GetNumClrEntries()
{
    return NumDIBColorEntries(m_pBMI);
}
```

We'll begin construction of the *CDIBPal* class by creating three functions. One function will create a palette from a *CDIB* object, another will return the number of colors in the palette, and the third will draw the colors of the palette to a device context (DC) so that we can see it. Here's the header file CDIBPAL.H:

```
class CDIBPal : public CPalette
{
public:
    CDIBPal();
    ~CDIBPal();
    BOOL Create(CDIB* pDIB);         // Create from a DIB.
    int GetNumColors();              // Get the number of colors
                                     // in the palette.
    void Draw(CDC* pDC, CRect* pRect);  // Draw to a DC.
};
```

Let's take the functions one at a time. First let's see how a palette is created from the color table in a *CDIB* object:

```
BOOL CDIBPal::Create(CDIB* pDIB)
{
    DWORD dwColors = pDIB->GetNumClrEntries();
    // Check to see whether the DIB has a color table.
    if (!dwColors) {
        TRACE("No color table");
        return FALSE;
    }

    // Get a pointer to the RGB quads in the color table.
    RGBQUAD* pRGB = pDIB->GetClrTabAddress();

    // Allocate a logical palette, and fill it with the color table info.
    LOGPALETTE* pPal = (LOGPALETTE*) malloc(sizeof(LOGPALETTE) +
                                 dwColors * sizeof(PALETTEENTRY));
    if (!pPal) {
        TRACE("Out of memory for logical palette");
        return FALSE;
    }
    pPal->palVersion = 0x300;            // Windows 3.0
    pPal->palNumEntries = (WORD) dwColors; // Table size
    for (DWORD dw=0; dw<dwColors; dw++) {
        pPal->palPalEntry[dw].peRed = pRGB[dw].rgbRed;
        pPal->palPalEntry[dw].peGreen = pRGB[dw].rgbGreen;
        pPal->palPalEntry[dw].peBlue = pRGB[dw].rgbBlue;
        pPal->palPalEntry[dw].peFlags = 0;
    }
    BOOL bResult = CreatePalette(pPal);
    free(pPal);
    return bResult;
}
```

First a call to the *GetNumClrEntries* function of the *CDIB* object confirms that the object has a palette and finds out how many colors are in it. If the DIB doesn't have a palette, *Create* simply returns.

A LOGPALETTE structure is allocated large enough for the header and all the color entries the palette will need. The structure is filled with data from the DIB's color table. Note that the organization of the red, green, and blue fields of a PALETTEENTRY structure is different from the organization of those fields in an RGBQUAD structure, so the fields have to be copied individually.

Once all the data has been copied, a call is made to *CreatePalette* to construct the actual Windows palette object. GDI copies the data from the LOG-PALETTE structure we supply when we call *CreatePalette*, so once the call returns, we can free the LOGPALETTE structure memory.

Later we will need to be able to get the number of colors in the palette when we draw it, so let's look at how that's done:

```
int CDIBPal::GetNumColors()
{
    int iColors = 0;
    if (!GetObject(sizeof(iColors), &iColors)) {
        TRACE("Failed to get the number of colors in the palette");
        return 0;
    }
    return iColors;
}
```

CDIBPal is derived from *CPalette*, which is in turn derived from *CGDI-Object*, and all *CGDIObject* objects support the *GetObject* function. *GetObject* returns different data for the various graphics device interface (GDI) objects, such as brushes, pens, and so on. For a palette object, *GetObject* returns an *int* value containing the number of colors in the palette. So a call to *GetObject* on a *CDIBPal* object could be used to get the number of colors in the palette, but it's a bit unwieldy to use because it returns data through a structure passed as a parameter to the call. To make it easy to get the number of colors in a *CDIBPal* object, the *GetNumColors* function does the dirty work for you. (Remember that *CDIBPal* inherits from *CPalette*, so the *GetObject* call used here is actually *CPalette::GetObject*.)

The *Create* function is really the only one we need to make *CDIBPal* useful in drawing a DIB with a palette, which is the main goal of the *CDIBPal* class, but I thought it would be fun to add a *Draw* function to the class so that we could see what the colors in a logical palette created from the color table in a DIB would look like when the palette was realized into the screen DC. Here's the *Draw* function:

```
void CDIBPal::Draw(CDC* pDC, CRect* pRect)
{
    int iColors = GetNumColors();
    CPalette* pOldPal = pDC->SelectPalette(this, FALSE);
```

```
    pDC->RealizePalette();
    int i, j, top, left, bottom, right;
    for (j=0, top=0; j<16 && iColors; j++, top=bottom) {
        bottom = (j+1) * pRect->bottom / 16 + 1;
        for (i=0, left=0; i<16 && iColors; i++, left=right) {
            right = (i+1) * pRect->right / 16 + 1;
            CBrush br (PALETTEINDEX(j * 16 + i));
            CBrush* brold = pDC->SelectObject(&br);
            pDC->Rectangle(left-1, top-1, right, bottom);
            pDC->SelectObject(brold);
            iColors--;
        }
    }
    pDC->SelectPalette(pOldPal, FALSE);
}
```

The palette is selected into the DC and realized, thus mapping its colors to the physical palette. Then, for every color entry in the palette, a rectangle is drawn and filled with a brush created in the color of the palette index. The boxes are arranged in a 16-by-16 grid, but only one box per palette entry is filled. If the palette has only 16 colors, only 16 boxes are filled.

NOTE

When a palette is selected into a DC, it must be realized before its colors can be used.

An Application for Viewing Palettes

So that we can test the *CDIBPal* class and see the palette in a DIB, let's create a simple single-document interface (SDI) application that will open a DIB file (.BMP), create a *CDIBPal* object from it, and draw the palette colors in the view window. See the box on the next page for the procedure we'll follow.

\anim32\showpal

The document has a single member variable to hold the palette and a function to return the current palette:

```
class CShowPalDoc : public CDocument
{
    :
    :
// Attributes
public:
    CDIBPal* GetPalette() {return m_pPal;}
    :
    :
private:
    CDIBPal* m_pPal;

};
```

Notice that we use a pointer to the object here because the wrapped GDI objects in MFC do not take kindly to being re-created. It is simplest to create an object when it's needed and destroy it when it's not needed.

NOTE

In general, the *Create* member functions of MFC's GDI objects can be called only once. Read up on the *Attach* and *Detach* member functions for information on how MFC objects wrap their GDI counterparts.

Procedure

1. Use AppWizard to create a simple SDI application.

2. Add the *CDIB* and *CDIBPal* .CPP files to the project make file.

3. Include DIB.H and DIBPAL.H in the application main .CPP file, the document .CPP file, and the view .CPP file.

4. Add a *CDIBPal m_pPal* member variable to the document header file.

5. Add constructor, destructor, and serialization code to the document file.

6. Add draw code to the view class.

7. Use App Studio to remove unused menu items and bitmaps and to create an icon.

8. Add handlers for the palette messages to the MAINFRM.CPP file and the view code.

The document file needs some simple code to handle construction, destruction, and document initialization:

```
CShowPalDoc::CShowPalDoc()
{
    m_pPal = NULL;
}


CShowPalDoc::~CShowPalDoc()
{
    if (m_pPal) delete m_pPal;
}


BOOL CShowPalDoc::OnNewDocument()
{
    if (!CDocument::OnNewDocument())
        return FALSE;
    if (m_pPal) {
        delete m_pPal;
        m_pPal = NULL;
    }
    return TRUE;
}
```

To support the idea of opening a palette from a DIB file, the serialization code for the document opens the DIB file and creates the palette object from it:

```
void CShowPalDoc::Serialize(CArchive& ar)
{
    if (ar.IsStoring()) {
        ASSERT(1); // We don't do this.
    } else {
        // Get the file from the archive.
        CFile* fp = ar.GetFile();
        ASSERT(fp);
        ar.Flush();
        // Load the DIB from the file.
        CDIB dib;
        if (!dib.Load(fp)) {
            AfxMessageBox("Failed to load DIB file");
            return;
        }
        // Create the palette from the DIB.
        if (m_pPal) delete m_pPal;
        m_pPal = new CDIBPal;
        ASSERT(m_pPal);
        if (!m_pPal->Create(&dib)) {
            AfxMessageBox("Failed to create palette from DIB file");
            delete m_pPal;
            m_pPal = NULL;
        }
    }
}
```

Notice that we don't keep the DIB around once the palette has been created. The palette creation will fail if the DIB has no palette—not too surprisingly! This will happen, for example, if you try to open a 24-bpp DIB.

Having created a palette in the document, we now need to add some code to the *OnDraw* function of the view to show the palette:

```
void CShowPalView::OnDraw(CDC* pDC)
{
    CShowPalDoc* pDoc = GetDocument();
    ASSERT(pDoc);
    CDIBPal* pPal = pDoc->GetPalette();
    if (!pPal) return;
    CRect rc;
    GetClientRect(&rc);
    pPal->Draw(pDC, &rc);
}
```

NOTE

A 16- or 24-bpp DIB file might contain a palette. Its colors would be a hint about the best set of colors to use on an 8-bpp display.

The palette is obtained from the document, and its *Draw* function is called to draw it into the entire client rectangle of the view window. Pretty simple stuff.

Not all palettes have 256 colors, and to make it obvious that only some boxes in the grid are drawn, I used ClassWizard to add a handler for the WM_ERASEBKGND message in the view class. The handler fills the background with a hatch brush pattern.

```
BOOL CShowPalView::OnEraseBkgnd(CDC* pDC)
{
    // Fill the background with a hatch brush so that it will show up
    // the areas not covered by palette entries.
    CBrush br;
    br.CreateHatchBrush(HS_FDIAGONAL, RGB(128,128,128));
    CRect rc;
    GetClientRect(&rc);
    pDC->FillRect(&rc, &br);
    return TRUE;
}
```

A brush is created and used to fill the entire client area. The diagonal hatch pattern differs greatly in appearance from the solid colors of the grid squares drawn by the *CDIBPal Draw* function, so the grid squares show up nicely against this background.

You could compile and test at this point. It would work quite well, but you'd notice that changing the currently active application to one that has its own palette wouldn't cause the ShowPal application to redraw its window. Instead, the ShowPal colors would simply change to some random set chosen by the other application. To fix this problem, we need to add handlers for the WM_PALETTECHANGED and WM_QUERYNEWPALETTE messages.

Unfortunately, although these messages are received by the application's frame window, they are not passed on to the view window, so we can't simply add the handlers to the view. The handlers must be added to the main frame window class. Adding the handlers to the frame isn't quite enough, though, because the frame doesn't know about the palette that the view needs to realize, so the frame must send the messages down to the view for processing.

We can use ClassWizard to add the handlers for processing the WM_PALETTECHANGED and WM_QUERYNEWPALETTE messages directly to the *CMainFrame* class. To use ClassWizard to add the handlers to the view class, we must temporarily change the class type of the view from child window to topmost frame window. By altering the filter ClassWizard uses in this way, we can then add handlers for the WM_PALETTECHANGED and WM_QUERYNEWPALETTE messages to the view class. If we don't change the window type, ClassWizard will show only messages that it thinks we might need for a child window. Since child windows don't normally handle palette messages, they wouldn't be visible in the list. Once we've added the handlers for the two palette messages, we can change the class type back to child window. Remember, the filter that ClassWizard uses has nothing to do with which messages the window will actually receive; the filter is just a convenience for you when you're creating the application framework.

The code in the frame window handlers simply passes the messages to the view. Unfortunately, the *On...* handlers in the view class that ClassWizard creates (*OnPaletteChanged* and *OnQueryNewPalette*, for example) are not public, so we can't call them directly from the frame class. I chose instead to simply send the palette messages to the view. Here's the code in MAINFRM.CPP that does this:

```
void CMainFrame::OnPaletteChanged(CWnd* pFocusWnd)
{
    CView* pView = GetActiveView();
    if (pView) {
        // OnPaletteChanged is not public, so send a message.
        pView->SendMessage(WM_PALETTECHANGED,
                        (WPARAM)(pFocusWnd->GetSafeHwnd()),
                        (LPARAM)0);
    }
}


// Note: Windows ignores the return value.
BOOL CMainFrame::OnQueryNewPalette()
{
    CView* pView = GetActiveView();
    if (pView) {
        // OnQueryNewPalette is not public, so send a message.
        return pView >SendMessage(WM_QUERYNEWPALETTE,
                        (WPARAM)0,
                        (LPARAM)0);
    }
    return FALSE;
}
```

In both cases, a pointer to the view is obtained and the message is forwarded. The view class handlers actually do the work, and the code looks like this:

```
void CShowPalView::OnPaletteChanged(CWnd* pFocusWnd)
{
    // See if the change was caused by us, and ignore it if not.
    if (pFocusWnd != this) {
        OnQueryNewPalette();
    }
}


// Note: Windows actually ignores the return value.
BOOL CShowPalView::OnQueryNewPalette()
```

(continued)

```
{
    // We are going active or the system palette has changed,
    // so realize our palette.
    CShowPalDoc* pDoc = GetDocument();
    ASSERT(pDoc);
    CDIBPal* pPal = pDoc->GetPalette();
    if (pPal) {
        CDC* pDC = GetDC();
        CPalette* pOldPal = pDC->SelectPalette(pPal, FALSE);
        UINT u = pDC->RealizePalette();
        ReleaseDC(pDC);
        if (u != 0) {
            // Some colors changed, so we need to do a repaint.
            InvalidateRect(NULL, TRUE); // Repaint the lot.
        }
    }
    return TRUE; // Windows ignores this.
}
```

If you refer back to the code in Chapter 3 (pages 49–50) that showed how this was done in C in a pre-MFC application, you'll see it's much the same, except that we can't conveniently fall through in the switch statement from one case to the next. Good thing too—I never did like that!

The *OnPaletteChanged* handler tests to see whether it was its own window that caused the palette to change, and if not, it calls *OnQueryNewPalette* to realize the palette. *OnQueryNewPalette* gets the current palette, selects it into the DC, and realizes it. If any of the colors are found to have changed, the whole image is redrawn to reflect the changes.

Now you can compile and test the code. Try running several instances of ShowPal at the same time as SysPal. Open different bitmaps in each of the ShowPal instances (with different palettes!), and click between the various applications to move the focus around. Watch what happens in the SysPal window as the system palette changes according to which logical palette is currently active in the foreground. Watch too what happens in each of the ShowPal windows. If you've followed the story so far, you should be able to explain what you see!

An Application for Viewing DIBs

\anim32\viewdib

Now that we have a class for DIBs and a class for their palettes, let's move right along and build a better DIB viewer. We'll take the concept of the BasicDIB application from Chapter 2 and add the *CDIB* and *CDIBPal* classes from this chapter to create a new version that shows 8-bpp DIBs with their correct colors. Remember that we added some code to *CDIB* to support palettes, so the

CDIB.CPP module here is not the older DIB.CPP from Chapter 2's BasicDIB sample. The new ViewDIB application will be able to show three different views for each DIB: the image, its palette, and its BITMAPINFO structure. See the box on pages 66 and 67 for an outline of the procedure.

The ViewDIB Application Code

We'll look at only the bits of ViewDIB that are concerned with palettes. The remainder of the code is fairly straightforward and uses the *CDIB* and *CDIBPal* classes we have used already. The *CDIBPal::Draw* function has to be modified slightly so that we can force the function to realize the palette in the background. The function acquires a new parameter to achieve this. Here are the new header description and code from CDIBPAL.H and CDIBPAL.CPP:

```
class CDIBPal : public CPalette
{
public:
    .
    .
    .
void Draw(CDC* pDC, CRect* pRect, BOOL bBkgnd = FALSE);
    .
    .
    .
};

void CDIBPal::Draw(CDC* pDC, CRect* pRect, BOOL bBkgnd)
{
    int iColors = GetNumColors();
    CPalette* pOldPal = pDC->SelectPalette(this, bBkgnd);
    pDC->RealizePalette();
    int i, j, top, left, bottom, right;
    for (j=0, top=0; j<16 && iColors; j++, top=bottom) {
        bottom = (j+1) * pRect->bottom / 16 + 1;
        for (i=0, left=0; i<16 && iColors; i++, left=right) {
            right = (i+1) * pRect->right / 16 + 1;
            CBrush br (PALETTEINDEX(j * 16 + i));
            CBrush* brold = pDC->SelectObject(&br);
            pDC->Rectangle(left-1, top-1, right, bottom);
            pDC->SelectObject(brold);
            iColors--;
        }
    }
    pDC->SelectPalette(pOldPal, FALSE);
}
```

The function prototype has a default condition for the new argument that will allow the function to behave as it did previously if the new argument is omitted. When the physical palette is shared among several images in a single application, the actual realization of the foreground palette is handled directly as the palette messages that establish which window is currently in the foreground are processed. The drawing operations are always realized in the background so that they don't affect the actual realization of the foreground palette by accident. For the current foreground window, the palette will be correctly realized by the message handling code before drawing takes place, so the rendering of the image will still come out right.

Let's look at the code that loads a document so that we can see how the DIB and palette for that document are created:

```
void CDibDoc::Serialize(CArchive& ar)
{
    if (ar.IsStoring()) {
        ASSERT(1); // We don't do this.
    } else {
        // Get the file from the archive.
        CFile* fp = ar.GetFile();
```

Procedure

1. Use AppWizard to create the framework of an MDI application. Name the application's document class *CDibDoc* and the view class *CDibImageView*. Make the default file extension .BMP.

2. Use App Studio to remove the unwanted menu items and bitmaps for File Save, Edit, and so on. Create an icon for the application and an icon for the image view class. Edit MAINFRM.CPP to delete support for any buttons you've removed. My application has only Open and About buttons on the toolbar. In VIEWDIB.CPP, remove the call to *OnFileNew*, which creates a new document at startup.

3. Do a full build, and check to see whether what you have done so far works.

4. Add the *CDIB* and *CDIBPal* .CPP and .H files from ShowPal to the project. Add DIB.H and DIBPAL.H to the .CPP files that need them.

5. In DIBDOC.H, add member variables for a *CDIB* pointer and a *CDIBPal* pointer. Add functions to return these pointers.

```
        ASSERT(fp);
        ar.Flush();
        // Load the DIB from the file.
        if (m_pDIB) delete m_pDIB;
        m_pDIB = new CDIB;
        if (!m_pDIB->Load(fp)) {
            AfxMessageBox("Failed to load DIB file");
            return;
        }
        // Create the palette from the DIB.
        if (m_pPal) delete m_pPal;
        m_pPal = new CDIBPal;
        ASSERT(m_pPal);
        if (!m_pPal->Create(m_pDIB)) {
            AfxMessageBox("Failed to create palette from DIB file");
            delete m_pPal;
            m_pPal = NULL;
        }
    }
}
```

6. In DIBDOC.CPP, add code for the constructor, destructor, initialization, and serialization of a document. Serialization creates a *CDIB* and a *CDIBPal*.

7. Add *OnDraw* code to IMAGEVW.CPP to draw the DIB using the DIB's palette.

8. Compile and test. The 8-bpp DIB should be OK now. Notice that we have no palette message handling yet, so the behavior as we change windows will be weird.

9. Add *GetWidth* and *GetHeight* functions to the *CDIB* class.

10. Convert the view class in IMAGEVW.CPP to be derived from *CScrollView*, implement *OnInitialUpdate* to resize the image to fit, and set the scroll range. Compile and test.

11. Add code to MAINFRM.CPP and IMAGEVW.CPP to handle palette messages and window activation. Compile and test with several DIBs that have different palettes. Notice that the *OnDraw* code changes to use TRUE in *SelectPalette* to force a background realization.

12. Add two more views, one to show the palette and one to show the DIB information. Note that the *CDIBPal::Draw* function is extended to allow the palette to be realized in the background.

The file associated with the archive is used to load a *CDIB* object. Then a new *CDIBPal* object is created from the data in the *CDIB* object. Pointers to the *CDIB* and *CDIBPal* objects are stored as the document data.

The Image View

Here's how the image view of the DIB is drawn:

```
void CDibImageView::OnDraw(CDC* pDC)
{
    CDibDoc* pDoc = GetDocument();
    // Select and realize the palette.
    // Note: always use TRUE to do a background
    // realization here.
    CPalette* pOldPal = pDC->SelectPalette(pDoc->GetPalette(),
                                           TRUE);
    pDC->RealizePalette();
    // Draw the DIB.
    pDoc->GetDIB()->Draw(pDC, 0, 0);
    // Restore the DC.
    pDC->SelectPalette(pOldPal, FALSE);
}
```

The palette is realized as it would be if the application were not the foreground application, and the *Draw* function for the DIB is called to draw it. The actual realization of the foreground palette is dealt with in *OnActivateView*, which is called when the view becomes active:

```
void CDibImageView::OnActivateView(BOOL bActivate,
                                   CView* pAcView,
                                   CView* pDeacView)
{
    if (bActivate) {
        // We are going active, so realize our palette in
        // the foreground and tell the frame to notify
        // all other windows of the change.
        SelRelPal(FALSE);
        CWnd* pMainFrame = AfxGetApp()->m_pMainWnd;
        pMainFrame->SendMessage(WM_PALETTECHANGED,
                                (WPARAM)GetSafeHwnd(),
                                0);
    }
}
```

The palette is realized in the foreground, which results in the physical palette's being changed. Now we get to do for our views what the Palette Manager does for applications—that is, tell everyone else that the physical palette has changed in case other windows need to redraw. We do this by sending a WM_PALETTECHANGED message to the main frame window so that it can pass the message on to the other views:

```
void CMainFrame::OnPaletteChanged(CWnd* pFocusWnd)
{
    // Tell all children to remap palettes.
    SendMessageToDescendants(WM_PALETTECHANGED,
                             (WPARAM)(pFocusWnd->GetSafeHwnd()),
                             (LPARAM)0,
                             TRUE);
}
```

Note that in order not to create a loop, we have to see to it that the window that originally causes the physical palette to be changed sends its window handle in the WM_PALETTECHANGED message. That way, when it receives the message itself, it won't try to remap the palette again in response.

A Note About Multiple Palettes

Creating an application that shows images that have different palettes is challenging, to say the least. Windows manages the palette at the application level, not at the window level, so if our application wants to display images with different palettes at the same time, it's going to have to manage the windows in much the same way that the Palette Manager manages applications. In practice, this means that the main frame window, which receives the palette messages from Windows, must distribute these messages in an intelligent way to the child windows it owns. Furthermore, the child windows that use palettes must respond to the palette messages correctly, and they must also change the way they realize palettes. It is not sufficient for each window to simply call *SelectPalette* with the *bForceBackground* parameter set to FALSE. In some cases, the parameter must be set to TRUE or the system will oscillate as palette messages get sent endlessly between the child windows and the frames that own them—fun to watch, but not terribly useful.

The simple, practical approach to using multiple palettes in a single application is to have the currently active image realize its palette as a foreground application would. If this causes the system palette to change, the image must be redrawn to remap the colors correctly. All other windows simply redraw (realizing their palettes in the background) to ensure that their colors get mapped as well as possible to the new system palette.

To the user, this means that a lot of repainting is going on as the window activation changes. There's not a lot we can do about this—it's a direct result of having to share one physical palette among multiple clients.

In many ways, computers and dogs are much alike—neither are very smart, and both can be made to go round in circles. For a dog to do this, you simply tie a bone to its tail. For a computer to do this, you have a novice programmer work with palette messages. The difference, of course, is that the computer is much faster than the dog, so it can be a bit hard to tell the difference between rapid looping and death.

The main frame window deals with activation of the application. As part of the activation process, Windows will send a WM_QUERYNEWPALETTE message to the application. The main frame window receives this message and passes it on to the currently active view.

```
BOOL CMainFrame::OnQueryNewPalette()
{
    // Tell the currently active view to realize in the foreground.
    CView* pView = GetActiveView();
    if (!pView) return FALSE;
    int i = pView->SendMessage(WM_QUERYNEWPALETTE,
                               (WPARAM)0,
                               (LPARAM)0);
    // If the mapping didn't change, tell all the other
    // windows that they might want to repaint anyway.
    if (!i) {
        SendMessageToDescendants(WM_PALETTECHANGED,
                                 (WPARAM)(pView->GetSafeHwnd()),
                                 (LPARAM)0,
                                 TRUE);
    }
    return (BOOL) i;
}
```

If the active view changes the palette, it will start the remap sequence by sending the WM_PALETTECHANGED message itself. If no change to the palette occurs, some windows may still need to repaint, so a WM_PALETTECHANGED message is sent to all the views to give them an opportunity to remap their colors to the new palette and repaint. Notice that the window handle for the currently active view is sent in the message to avoid a loop.

A view processes the WM_PALETTECHANGED message by remapping its palette:

```
BOOL CDibImageView::OnQueryNewPalette()
{
    return SelRelPal(FALSE); // Realize in foreground.
}
```

The helper function *SelRelPal* selects and realizes the palette:

```
BOOL CDibImageView::SelRelPal(BOOL bForceBkgnd)
{
    // We are going active, so realize our palette.
```

```
CDC* pdc = GetDC();
CDibDoc* pDoc = GetDocument();
CPalette* poldpal = pdc->SelectPalette(pDoc->GetPalette(),
                                       bForceBkgnd);
UINT u = pdc->RealizePalette();
pdc->SelectPalette(poldpal, TRUE);
pdc->RealizePalette();
ReleaseDC(pdc);
// If any colors have changed or we are in the
// background, repaint the lot.
if (u || bForceBkgnd) {
    InvalidateRect(NULL, TRUE); // Repaint.
}
return (BOOL) u; // TRUE if some colors changed.
}
```

Note that if either the system palette is detected as changing—that is, the result of calling *RealizePalette* is nonzero—or the realization is being done in the background, the window is marked for repainting to ensure that the color information will be remapped.

The Palette View

The image view and the palette view of the document have similar code for handling the palette messages. The *OnDraw* function in the palette view uses the *CDIBPal::Draw* function to do most of the work:

```
void CPalView::OnDraw(CDC* pDC)
{
    CDibDoc* pDoc = GetDocument();
    ASSERT(pDoc);
    CDIBPal* pPal = pDoc->GetPalette();
    if (!pPal) return;
    CRect rc;
    GetClientRect(&rc);
    pPal->Draw(pDC, &rc, TRUE);
}
```

Remember that the *CDIBPal::Draw* function is told to map the palette into the background so that it won't disturb the current foreground mapping set up by the palette messages.

The View of the BITMAPINFO Structure

Just for completeness, a third view of the document displays information about the DIB. The *CInfoView* class is based on *CScrollView* and uses a fixed pitch font for a nice regular-looking text display. I won't show the code for the info view here since it doesn't have anything to do with palettes. Please refer to the ShowPal sample code if you want to see how the *CInfoView* class was implemented.

Confused?

OK, so you didn't quite follow the story about what happens when we have multiple palettes. You're not alone. I didn't follow it either for the first year or so. It's a tricky business, and the best thing to do when we don't understand this particular thing fully is... to ignore it! That's not usually my line at all, but in this case, it's really a valid approach. As you'll see a little later when we create an animated image, we have to stick to only one palette for the simple reason that remapping the system palette is a slow operation and we can't afford the time it takes. So all of our animation code will be concerned with only one palette, and we can leave the vagaries of multiple palette management to the Palette Manager to deal with.

You might also be a bit confused about multiple views in MFC applications. The *C++ Tutorial* that comes with Visual C++ has more information about creating multiple views of a single document.

5

CHAPTER

Sprites,
Rendering,
and All That Jazz

n order to understand the chapters that follow, we need to take a little time out here and look at just how animation is done on a computer screen. While we'll focus mainly on how to do animation in Microsoft Windows, we'll touch briefly first on what happens in a non-Windows environment.

Animation in Simple Computer Environments

In a simple environment such as MS-DOS, only one application runs at a time, and it has complete freedom to do whatever it likes. In such an environment, animation is done with code that works very closely with the computer display hardware. Writing code that talks directly to the hardware ensures the best possible performance for the application, and if the code is written well (that is, with a good understanding of how the hardware works), the results can be stunning, even on machines with mediocre processors. The great disadvantage of writing directly to the hardware is that the application must deal directly with all the idiosyncrasies of the various display adapters it runs on. Some generality is possible since many devices support a fixed set of features. All VGA adapters are supposed to behave the same way, for instance, so generic VGA code should run on all VGA-compatible devices. This uniformity gives us some degree of portability but limits the application to using only the generic capabilities of the class of device.

Because writing animated games is such a cutthroat business, companies engaged in this work don't want to limit themselves to the generic performance they get with generic drivers. They would much rather go to the trouble of creating many different display drivers in order to wring the last bit of performance from each device.

Animation in the Windows Environment

Creating an animated application in the Windows environment is quite different from creating an animated application in the MS-DOS world. On the upside, the application has access to the entire memory space of the machine without having to use a DOS extender or expanded memory specification (EMS) support. Windows provides a display driver to do the direct hardware access, so the application is assured of the best performance with a generic function set—or so the party line goes. On the downside, the Windows-based application has to share its environment with other applications and consequently isn't permitted direct access to anything. An application for Windows must be content with the system-provided functions and the performance they give.

I'll forgive you your "Well, I'm hosed, then" conclusion here. That's not an uncommon reaction. At first glance, it seems that Windows will prevent us from doing what we think we want to do and that we will be entirely dependent on the implementation of the system functions—good or bad. Since we have no alternative, we expect that our application will perform no better and no worse than all the other Windows-based applications and that the performance is likely to be much worse than that of its MS-DOS–based cousins.

Well, things aren't necessarily like that in development for Windows. To be sure, the conservative instruction in Windows Programming 101 advocates always using graphics device interface (GDI) functions for drawing to ensure portability and consistent behavior. But with a little more understanding of how Windows works and, in particular, of how GDI uses the device drivers, it is possible to get performance close to what we would expect of an MS-DOS–based application using the same animation technique.

What do I mean by "using the same animation technique"? Typically, MS-DOS–based applications use some form of double buffering and flip buffer pages on the display hardware in order to get screen updates that seem, for all intents and purposes, to be instantaneous. In Windows development, we can't do that because the display drivers won't work that way. What we can do is be smart about how we create the scenes we want to show and use the fastest possible *software* technique to update the screen. If we wrote an MS-DOS–based application using the same technique, the performance would be the same.

Yes, MS-DOS–based applications can always be faster, but a Windows-based application can be almost as fast. In fact, the difference can be so small as to be insignificant in a wide range of animated applications.

One other aspect to note about working on animation in the Windows environment is that the screen resolution is usually much finer than it is for applications that run under MS-DOS. A typical MS-DOS–based game might run on a screen that is 320 by 200 pixels or 320 by 240 pixels with 256 colors. A typical Windows-based application runs on a screen that is at least 640 by

480 and possibly much larger, so to fill a screen with a single image will involve updating at least four times as many pixels as for the low-resolution MS-DOS case.

So when we compare performance between applications written for MS-DOS and for Windows, we must be careful to compare apples with apples and not with heffalumps. Ha ha, you thought I'd say oranges there, didn't you? Just shows how much you have to learn about Windows programming!

Cast-Based and Frame-Based Animation

You will see two basic types of animation on a computer: cast-based animation, which makes use of sprites, and frame-based animation, which operates more like a movie, consisting of a series of fixed images played in sequence. Cast-based animation is more interesting as a programming topic because it calls for dealing with concepts such as transparency and may involve interaction with the user. You can convert a cast-based animation into a frame-based animation by shooting each step in each scene and connecting the snapshots as a sequence of frames in a single file.

Naming of Parts

There's not much point in lying down and sliding under the car if you don't know the difference between the large round thing with two holes in it and the sort of square thing with five hex bolts and a cable coming out of it, is there? Knowing that they are called the widget adapter plate and the adjustable interflange compressor strut makes it all so much clearer, doesn't it?

OK, so knowing the names doesn't help much when you're on your own, but it sure helps when you want to tell the mechanic on the phone which bit of the car has stuff oozing from it. To understand how animation is done, we need to have a few common terms for common things. These terms will be used a lot in the next few chapters: *sprites*, *rendering*, and *drawing* or *painting*.

Sprites

A *sprite* is an irregularly shaped picture that can be moved anywhere on the screen. A sprite can be in front of or behind another sprite. A character in an animation could be a sprite. To make the character move around in a scene, we move the sprite for that character and change its image to simulate changes in the appearance of the character as it moves.

We can implement a sprite from some image class, such as *CDIB*, by adding to the class a way to define which areas of the image are transparent (not solid) and what the image's *x*, *y*, and *z* screen coordinates are. The simplest way to define transparency is to select a color not used elsewhere in the image and paint all the transparent areas with that color. When the sprite image is drawn, the transparent-colored pixels won't be copied to the screen.

Rendering, Drawing, and Painting

The *rendering, drawing,* and *painting* terms are generally used interchangeably; however, I use *rendering* to mean one thing and *painting* and *drawing* to mean something else.

As you will see later when we look at using a buffer for constructing a scene for an animation, getting an image on the screen is a two-stage process. The first part of the process is to build the image of the new scene in the buffer—I call this *rendering*. The second part of the process is to copy the buffer image to the screen—I call this *drawing* or *painting*.

How Moving Images Are Created

In Nigel's ideal world, all video adapters would offer direct hardware support for sprites, and all we would need to do as programmers is tell the hardware where the image for a sprite is in memory and what x, y, and z coordinates we wanted the sprite to be moved to on the screen. Today some video adapters support one sprite of limited size, and that support is used to implement a cursor that moves over the top of the screen in response to the user's pushing a mouse around. Adapters that don't have hardware support for a cursor have to have cursor support emulated by software in the device driver.

NOTE

The ideal video adapter would also be a 24-bpp adapter with huge resolution and would have the ability to blt a rectangle in one clock cycle. Unrealistic? Maybe, but look at where DSP technology is now.

Significantly, the machines used to run games in video arcades are filled with hardware sprite engines, hardware support for scrolling regions, and much more. The typical PC owner wouldn't want to pay the price of a video adapter capable of the same stuff that the quarter-gobbling arcade machines can do, and, consequently, video adapters for the PC market come without these useful additions.

Since PC video adapters don't offer hardware support for sprites, we'll have to implement the support in the software ourselves, and that means we'll have to understand how to render the image of a scene containing multiple overlapping sprites and repaint the screen as the sprites move without having the screen flicker.

That last point—without having the screen flicker—is most important. If we didn't care about flickering, we could simply render each sprite directly to the screen device context (DC) to create the new image each time something in our scene changed. Unfortunately, the result would be quite unacceptable—to even the most tolerant of users. Every time a sprite moved, the user would watch as the area it occupied was erased and all the sprites that overlapped that area were redrawn one at a time—hardly a simulation of real life.

Creating moving images without flickering involves the use of some intermediate place in memory where the new image can be constructed while the previous image remains displayed on the screen. When the composition of the new image is done, the screen can be updated with the new image while composition of the next image can begin.

Let's return to the simple MS-DOS world for a moment. The simplest buffering scheme involves setting the video card to a mode that uses less than half of the card's video memory for the displayed image and leaves the remainder of the memory for the application to use. The application constructs a new image in a part of the video memory not currently being used for display. When the new image has been built, the hardware register containing the video memory start address is altered so that the register now points to the memory containing the new image. On the screen, the image then changes (almost) instantly to the new view. The application then uses the memory from the previous display for rendering the next frame. This Ping-Pong buffering technique is simple and very effective. The time at which the buffer is changed is usually synchronized with the time at which a new frame is being refreshed by the hardware to avoid the visible tearing effects that can occur in unsynchronized updates. *Figures 5-1* and *5-2* show how the video memory is used in the Ping-Pong buffering scheme.

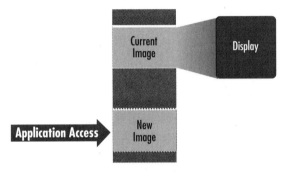

Figure 5-1 *In the simple Ping-Pong buffering technique, part of the video memory is used as a buffer for the display while another part is used as a buffer for the updated image.*

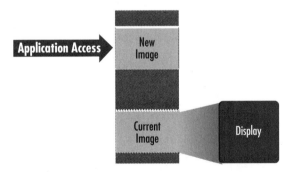

Figure 5-2 *The address in the hardware register is changed to show the new image, and the application uses the previous display buffer to render the next frame.*

In Windows, we don't have the luxury of either direct access to the video hardware or (usually) enough video memory that we can use only half of it for the display, so we have to buffer the image updates in a different way. The technique we use involves a buffer created in main memory into which the new image is rendered each time and a technique for getting just the bits that have changed from the buffer to the screen. It's getting the updates from the buffer to the screen that requires the most work if the technique is to be efficient. More of that later.

To understand how rendering through an off-screen buffer works, we'll take a step-by-step look at what happens when a sprite moves in a scene and the screen image is updated. The scene we'll use as an example consists of a background underwater image in front of which are two fish sprites—a goldfish sprite and an angel fish sprite. We'll start by looking at the state of the images, the buffer, and the screen before anything moves. *Figure 5-3* shows the start condition.

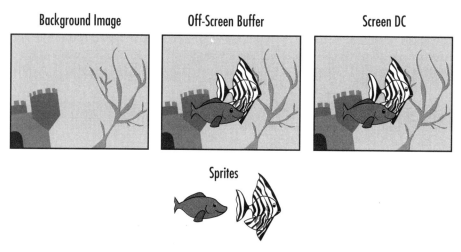

Figure 5-3   *The initial state of the background and sprite images, the off-screen buffer, and the screen device context.*

Let me explain what you're seeing in Figure 5-3 in a bit more detail. The memory space of the application contains an image of the underwater background (a *CDIB* object, perhaps), an image of each fish sprite, and a buffer into which the new images are rendered. Typically, the buffer is the same size as the application's window. In other words, a 640-by-480 window needs a 640-by-480-byte buffer. The background image will usually be the same size as the window too. The only thing not present in the memory space is the screen DC.

Figure 5-4 on the next page shows what we're going to do to the off-screen buffer as the goldfish sprite moves out ahead of the angel fish sprite.

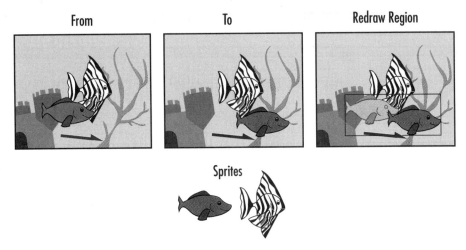

Figure 5-4 *Changes that will be made to the off-screen buffer as the goldfish sprite moves out ahead of the angel fish sprite.*

In Figure 5-4, the picture on the far right shows which bits of the buffer and screen are affected by the move. Knowing which bits have changed is a key part of efficiently updating the screen since the less data we move, the shorter the time the update will take. Let's look at the individual steps taken to move the goldfish sprite image. **Figure 5-5** shows the first step, in which the relevant part of the off-screen buffer is erased.

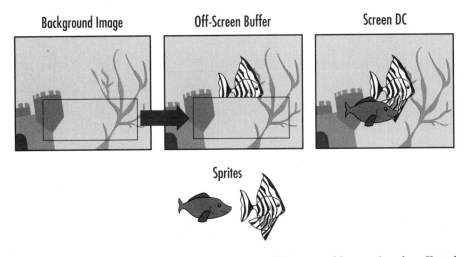

Figure 5-5 *The affected area of the off-screen buffer is erased by copying the affected part of the background image from the background image to the buffer.*

In order to move the goldfish sprite, we must erase it from its old position and draw it in the new one. The sense of depth in the scene and the placement of images in the scene must be maintained. We do this by rendering the new image in the off-screen buffer, starting with the backmost parts of the picture, so the first image to be rendered to the update area of the off-screen buffer is the background image. Note that we copy only the update rectangle from the background image, not the whole background image. Small updates mean better performance.

Having rendered the background, we can render each sprite that overlaps the update area in turn, starting with the backmost, angel fish, sprite. **Figure 5-6** shows the backmost sprite being rendered to the buffer.

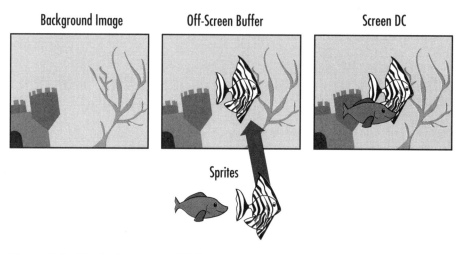

Figure 5-6   *The backmost, angel fish, sprite is rendered to the off-screen buffer.*

Note that the backmost sprite is rendered to the buffer in such a way as to maintain the transparency areas of its image—only the solid parts are copied, so this is a bit more complex than the simple copying of the background image rectangle we saw in Figure 5-5.

Figure 5-7 shows the next (and final) sprite being rendered to the off-screen buffer.

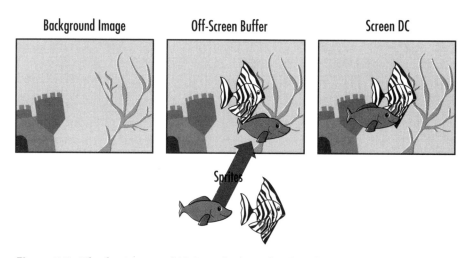

Figure 5-7   *The frontmost, goldfish, sprite is rendered to the off-screen buffer. The screen DC remains unchanged.*

Notice now that the off-screen buffer has been completely updated with the changes while the screen image has been unaffected.

The next task is to paint the changed area of the buffer to the screen. **Figure 5-8** shows this step.

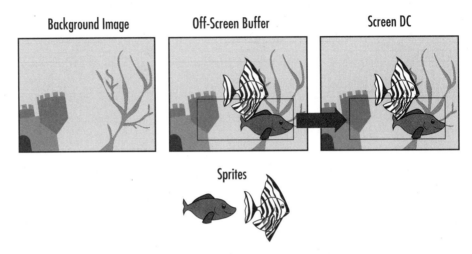

Figure 5-8 *The screen is updated with the changes from the buffer.*

Notice that we copy only the bits that have changed. I know I keep repeating this point, but it's very important. In fact, it's so important that we'll be spending a whole chapter on looking at how to make that copying more efficient.

The final state is shown in **Figure 5-9**. Compare this figure to Figure 5-3 back on page 79 to see the overall change.

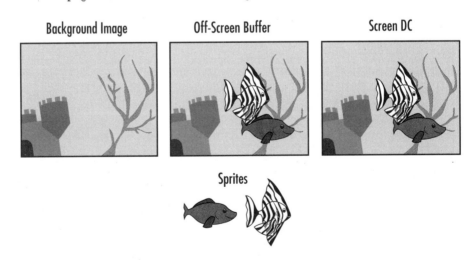

Figure 5-9 *The final state of the off-screen buffer and screen DC with all the changes complete.*

Key Points for Efficient Animation

An efficient way to render a sprite with transparency and an efficient way to get updated areas to the screen are the key aspects of efficient animation by means of the off-screen buffer technique. If you were to use a profiler to examine the execution time of the code used to render and paint a scene from an animation, you would find that the code used to render a section of the scene executed much faster than the code used to paint the same area of the scene to the screen. From this observation, it's clear that effort spent on optimizing the screen updates will provide the greatest wins in overall animation performance.

We'll be covering ways to track the update areas and minimize the screen update time later, in Chapter 10, "Efficient Repainting."

The Images in Memory

We need to keep the image of our background scene and the images of our sprites in memory, and we can do this by one of two means: we can use the *CBitmap* class to keep the images as device-dependent bitmaps (DDBs), or we can use the *CDIB* class to keep the images as DIBs. OK, no big prize for guessing that I'm going to use DIBs, but why?

There are two reasons for using DIBs. The first is that using DIBs allows us to modify the image of a sprite directly in memory if we choose, and that could be advantageous if we wanted to fade the image in or out, for example. The second reason is that, if we also use a DIB for the off-screen buffer, we can write the transparency rendering code ourselves and avoid having to use the raster operations (and thus GDI functions) required to draw DDBs with transparency. We already know from Chapter 2 that we can use *StretchDIBits* to copy a DIB from memory to the screen, so we already know of at least one way to perform the screen updates from an off-screen DIB buffer. The next step will be to see how we implement the buffer using the *CDIB* class, but first we need to look at how screen updates are done, in a little more detail.

What's a Raster Operation?

I should expand a little on what raster operations are in case you're not familiar with them. GDI provides a set of operations that can be performed on bitmaps (and in some cases with brushes). Since they deal with rasterized images, these operations are called raster operations. We could use the logical AND operation, for example, to combine a color bitmap with a monochrome bitmap. The effect would be to mask the color image with the shape defined in the monochrome image. By using combinations of various logical operations—raster operations—we can draw bitmaps with transparent areas. This process typically requires three calls to *BitBlt* to perform what is in effect a transparent blt. Being able to access the bits of a DIB directly means that we can write some clever code (OK, maybe not that clever) that simply copies pixels from one DIB to another, ignoring any pixels we have decided will be transparent. If we do a reasonable job of writing this code (which isn't hard), we can easily get the job of rendering a sprite built from a DIB with its irregular shape done faster than by making all the GDI calls we would need in order to render a sprite built from a DDB. Since speed in rendering and drawing is vital to an animation, DIBs give us a better solution than DDBs do.

CHAPTER

StretchDIBits,
CreateDIBSection,
and Color Mapping

StretchDIBits

Creating an Identity Palette

Getting the Most from the Host

ften the tasks that look simplest in Microsoft Windows turn out to be full of technical complexity or they're just plain confusing. In fact, learning about Windows is rather like learning about physics at school. The first year you learn a set of laws, and you are told that they govern the universe. The next year you learn that what you were told last year is not exactly true, that actually, the universe is a bit more complex than the mechanics of a simple inclined plane might suggest. The year after that, this dude called Heisenberg shows you that, no matter what you think you know, you really can't be sure exactly where you learned it—or something like that. (If you don't get the joke here, don't worry—you might understand it tomorrow or the next day <grin>.)

StretchDIBits

In Chapter 2, we created a *Draw* routine for the *CDIB* class that would call *StretchDIBits* to do the work of copying the DIB image to the screen. Using *StretchDIBits* to render a device-independent bitmap (DIB) to a device context (DC) is rather like using the laws of physics—it's fine so long as we don't dig too deeply into how it works. Unfortunately, it's Heisenberg time for *Stretch-DIBits*. We can't just use it and ignore how it works because if we do, we'll pay a dreadful performance penalty that we don't want and don't have to pay. So we are going to look at *StretchDIBits* a little more closely and see how color mapping in the graphics device interface (GDI) affects *StretchDIBits*'s performance. We'll confine our consideration to what happens when *StretchDIBits* is used to copy a rectangle from an 8-bpp DIB to a palettized device since that's the case we're most interested in. *StretchDIBits* can also be used to copy other DIB formats, of course, and can also copy a DIB to a nonpalettized device. The details of how these other variations work would just add to the confusion, so we'll leave them out of our consideration. Having looked at just how *StretchDIBits* works, we'll be able to go on to look at what needs to be done to ensure that the call we make to *StretchDIBits* will work as fast as possible.

Let's begin by reviewing the short piece of code (we saw in Chapter 2) that draws a DIB in *CDIB::Draw*:

```
void CDIB::Draw(CDC* pDC, int x, int y)
{
    ::StretchDIBits(pDC->GetSafeHdc(),      // 1 Destination DC
                    x,                       // 2 Destination x
                    y,                       // 3 Destination y
                    DibWidth(),              // 4 Destination width
                    DibHeight(),             // 5 Destination height
                    0,                       // 6 Source x
                    0,                       // 7 Source y
                    DibWidth(),              // 8 Source width
                    DibHeight(),             // 9 Source height
                    GetBitsAddress(),        // 10 Pointer to bits
                    GetBitmapInfoAddress(),  // 11 BITMAPINFO
                    DIB_RGB_COLORS,          // 12 Options
                    SRCCOPY);                // 13 Raster operation code
}
```

This looks very simple—a single function call does the whole job—but what's going on inside? Let's look at some of the parameters and see what each of them does. The first parameter is a DC. We know that the DC will have a logical palette of some sort associated with it even if it's only the default logical palette. The tenth parameter is a pointer to the bits in the DIB. For an 8-bit-per-pixel DIB, the kind we are most interested in, this is a pointer to a large array of bytes, in which each byte holds an index into the color table of the DIB. The eleventh parameter is a pointer to the DIB BITMAPINFO structure, which contains width, height, and color depth information for the DIB and the DIB's color table. The twelfth parameter controls how the other parameters will be interpreted. In the case shown here, the parameter is *DIB_RGB_COLORS*, which tells GDI that the DIB bits contain index values into the DIB color table supplied through parameter 11 and that the colors in the table should be used to draw the image. If the DC is for an 8-bpp palettized display, the colors in the DIB color table will be matched against entries in the logical palette in the DC, and the index value for the current hardware palette entry for the matching color will be placed in the video hardware memory. See, I told you it was more complex than it looks. *Figure 6-1* on the next page shows the data flow.

Figure 6-1 depicts the *CDIB::Draw* case. GDI takes the pixel values from the DIB and converts them to RGB values by looking them up in the DIB's color table. Having obtained the RGB values from the DIB, GDI then tries to match those colors to ones that are defined in the currently selected logical palette. GDI does this by calling a function similar to *GetNearestPaletteIndex*. The logical palette index values are then translated to physical palette index values, and the resulting physical palette index values are passed to the device driver to be written to the display video memory. Do you see why we want to understand what's going on here? We know this works—we've been using it—

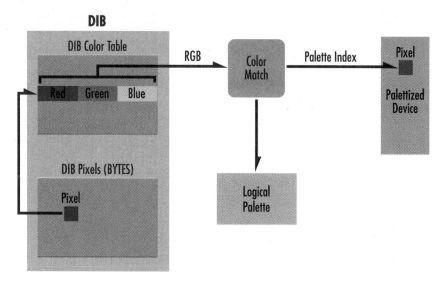

Figure 6-1 *Using* StretchDIBits *with* DIB_RGB_COLORS *to draw a DIB to a palettized device.*

but look at all the conversions going on. And remember that this conversion process is done for every pixel *every time we call* StretchDIBits.

Obviously, having to color-match every pixel is very time consuming and seems a little pointless given that we have already taken the trouble to create a logical palette from the DIB's color table. It would be nice if we could just say that the pixel values in the DIB are index values into the logical palette and prevent GDI from doing any color matching at all. Happily, we can do exactly this by calling *StretchDIBits* with the *DIB_PAL_COLORS* option. *Figure 6-2* shows what happens if we do.

GDI takes the pixel values in the DIB and translates them through an index translation table in the DIB header that replaces the RGB color table. These logical palette index values are then mapped to the physical palette index values so that the physical color selected matches the color in the logical palette. GDI builds the logical-to-physical palette index translation table when the logical palette is first realized in the DC. You might be wondering why we need a translation table in the DIB. Good question. Since the DIB pixel values are already index values into the current logical palette, we don't need to translate them at all, and in fact the table can simply have 0 in location 0, 1 in location 1, and so on, and thus provide an identity table that does no translation. Actually, the logical-to-physical translation table that GDI sends to the device driver is built by combining the DIB translation table with GDI's own logical-to-physical translation table, so the device driver actually does only one lookup per pixel.

Score 1000 bonus points here if you wondered what it would take to get rid of the logical-to-physical index translation table altogether and just have the DIB pixel values written directly to the video memory. In fact, the device

NOTE

In practice, GDI uses *GetNearestPaletteIndex* to construct a lookup table that translates the colors in the DIB header to the final palette indices. Translation of the pixels is then done by a lookup of the new color in the translation table.

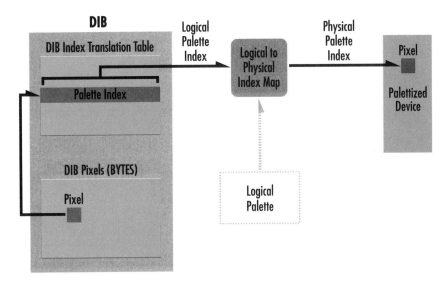

Figure 6-2 Using StretchDIBits *with* DIB_PAL_COLORS *to draw a DIB to a palettized device.*

driver contains code to detect when the translation table is an exact 1-to-1 mapping (that is, is an identity table) and in such a case simply copies the pixel values to the display memory without translating them at all, which results in a massive improvement in performance. So how do we get a 1-to-1 translation table? The answer: the logical and physical palettes must be exactly the same.

It's a shame, but not all Windows version 3.1 display drivers do this 1-to-1 table detection correctly. Work is underway to fix this, so we'll press on in hopes that by the time our application is written all will be well in Device Driver–land. If you're targeting Windows NT version 3.1, there is sadness in store for you. The device driver interface in Windows NT's GDI is slightly different from the one in Windows 3.1. In Windows NT, GDI passes a pointer to the translation table with a rule that, if the pointer is NULL, the driver doesn't have to do any translation. (It's going to find that hard to do with a NULL pointer anyway, of course.) So *all* of the Windows NT GDI drivers do the right thing, *but*—and this exception is a biggie—GDI in Windows NT 3.1 never sends a NULL translation table pointer even if the table is a 1-to-1. Someone forgot to add the code. Oh, woe! The good news is that Windows NT version 3.5 has fixed this omission, but the even better news is that Windows NT 3.5 and Windows 95 both have an entirely new function called *CreateDIBSection* that makes *StretchDIBits* redundant and provides the best possible performance in the simplest possible way.

What this means to us is that, in order to get the best possible performance from *StretchDIBits* (or from *CreateDIBSection*), we'll have to adjust the run-time code according to the operating system the application is running on. As you'll see in the next chapter, this amounts to a very few lines of code that, once written, can be forgotten.

Let's stay with *StretchDIBits* for the moment and look at exactly what is required to get a 1-to-1 translation table for the palette index values. For this to happen, we have to create an *identity palette*, which is a logical palette that maps exactly to the system palette. Furthermore, we're going to have to mess with the DIB pixel values and the color table to get them to work with this wonderful new palette.

Creating an Identity Palette

We want to create a palette such that, when it is realized into a screen DC, the order and placement of the colors in the logical palette will be exactly the same as the order and placement in the physical palette. If we can achieve this identity, a DIB's pixel values will become index values into the hardware palette, requiring no translation before they can be copied to the video memory.

There are two ways to create an identity palette. The first is easy to do, but it doesn't work for every case. The second way is a bit more complex, but it works fairly reliably. There's no way to be 100 percent certain that things will go your way because Windows is a sharing, caring environment. Some other application might have recently reserved half the system palette for animation (palette animation, that is). When I say that the second way to create an identity palette works fairly reliably, I mean that, if no one else is doing anything wrong, you'll get what you expect in the foreground application.

Grabbing the System Colors

We use the *GetSystemPaletteEntries* function to copy the first 10 and the last 10 system colors to our DIB color table so that they occupy the first and last 10 positions of the DIB color table, respectively. For all the other 236 entries, we set the PC_NOCOLLAPSE flag and create a palette from the table. When this palette is realized into a screen DC, what should happen is that the system color entries get mapped to their counterparts in the system palette, and the 236 middle entries get dropped into the system palette directly, starting at location 10.

This scheme works very well, provided that the original DIB color table contains colors similar to the system set in its first and last 10 slots. If it doesn't, the DIB loses color information and, what's worse, the pixels of the DIB that referenced the first and last 10 positions of the color table are now mapped to the ghastly Day-Glo system colors, which results in a generally trashed image.

If you are prepared to guarantee that your DIB color tables will always be authored to have the system colors in the first and last 10 positions, this is a possible way to go. ***Figure 6-3*** shows the data flow.

Authoring every DIB with 10 empty slots at each end of its color table is not always convenient or possible, though, so a more general solution might be more practical.

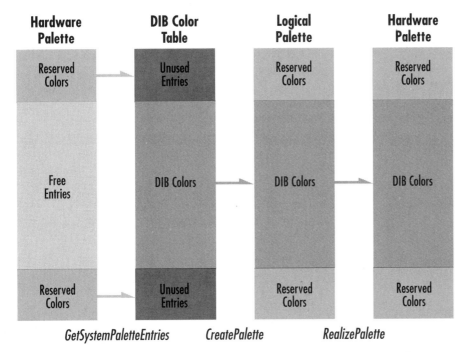

Hardware Palette	DIB Color Table	Logical Palette	Hardware Palette
Reserved Colors	Unused Entries	Reserved Colors	Reserved Colors
Free Entries	DIB Colors	DIB Colors	DIB Colors
Reserved Colors	Unused Entries	Reserved Colors	Reserved Colors

GetSystemPaletteEntries   CreatePalette   RealizePalette

Figure 6-3   *Creating an identity palette by grabbing the reserved system colors.*

The More General Solution

If you want to be able to use any DIB and still guarantee a 1-to-1 palette match, you will have to do a little more work. The problem here is that, in general, the first entry in the DIB color table is considered to be the most important color, the second the next most important, and so on. This means that we can't just blow these entries away—we have to find a way to get them into the physical palette.

The way to do this is to first create a logical palette for the entire DIB color table and then select the palette into the screen DC and realize it. GDI will take your set of colors and map them or insert them into the system palette as it sees fit. Now comes the clever bit.

Use *GetSystemPaletteEntries* to grab the entire 256 system color entries, and put these values into your logical palette by calling *SetPaletteEntries*. Your logical palette now matches the system palette exactly. The only problem is that the DIB is all messed up because its pixel values no longer index the correct colors in the logical palette.

To fix the DIB pixel values, take the colors in the DIB color table, and for each one, use the GDI function *GetNearestPaletteColor* to find an entry in your new logical palette that matches (or is close to) the color in the DIB color table. Use this information to create a translation table for the DIB pixel values. Then walk through the DIB, and for every pixel, look up its new index value in the translation table and write it back to the DIB. The DIB pixels will now map correctly to the logical palette, but some color information might be lost if the original logical palette does not map well to the system palette (unlikely).

The final step is to reset the DIB color table to have the same RGB values as the new logical palette so that the DIB and its header are once more in sync. You need to worry about doing this only if you will want to use the RGB values in the header later, which is not often the case for animation use of DIBs. Usually, we simply want to get the right palette, and that's it. The DIB is never saved, so we don't care if it gets a bit mixed up along the way. Do beware, though: if the DIB is saved back to the file it came from, it won't necessarily be quite the same beastie it once was.

Because creating an identity palette is such a useful thing to do, I added a function to the *CDIBPal* class to do this:

```
BOOL CDIBPal::SetSysPalColors()
{
    BOOL bResult = FALSE;
    int i, iSysColors, iPalEntries;
    HPALETTE hpalOld;

    // Get a screen DC to work with.
    HWND hwndActive = ::GetActiveWindow();
    HDC hdcScreen = ::GetDC(hwndActive);
    ASSERT(hdcScreen);

    // Make sure we are on a palettized device.
    if (!GetDeviceCaps(hdcScreen, RASTERCAPS) & RC_PALETTE) {
        TRACE("Not a palettized device");
        goto abort;
    }

    // Get the number of system colors and the number of palette
    // entries. Note that on a palettized device the number of
    // colors is the number of guaranteed colors, i.e., the number
    // of reserved system colors.
    iSysColors = GetDeviceCaps(hdcScreen, NUMCOLORS);
    iPalEntries = GetDeviceCaps(hdcScreen, SIZEPALETTE);

    // If there are more than 256 colors, we are wasting our time.
    if (iSysColors > 256) goto abort;

    // Now we force the Palette Manager to reset its tables so that
    // the next palette to be realized will get its colors in the order
    // in which they appear in the logical palette. This is done by
    // changing the number of reserved colors.
    SetSystemPaletteUse(hdcScreen, SYSPAL_NOSTATIC);
    SetSystemPaletteUse(hdcScreen, SYSPAL_STATIC);
```

```
// Select our palette into the screen DC and realize it so that
// its colors will be entered into the free slots in the physical
// palette.
hpalOld = ::SelectPalette(hdcScreen,
                          (HPALETTE)m_hObject, // Our hpal
                          FALSE);
::RealizePalette(hdcScreen);
// Now replace the old palette (but don't realize it).
::SelectPalette(hdcScreen, hpalOld, FALSE);

// The physical palette now has our colors set in place and its own
// reserved colors at either end.  We can grab the lot now.
PALETTEENTRY pe[256];
GetSystemPaletteEntries(hdcScreen,
                        0,
                        iPalEntries,
                        pe);

// Set the PC_NOCOLLAPSE flag for each of our colors so that GDI
// won't merge them. Be careful not to set PC_NOCOLLAPSE for the
// system color entries so that we won't get multiple copies of
// these colors in the palette when we realize it.
for (i = 0; i < iSysColors/2; i++) {
    pe[i].peFlags = 0;
}
for (; i < iPalEntries-iSysColors/2; i++) {
    pe[i].peFlags = PC_NOCOLLAPSE;
}
for (; i < iPalEntries; i++) {
    pe[i].peFlags = 0;
}

// Resize the palette in case it was smaller.
ResizePalette(iPalEntries);

// Update the palette entries with the entries that are now in the
// physical palette.
SetPaletteEntries(0, iPalEntries, pe);
bResult = TRUE;

abort:
    ::ReleaseDC(hwndActive, hdcScreen);
    return bResult;
}
```

Having altered the palette so that it will be an identity palette when it is next realized in the screen DC, we need to adjust the pixels of the DIB using the palette. Here's the function added to the *CDIB* class that maps the DIB pixel values to match a given palette:

```
BOOL CDIB::MapColorsToPalette(CPalette* pPal)
{
    if (!pPal) {
        TRACE("No palette to map to");
        return FALSE;
    }
    ASSERT(m_pBMI->bmiHeader.biBitCount == 8);
    ASSERT(m_pBMI);
    ASSERT(m_pBits);
    LPRGBQUAD pctThis = GetClrTabAddress();
    ASSERT(pctThis);
    // Build an index translation table to map this DIB's colors
    // to those of the reference DIB.
    BYTE imap[256];
    int iChanged = 0; // For debugging only
    for (int i = 0; i < 256; i++) {
        imap[i] = (BYTE) pPal->GetNearestPaletteIndex(
                        RGB(pctThis->rgbRed,
                            pctThis->rgbGreen,
                            pctThis->rgbBlue));
        pctThis++;
        if (imap[i] != i) iChanged++; // For debugging
    }
    // Now map the DIB bits.
    BYTE* pBits = (BYTE*)GetBitsAddress();
    int iSize = GetStorageWidth() * DibHeight();
    while (iSize--) {
        *pBits = imap[*pBits];
        pBits++;
    }
    // Now reset the DIB color table so that its RGB values match
    // those in the palette.
    PALETTEENTRY pe[256];
    pPal->GetPaletteEntries(0, 256, pe);
    pctThis = GetClrTabAddress();
    for (i = 0; i < 256; i++) {
        pctThis->rgbRed = pe[i].peRed;
        pctThis->rgbGreen = pe[i].peGreen;
        pctThis->rgbBlue = pe[i].peBlue;
        pctThis++;
    }
    return TRUE;
}
```

Please note that this code is rather dependent on the DIB's being 8 bits per pixel and having a 256-entry color table. A more general solution that handles 1-, 4-, and 8-bpp DIBs would be better.

Being able to map a DIB's colors to a given palette turns out to be useful, not only because we care about the identity palette performance in the case of using *StretchDIBits*, but, as we'll see later, also because the mapping capability can be used when several DIBs have to share a single palette.

Getting the Most from the Host

A little while back I mentioned that Windows NT version 3.5 and Windows 95 have a new function called *CreateDIBSection*, which allows an application to either create a section of memory or provide a chunk of memory of its own that GDI will treat as a DIB. The way this is set up means that the application can have direct access to the bits, which is nice, but the application can also effectively select the DIB section into a DC and perform GDI operations on it. To update the screen from the section is simply a matter of calling *BitBlt*. This is a great improvement over using *StretchDIBits* because it provides so much more flexibility.

The reason for providing *CreateDIBSection* is that using *StretchDIBits* on Windows NT can be rather slow because of the way the client-server architecture works. Let's finish up this chapter by looking at how *StretchDIBits* works on Windows 3.1 and Windows NT 3.1, and then we'll look at how *CreateDIBSection* improves things. We'll assume that we know what we're doing with palettes and have taken the necessary steps to ensure that the palette we are using is an identity palette, so no pixel translation will be required. *Figure 6-4* shows what effectively happens when we do the right thing with *StretchDIBits* on Windows 3.1.

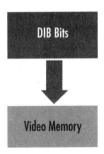

Figure 6-4 StretchDIBits(DIB_PAL_COLORS) *on Windows 3.1.*

The DIB pixels go straight from the DIB memory to the screen memory. This is almost as good as what an MS-DOS–based application can do. We can't get quite the same performance an MS-DOS–based application that does video memory page swapping can, but it's very close. Now let's look at ***Figure 6-5*** on the next page to see what happens when we call *StretchDIBits* on Windows NT 3.1.

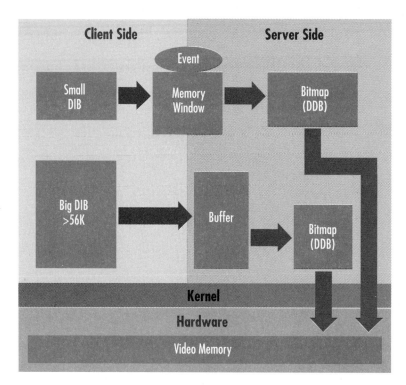

Figure 6-5 StretchDIBits(DIB_PAL_COLORS) *on Windows NT.*

As you can see, this is just a bit more complicated than on Windows 3.1 and is consequently somewhat slower.

Memory for the DIB is allocated on the client side. To execute a call to *StretchDIBits*, GDI needs to create a device-dependent bitmap (DDB) on the server side. Actually, DDBs are implemented as DIBs on the server side, but we still need to copy the bits because of process address space isolation. If the DIB is less than about 56K, it gets copied through the shared memory window. If it is larger than 56K, the Windows NT kernel is used to create a buffer on the server side and copy the DIB bits to the buffer. The server then creates a DDB from the buffer. Either way, the DIB is copied. In order to move the DDB to the screen, a blt function then gets called in the device driver that copies the bits in the server-side buffer directly to the physical memory of the device. The Windows NT kernel provides a way to map the physical memory of the display device into the process address space of the server but is not otherwise involved in the blt operation at all. The video device driver runs in the server process address space.

Just for comparison: if the application creates a DDB, the memory for the DDB is allocated on the server side and *BitBlt* can be used to transfer the bits directly to the video memory.

Copying the bits of large DIBs is obviously a waste of time and memory space. Let's look in **Figure 6-6** at how the *CreateDIBSection* function on Windows NT 3.5 and Windows 95 fixes this problem.

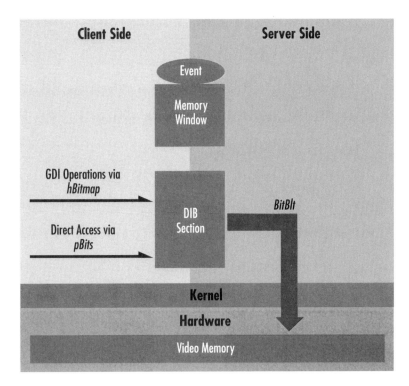

Figure 6-6 CreateDIBSection *on Windows NT 3.5 and Windows 95.*

As you can see, things are much simpler. A common memory window is created to hold the DIB bits. The application on the client side can use the bitmap handle returned to select the bitmap into a DC and perform GDI operations on it, or it can use the pointer to the bits to access the DIB memory directly. Total control!

Now we can simply use *BitBlt* to transfer the DIB section bits to the display device memory as with DDBs. Note that using *StretchDIBits* won't work as well since there is no way to differentiate between one of the shared memory buffers and a chunk of memory allocated on the client side. *StretchDIBits* will still have to copy the buffer to a separate buffer on the server side and call *BitBlt* from there, much as it does now on Windows NT 3.1.

Let's end with a look at the *Draw* function taken from the off-screen buffer view class we'll develop in the next chapter in order to see how drawing is done with either *StretchDIBits* or *BitBlt* (with a DIB section). I'll leave the explanation of the code until later. For now I want to show how trivial it is to select which technique to use at run time.

```
if (m_bUseCreateDIBSection) {
        HDC dcMem = ::CreateCompatibleDC(pdc->GetSafeHdc());
        HBITMAP hbmOld = (HBITMAP) ::SelectObject(dcMem, m_hbmSection);
```

(continued)

```
    // Note: you do not need to select the palette into
    // the memory DC because the DIB section is using palette
    // index values, not colors.
    ::BitBlt(pdc->GetSafeHdc(),
            xd, yd,
            w, h,
            dcMem,
            xs, ys,
            SRCCOPY);
    ::SelectObject(dcMem, hbmOld);
    ::DeleteDC(dcMem);
} else {
    pBits = m_pDIB->GetBitsAddress();
    StretchDIBits(pdc->GetSafeHdc(),
                    xd,                 // Destination x
                    yd,                 // Destination y
                    w,                  // Destination width
                    h,                  // Destination height
                    xs,                 // Source x
                    ys,                 // Source y
                    w,                  // Source width
                    h,                  // Source height
                    pBits,              // Pointer to bits
                    m_pOneToOneClrTab,  // BITMAPINFO
                    DIB_PAL_COLORS,     // Options
                    SRCCOPY);           // ROP
}
```

Of course, I have omitted showing how the DIB section gets created and so on. We'll look at all of that in the next chapter.

CHAPTER

Creating an Off-Screen Buffered View Class

The Long Road to the Final Application

An Off-Screen Buffered View

Direct Pixel Manipulation
but No GDI Calls

The *COSBView* Class

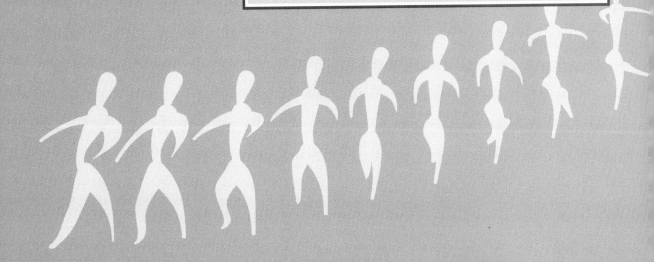

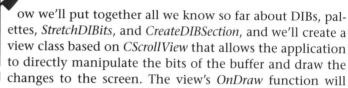

ow we'll put together all we know so far about DIBs, palettes, *StretchDIBits*, and *CreateDIBSection*, and we'll create a view class based on *CScrollView* that allows the application to directly manipulate the bits of the buffer and draw the changes to the screen. The view's *OnDraw* function will automatically redraw the entire view.

The Long Road to the Final Application

For each of most of the chapters so far, I have created a unique sample application that illustrated the ideas contained in that chapter. From this point on, we'll do something a little different. Instead of coming up with a new sample for each idea we go into, I'll keep the name of the application and all of its source files constant over several chapters and simply add features to the sources as we need them. In this way, I hope that you will be able to follow where things go in the code by becoming familiar with the names of the source code files and so on.

As the application gains features, existing classes will gain new member functions and a few new classes will be created. In some cases, a function in a class—*CDIB::Draw*, for instance—may become redundant. In these cases, the old function will remain in the class just in case you find a use for it. The code developed in each chapter after this one will thus include all the code from the classes developed in the earlier chapters.

Please remember that the focus is on 8-bit-per-pixel (bpp) DIBs and palettized displays. While the code may also work with other DIB formats and other display variants, my energies have been directed toward making the 8-bpp case work because this is the most popular. In some cases, the work to support other formats would be too great to warrant inclusion, and in those cases an ASSERT statement makes a check to ensure that the code is being called to process only an 8-bpp DIB. You can enhance these sections of code yourself to support other DIB formats.

An Off-Screen Buffered View

Let's go back to Chapter 5 for just a moment. You might remember that in order to do flicker-free updates of the screen we need a buffer somewhere in memory in which we can compose each frame of the animation before drawing it to the screen. The MFC application architecture is based (roughly) on having a document class that describes the data and a view class that deals with displaying the data. What we are going to do now is create a special kind of view class that uses an off-screen buffer. The buffer we'll use will actually be a *CDIB* object.

Direct Pixel Manipulation but No GDI Calls

You'll remember that one reason for using DIBs is that we can directly access the pixels in a DIB image. Because a buffered view class object is created from a DIB, we'll be able to directly access the pixels in the buffer. Unfortunately, there is no device context (DC) associated with the buffer, so we can't use graphics device interface (GDI) calls to draw to it.

If you inspect the code that uses *CreateDIBSection*, you'll see that a handle to the section bitmap is retained. This handle could be selected into a DC so that GDI operations could be used to draw to the DIB section—this is a major feature of *CreateDIBSection*. If you plan to have your code run only on Windows 95 or Windows NT version 3.5, you could modify what I've done here so that the *StretchDIBits* code is removed and the drawing operations rely solely on *CreateDIBSection*. In that case, you could slightly change the way the class works so that you could create a DC and use GDI operations to draw to the buffer. Appendix A includes a short discussion of how the WinG library can also be used to implement the off-screen buffered view class. Using WinG is exactly like using *CreateDIBSection* and thus will allow you to expose a DC to the buffer, which can be drawn to with GDI operations.

> **NOTE**
>
> If you use a combination of GDI calls and direct pixel access to a DIB section, you must call *GdiFlush* after the GDI operations to ensure that they are executed (not left in the operations cache) before you do direct pixel access to the DIB section.

The *COSBView* Class

The *COSBView* (off-screen buffered view) class uses a *CDIB* object as a buffer to a Microsoft Foundation Class Library (MFC) *CScrollView* class. The application manipulates the DIB buffer pixels directly, and the results can be painted on the view's client area by a call to *COSBView::Draw*. In order to draw a DIB, we need an associated palette, so the *COSBView* class includes one. The essential component, then, is a new class derived from *CScrollView* that has *CDIB* and *CDIBPal* objects as members. In fact, the implementation of *COSBView* uses pointers to the *CDIB* and *CDIBPal* objects because, although we could embed a *CDIB* object, we could not embed a *CDIBPal* object and reuse it very easily. Remember, it's essentially a wrapper around a GDI palette object, and most of these can't be initialized more than once. In the interests of consistency, I decided to use a pointer to both the *CDIB* and the *CDIBPal* objects.

\anim32\osbview

Because the creation of large objects such as DIBs in the constructor code for a class can lead to low-memory failures and they're a pain to deal with in the code, I chose to use a two-stage construction for *COSBView*. The constructor simply sets the member variables to defined values. A *Create* member function actually creates the buffer later.

In order to use *CreateDIBSection* in this code, I was forced to dynamically link to it at run time because no import library was available when this code was developed. For that matter, the actual definition of *CreateDIBSection* was somewhat volatile for a while, so the header file for *COSBView* includes a definition for *CreateDIBSection* and the constructor code makes the run-time link if the function is present in the system. Although this may look a little ugly, it has the advantage of having the *COSBView* class automatically use *CreateDIBSection* if the system supports it and fall back on using *StretchDIBits* if the system doesn't.

Creation of a *COSBView* Object

Let's begin by looking at the entire header file for the *COSBView* class:

NOTE

The funny-looking *typedef* statement is a function prototype for the *CreateDIBSection* function, which was not included in WINDOWS.H at the time this book was written.

```
// Define the CreateDIBSection function.
typedef HBITMAP (APIENTRY CDSPROC)
                (HDC hDC,
                 BITMAPINFO* pbmi,
                 UINT iUsage,
                 VOID ** ppvBits,
                 HANDLE hSection,
                 DWORD dwOffset);

class COSBView : public CScrollView
{
protected: // Create from serialization only.
    COSBView();
    DECLARE_DYNCREATE(COSBView)

// Attributes
public:
    CAnimDoc* GetDocument();
    CDIB* GetDIB() {return m_pDIB;}
    CDIBPal* GetPalette() {return m_pPal;}

// Operations
public:
    BOOL Create(CDIB* pDIB);            // Create a new buffer.
    void Draw(CDC* pDC = NULL,
             RECT* pClipRect = NULL);   // Draw off-screen buffer
                                        // to screen.
```

```
// Implementation
public:
    virtual ~COSBView();
    virtual void OnDraw(CDC* pDC);  // Overridden to draw this view
    virtual void OnInitialUpdate(); // First time after construction


#ifdef _DEBUG
    virtual void AssertValid() const;
    virtual void Dump(CDumpContext& dc) const;
#endif

protected:
    CDIB* m_pDIB;           // The DIB buffer
    CDIBPal* m_pPal;        // Palette for drawing

private:
    BITMAPINFO* m_pOneToOneClrTab;  // Pointer to 1-to-1 color table
    BOOL m_bUseCreateDIBSection;    // Flag
    CDSPROC* m_pCDSProc;            // Pointer to CreateDIBSection
    HBITMAP m_hbmSection;           // Bitmap from section

// Generated message map functions
protected:
    //{{AFX_MSG(COSBView)
    afx_msg void OnPaletteChanged(CWnd* pFocusWnd);
    afx_msg BOOL OnQueryNewPalette();
    //}}AFX_MSG
    DECLARE_MESSAGE_MAP()
};

#ifndef _DEBUG  // Debug version in osbview.cpp
inline CAnimDoc* COSBView::GetDocument()
    { return (CAnimDoc*) m_pDocument; }
#endif
```

As you can see, *COSBView* is based on *CScrollView*. Its member variables include pointers for the DIB buffer object, a palette, and a 1-to-1 palette index translation table to be used with *StretchDIBits*. There are also some member variables used for the run-time link to *CreateDIBSection*, and we'll see how those are used when we look at the constructor and the drawing code.

Public member functions are provided to return pointers to the DIB and palette objects. Remember—we are going for maximum performance here, not maximum encapsulation. The class also has public *Create* and *Draw* functions. Let's look at the various functions in turn, beginning with the constructor code.

```
COSBView::COSBView()
{
    m_pDIB = NULL;
    m_pPal = NULL;
    m_pOneToOneClrTab = NULL;
    m_bUseCreateDIBSection = FALSE;
    m_hbmSection = NULL;

    // Try to get the CreateDIBSection process address.
    HANDLE hMod = ::GetModuleHandle("gdi32");
    if (hMod) {
        m_pCDSProc = (CDSPROC*) GetProcAddress((HMODULE) hMod,
                                            "CreateDIBSection");
        if (m_pCDSProc) {
            m_bUseCreateDIBSection = TRUE;
        }
    }
}
```

The constructor initializes most of the member variables trivially and then goes on to see if the system supports *CreateDIBSection*. An attempt is made to get the module handle for GDI32.DLL, the system component in Windows 95 and Windows NT 3.5 that contains the *CreateDIBSection* function. If the module is found, the entry point for *CreateDIBSection* is requested and stored in *m_pCDSProc*. Because I prefer my code to be obvious (well, sometimes I do), I also include the Boolean variable *m_bUseCreateDIBSection*, which is set to TRUE if the function is found.

The destructor simply deletes any objects we have valid pointers to:

```
COSBView::~COSBView()
{
    if (m_pDIB) delete m_pDIB;
    if (m_pPal) delete m_pPal;
    if (m_pOneToOneClrTab) free(m_pOneToOneClrTab);
    if (m_hbmSection) ::DeleteObject(m_hbmSection);
}
```

Let's look at how the *Create* function is used to actually create a DIB buffer. This could have been done in many different ways; what you see here is the result of my experience in creating the final animation engine. I chose to make it easy to create the buffer the same size as a given DIB and, furthermore, to have a palette based on that DIB. The background scene in my animations was always the largest image and was also used to define the current palette, so basing the creation of the buffer on the background image DIB made a lot of sense. As you read through the code, you'll see that it's fairly simple to come up with many variants of this scheme to accommodate your own needs. Here's the *Create* function:

```
BOOL COSBView::Create(CDIB* pDIB)
{
    // Create the 1-to-1 palette index table.
    if (m_pOneToOneClrTab) free(m_pOneToOneClrTab);
    m_pOneToOneClrTab =
        (LPBITMAPINFO) malloc(sizeof(BITMAPINFOHEADER) +
                              256 * sizeof(WORD));
    if (!m_pOneToOneClrTab) {
        TRACE("Failed to create color table");
        return FALSE;
    }

    // Set up the table header to match the DIB
    // by copying the header and then constructing the 1-to-1
    // index translation table.
    memcpy(m_pOneToOneClrTab,
           pDIB->GetBitmapInfoAddress(),
           sizeof(BITMAPINFOHEADER));
    m_pOneToOneClrTab->bmiHeader.biClrUsed = 0;
    WORD* pIndex;
    pIndex = (LPWORD)((LPBYTE)m_pOneToOneClrTab +
                      sizeof(BITMAPINFOHEADER));
    for (int i = 0; i < 256; i++) {
        *pIndex++ = (WORD) i;
    }

    // Create a palette from the DIB so that
    // we can use it to do screen drawing.
    if (m_pPal) delete m_pPal;
    m_pPal = new CDIBPal;
    ASSERT(m_pPal);
    if (!m_pPal->Create(pDIB)) {
        TRACE("Failed to create palette");
        delete m_pPal;
        m_pPal = NULL;
        return FALSE;
    } else {
        // Map the colors so that we get an identity palette.
        m_pPal->SetSysPalColors();
    }

    // Delete any existing DIB and create a new one.
    if (m_pDIB) delete m_pDIB;
    m_pDIB = new CDIB;
    BOOL bResult = FALSE;
    if (m_bUseCreateDIBSection) {
        if (m_hbmSection) ::DeleteObject(m_hbmSection);
```

(continued)

```
        ASSERT(m_pCDSProc);
        CDC* pDC = GetDC();
        CPalette* pPalOld = pDC->SelectPalette(m_pPal, FALSE);
        pDC->RealizePalette();
        BYTE* pBits = NULL;
        m_hbmSection = (*m_pCDSProc)(pDC->GetSafeHdc(),
                                     m_pOneToOneClrTab,
                                     DIB_PAL_COLORS,
                                     (VOID**) &pBits,
                                     NULL,
                                     0);
        pDC->SelectPalette(pPalOld, FALSE);
        ASSERT(m_hbmSection);
        ASSERT(pBits);
        ReleaseDC(pDC);
        bResult = m_pDIB->Create(pDIB->GetBitmapInfoAddress(), pBits);
    } else {
        bResult = m_pDIB->Create(pDIB->GetWidth(), pDIB->GetHeight());
    }
    if (!bResult) {
        TRACE("Failed to create off-screen DIB");
        delete m_pDIB;
        m_pDIB = NULL;
        return FALSE;
    }

    CSize sizeTotal;
    sizeTotal.cx = m_pDIB->GetWidth();
    sizeTotal.cy = m_pDIB->GetHeight();
    SetScrollSizes(MM_TEXT, sizeTotal);
    return TRUE;
}
```

Starting from the top, the first step is to create a 1-to-1 palette index translation table that can be used with calls to *StretchDIBits*. Memory is allocated for a table with 256 entries. The BITMAPINFO structure of the table is copied directly from the BITMAPINFO structure of the DIB, and the translation table values are filled in.

A *CDIBPal* object is created from the color table in the DIB, and a call is made to *SetSysPalColors* to make an identity palette. Note that the header file included *GetPalette* to retrieve the current palette for use outside the *COSBView* class.

A new *CDIB* object is created for the buffer, and what follows next is determined by whether we will be using *CreateDIBSection*. If not, then *CDIB::Create* is called with width and height parameters to create a default *CDIB* object of that size. Remember that this will create an 8-bpp DIB with a 256-entry color table. If we are going to use *CreateDIBSection*, a little more work is required.

A DC is created, and the palette is selected and realized in it. *CreateDIBSection* is called and, if successful, returns a handle to a device-dependent bitmap that we save in *m_hbmSection*. We also get back a pointer to the pixels in the DIB section, and this pointer is saved in *pBits*. If the section was created successfully, *CDIB::Create* is called and is passed pointers to the source DIB BITMAPINFO and the bits of the DIB section. Note that this is a new function in the *CDIB* class, which we'll look at in just a moment.

Once the DIB buffer has been created, the scroll range of the view window is set to be the size of the DIB buffer.

In order to function with *CreateDIBSection*, it was necessary to be able to create a *CDIB* object from an existing piece of memory, such as the one *CreateDIBSection* creates. A later version of *CreateDIBSection* was to have an option for creating the section from a supplied block of memory, but this option wasn't available when I wrote the first samples, so I modified *CDIB* to handle the problem.

The modifications to *CDIB* include a Boolean member variable that keeps track of whether the *CDIB* object owns the pixel memory or not. This is very important because the *CDIB* object must not attempt to destroy a memory section created by *CreateDIBSection*. The tracking makes some of the code inside *CDIB* a little messy, but the solution works well. Here's the new *CDIB::Create* function, which allows you to supply the pixel memory:

```
BOOL CDIB::Create(BITMAPINFO* pBMI, BYTE* pBits)
{
    ASSERT(pBMI);
    ASSERT(pBits);
    if (m_pBMI != NULl) free(m_pBMI);
    m_pBMI = (BITMAPINFO*) malloc(sizeof(BITMAPINFOHEADER) +
                        256 * sizeof(RGBQUAD));
    ASSERT(m_pBMI);
    memcpy(m_pBMI, pBMI, sizeof(BITMAPINFOHEADER) +
                        NumDIBColorEntries(pBMI) * sizeof(RGBQUAD));

    if (m_bMyBits && (m_pBits != NULL)) free(m_pBits);
    m_pBits = pBits;
    m_bMyBits = FALSE; // We can't delete the bits.
    return TRUE;
}
```

Note that the BITMAPINFO structure is copied but the bits are not. The *m_bMyBits* flag is set to TRUE to prevent the bits' memory from being deleted by code elsewhere in the *CDIB* class.

Drawing Functions

Since *COSBView* is a view class, it includes an *OnDraw* function, which is trivial to implement.

```
void COSBView::OnDraw(CDC* pDC)
{
    Draw(pDC);
}
```

OK, so you haven't seen the *Draw* function yet, but it's looking good so far, isn't it? Because we are using a palette, we need to include code to handle palette messages to the application; this is a two-step process. The main frame module must handle the WM_PALETTECHANGED and WM_QUERYNEW-PALETTE messages, which it forwards to the view. It does this with two handler functions:

```
void CMainFrame::OnPaletteChanged(CWnd* pFocusWnd)
{
    // Pass this message on to the active view.
    CView* pview = GetActiveView();
    if (pview) {
        // OnPaletteChanged is not public.
        pview->SendMessage(WM_PALETTECHANGED,
                        (WPARAM)(pFocusWnd->GetSafeHwnd()),
                        (LPARAM)0);
    }
}
```

and

```
BOOL CMainFrame::OnQueryNewPalette()
{
    // Pass this message on to the active view.
    CView* pview = GetActiveView();
    if (pview) {
        return pview->SendMessage(WM_QUERYNEWPALETTE,
                            (WPARAM)0,
                            (LPARAM)0);
    }
    return FALSE; // Did nothing.
}
```

Please note that we handle only the case in which there is one view attached to the document. This is quite reasonable for most animation requirements, but take note of it in case you want to have more than one view. The palette messages are passed from the main frame window to the view class and handled there by the two complementary functions *OnPaletteChanged* and *OnQueryNewPalette*:

```
void COSBView::OnPaletteChanged(CWnd* pFocusWnd)
{
    // See if the change was caused by us and ignore it if not.
    if (pFocusWnd != this) {
        OnQueryNewPalette();
    }
}
```

```
BOOL COSBView::OnQueryNewPalette()
{
    // We are going active, so realize our palette.
    if (m_pPal) {
        CDC* pdc = GetDC();
        CPalette* poldpal = pdc->SelectPalette(m_pPal, FALSE);
        UINT u = pdc->RealizePalette();
        ReleaseDC(pdc);
        if (u != 0) {
            // Some colors changed, so we need to do a repaint.
            InvalidateRect(NULL, TRUE); // Repaint the lot.
            return TRUE; // Say we did something.
        }
    }
    return FALSE; // Say we did nothing.
}
```

What these functions are doing was covered earlier. If you've forgotten, go back to Chapters 3 and 4, which discuss palettes.

The real guts of the drawing code are in the *Draw* function:

```
void COSBView::Draw(CRect* pRect)
{
    CClientDC dc(this);
    CRect rcDraw;

    // Make sure we have what we need to do a paint.
    if (!m_pDIB || !m_pOneToOneClrTab) {
        TRACE("No DIB or color table to paint from");
        return;
    }

    // See if a clip rect was supplied, and use the client area if not.
    if (pRect) {
        rcDraw = *pRect;
    } else {
        GetClientRect(rcDraw);
    }

    // Get the clip box.
    CRect rcClip;
    dc.GetClipBox(rcClip);

    // Create a rect for the DIB.
    CRect rcDIB;
    rcDIB.left = rcDIB.top = 0;
    rcDIB.right = m_pDIB->GetWidth() - 1;
    rcDIB.bottom = m_pDIB->GetHeight() - 1;
```

(continued)

```
// Find a rectangle that describes the intersection of the draw
// rect, clip rect, and DIB rect.
CRect rcBlt = rcDraw & rcClip & rcDIB;

// Copy the update rectangle from the off-screen DC to the
// window DC. Note that the DIB origin is the bottom-left corner.
int w, h, xs, xd, yd, ys;
w = rcBlt.right - rcBlt.left;
h = rcBlt.bottom - rcBlt.top;
xs = xd = rcBlt.left;
yd = rcBlt.top;
if (m_bUseCreateDIBSection) {
    ys = rcBlt.top;
} else {
    ys = m_pDIB->GetHeight() - rcBlt.bottom;
}

// If we have a palette, select and realize it.
CPalette* ppalOld = NULL;
if (m_pPal) {
    ppalOld = dc.SelectPalette(m_pPal, 0);
    dc.RealizePalette();
}


BYTE* pBits;
if (m_bUseCreateDIBSection) {
    HDC dcMem = ::CreateCompatibleDC(dc.GetSafeHdc());
    HBITMAP hbmOld = (HBITMAP) ::SelectObject(dcMem, m_hbmSection);
    // Note: you do not need to select the palette into
    // the memory DC because the DIB section is using palette
    // index values, not colors.
    ::BitBlt(dc.GetSafeHdc(),
            xd, yd,
            w, h,
            dcMem,
            xs, ys,
            SRCCOPY);
    ::SelectObject(dcMem, hbmOld);
    ::DeleteDC(dcMem);
} else {
    pBits = (BYTE*)m_pDIB->GetBitsAddress();
    ::StretchDIBits(dc.GetSafeHdc(),
                    xd,              // Destination x
                    yd,              // Destination y
                    w,               // Destination width
                    h,               // Destination height
                    xs,              // Source x
```

```
    ys,                  // Source y
    w,                   // Source width
    h,                   // Source height
    pBits,               // Pointer to bits
    m_pOneToOneClrTab,   // BITMAPINFO
    DIB_PAL_COLORS,      // Options
    SRCCOPY);            // Rop
    }


    // Select old palette if we altered it.
    if (ppalOld) dc.SelectPalette(ppalOld, 0);
}
```

Draw takes one parameter: a pointer to a rectangle to be used for clip-ping the drawing operation to within a given area. The rectangle pointer is optional and may be NULL, so the first part of the function deals with calcu-lating the rectangle that will be drawn into.

If a palette is available, it is selected and realized into the DC. If we are using *CreateDIBSection*, *BitBlt* is called to copy the rectangle from the buffer memory to the screen DC. If *CreateDIBSection* is not available, we use *StretchDIBits* to do the same thing.

The palette is restored in the DC, completing the operation.

There are quite a few lines of code here, but the functionality is really quite simple: work out the rectangle to copy, and copy it. Of course, it's the details that make it all work so well, and if you followed the earlier chapters, you'll understand why. If you didn't, I guess you can cut and paste the code and just use it!

The Testing Phase

Writing this sort of code isn't really very exciting. It contains lots of important little details that make it work, but when we get down to seeing what it does, it's not at all impressive. Still, we need to test whether we can create a *COSBView* object, draw to its buffer, and see the results in the view window. To do this, I added some code to the document module that creates a view and draws a red rectangle into its center:

```
BOOL CAnimDoc::OnNewDocument()
{
    if (!CDocument::OnNewDocument())
        return FALSE;

    // Just to test the off-screen buffered view Draw function,
    // create a DIB and create the off-screen buffer
    // to match it.
    CDIB dib;
    dib.Create(320, 240);  // A classic size
```

(continued)

```
POSITION pos;
pos = GetFirstViewPosition();
ASSERT(pos);
COSBView* pView = (COSBView*)GetNextView(pos);
ASSERT(pView);
ASSERT(pView->IsKindOf(RUNTIME_CLASS(COSBView)));
if (!pView->Create(&dib)) {
    TRACE("Failed to create buffered view");
    return FALSE;
}

// Just for fun, fill a chunk of the view buffer
// with a red rectangle.
CDIB* pDIB = pView->GetDIB();
ASSERT(pDIB);
int iWidth = pDIB->GetWidth();
int iHeight = pDIB->GetHeight();
BYTE bIndex =
    pView->GetPalette()->GetNearestPaletteIndex(RGB(255,0,0));
for (int j = iHeight / 4; j < iHeight * 3 / 4; j++) {
    BYTE* pBits = (BYTE*)pDIB->GetPixelAddress(iWidth / 4, j);
    for (int i = 0; i < iWidth / 2; i++) {
        *pBits++ = bIndex;
    }
}

return TRUE;
}
```

A new *CDIB* object that is 320 by 240 pixels is created. A pointer to the view is obtained, and we use an ASSERT statement to test that it really is a *COSBView* object. Having assured ourselves that we have what we expected, we call *COSBView::Create* to create a buffer to match the DIB. Notice that in order to get a pointer to the view we need to use calls to *GetFirstViewPosition* and *GetNextView*. This seems a little complex given that we have only one view, but that's the way it has to be done.

So that we have something to look at, a red rectangle is rendered into the center of the buffer DIB, and we use another new function in *CDIB*. The *GetPixelAddress* function finds the start address of each line of the rectangle. Here's the code for *CDIB::GetPixelAddress*:

```
void* CDIB::GetPixelAddress(int x, int y)
{
    int iWidth;
    // This version deals only with 8-bpp DIBs.
    ASSERT(m_pBMI->bmiHeader.biBitCount == 8);
    // Make sure it's in range, and if it isn't, return NULL.
    if ((x >= DibWidth())
```

```
        !! (y >= DibHeight())) {
            TRACE("Attempt to get out-of-range pixel address");
            return NULL;
        }
        iWidth = StorageWidth();
        return m_pBits + (DibHeight()-y-1) * iWidth + x;
}
```

Note that this function handles only 8-bpp DIBs, but that's fine for now.

Having gotten this far, we can compile and run the application. What you should see is shown in black and white in **Figure 7-1**.

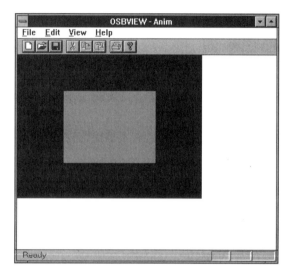

Figure 7-1   *The result of running the* OSBView *version of ANIM.EXE.*

The view window shows the buffered area as a black rectangle—remember that this is the initial state of the *CDIB* image pixels—with the "red" rectangle drawn in its center. Outside the buffered area, the view window is painted with whatever you have set for your window background color.

Obviously, we could resize the window to fit the buffer or use a WM_ERASEBKGND message handler to paint the extra area black too, but leaving things as they are allows for very simple testing of the redraw code. Resize the application and watch it redraw—it should be very fast.

The code in this chapter doesn't look very complicated, but it does embody all that we've learned so far about DIBs, palettes, *StretchDIBits*, and so on. In the next chapter, we'll get back to looking at real images by creating a background picture for the animation scene.

Dog strip

RunDog background

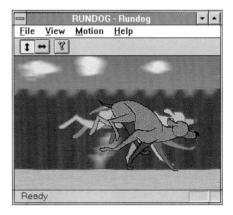

Dog running in place

Dog running and moving

In the RunDog sample, the strip of dog images on the left is combined with the background scene at the top to give either a scene in which the dog runs in place as the background goes by or a scene with a static background in which the dog runs by.

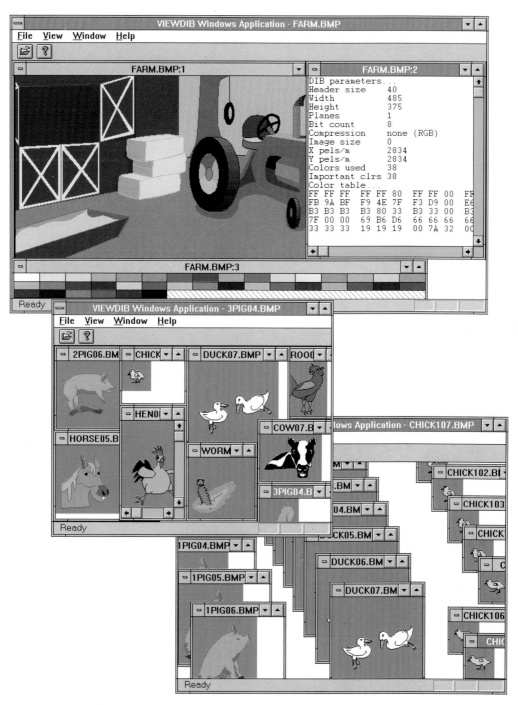

ViewDIB with a few DIB files open
The ViewDIB sample is shown here with a number of bitmaps (DIBs) open. ViewDIB can show the image of a DIB, the DIB's palette, and a data dump of the DIB's header and color table.

```
─                    Microsoft Visual C++ - RUNDOG.MAK                    ▼ ▲
 File   Edit   View   Project   Browse   Debug   Tools   Options   Window   Help
  ┌──┐ ┌──┐ ┌──┐ ┌─────────────────────┐ ▼ ┌──┐ ┌──┐┌──┐┌──┐  ┌──┐  ┌──┐┌──┐┌──┐┌──┐
  │  │ │  │ │  │ │                     │   │  │ │  ││  ││  │  │  │  │  ││  ││  ││  │
  └──┘ └──┘ └──┘ └─────────────────────┘   └──┘ └──┘└──┘└──┘  └──┘  └──┘└──┘└──┘└──┘
  ┌──────────────────────────────────────────────────────────────────────┐
  │ ─            <1> C:\ANIM32\RUNDOG\RUNDGVW.CPP                    ▼ ▲ │
  │ CDIB* pdibBkgnd = pDoc->GetBackground();                          ▲ │
  │ int iBkgndWidth = pdibBkgnd->GetWidth();                            │
  │ if (! pDoc->IsInPlace()) {                                          │
  │     // Move the dog to a new position.                             │
  │     int iX = pSprite->GetX();                                       │
  │     int iSpriteWidth = pSprite->GetWidth();                        │
  │     iX += 50;                                                       │
  │     if (iX > iBkgndWidth) {                                         │
  │         iX = -iSpriteWidth;                                         │
  │         if ((rand() % 10) == 1) pDoc->Woof();                     ▼ │
  │     }                                                               │
  │ ◄                                                                ► │
  │──────────────────────────────────────────────────────────────────│
  │ ─            <2> C:\ANIM32\RUNDOG\MAINFRM.CPP                    ▼ ▲ │
  │     if (!m_wndToolBar.Create(this) ||                             ▲ │
  │         !m_wndToolBar.LoadBitmap(IDR_MAINFRAME) ||                  │
  │         !m_wndToolBar.SetButtons(buttons,                           │
  │           sizeof(buttons)/sizeof(UINT)))                            │
  │     {                                                               │
  │         TRACE("Failed to create toolbar\n");                       │
  │         return -1;        // fail to create                        │
  │     }                                                               │
  │                                                                     │
  │     if (!m_wndStatusBar.Create(this) ||                            │
  │         !m_wndStatusBar.SetIndicators(indicators,                ▼ │
  │ ◄                                                                ► │
  └──────────────────────────────────────────────────────────────────┘
                                                        ┌──────┐┌────┐
                                                        │00065 ││001 │
                                                        └──────┘└────┘
```

Using Visual C++ to help with the animation process
Just to prove that it's not all smoke and mirrors—here's a screen shot of Visual C++ being used to develop one of the sample applications.

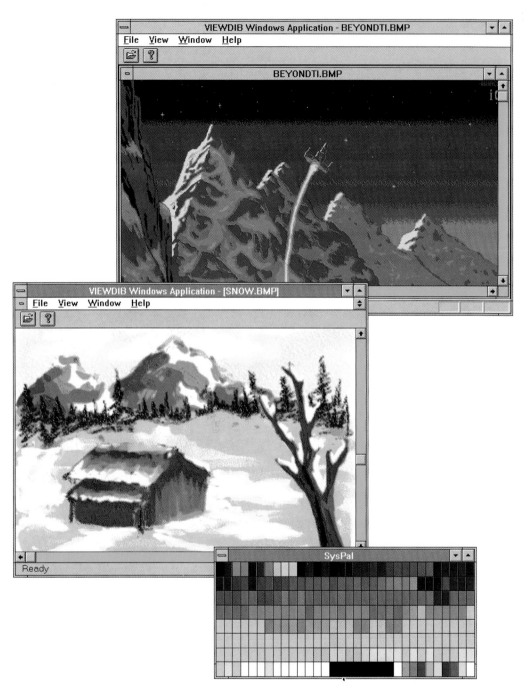

SysPal inspection of a DIB
This screen shot shows the SysPal sample being used to display the current state of the
system (hardware) palette. The ViewDIB sample has several images open. The currently
active image is being used to set the system palette.

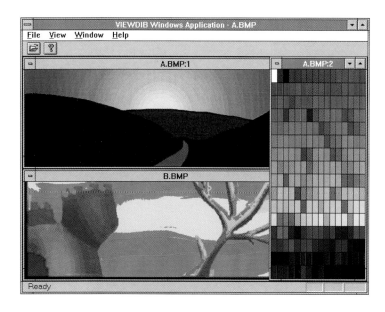

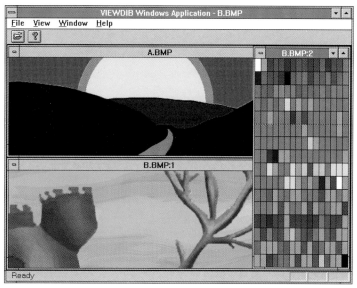

The difference between the palette for an active application and the palette for an inactive application

These two screen shots show what happens when two very different images compete for the limited system palette. Notice in the first that the active A application has its colors rendered correctly but that the inactive B application has to make do with what it's given. In the second, the active B application has control and the inactive A application has to make do.

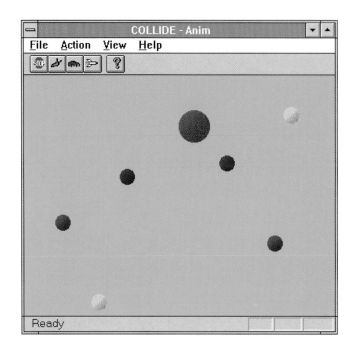

Collide
The picture shows a screen shot of the Collide sample, which simulates the physics of perfect
inelastic collision on a frictionless surface.

Herman's Farm Yard
This screen shot from the Farm sample shows a typical scene from a typical children's application.
Each animal responds to a mouse click with a sound and a short animation sequence.

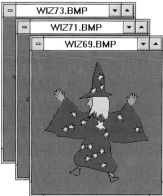

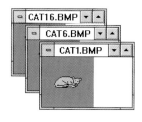

The wizard's lair
This screen shot from the Wizard sample shows a characteristic scene from another type of game. Click-sensitive areas of the scene start up animation sequences involving the wizard character.

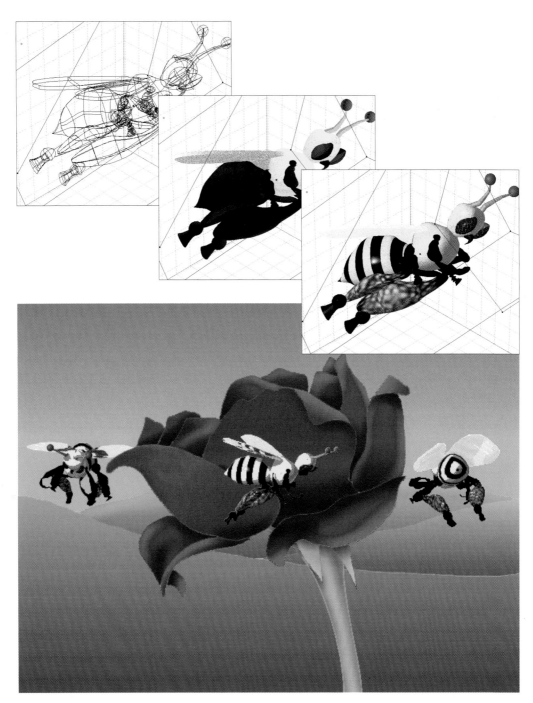

Doin' the Bee Buzz Bop
This composite picture is made from some of the frames in the Bee sample. The Bee application's sprite images were created with 3D modeling software. Using prerendered 3D images as sprites enables you to manipulate spectacular-looking characters with good performance.

Creating a Background Image

CHAPTER

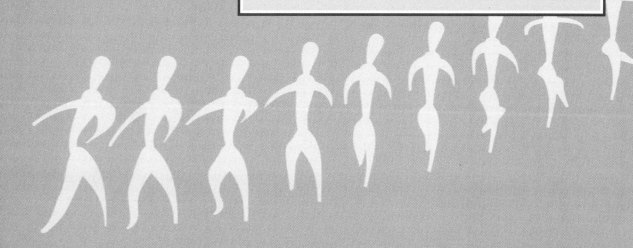

n this chapter, we'll begin to create an animated scene by creating a background image. Later we'll see how to add sprites on top of the background to complete the scene. The sample code so far has been reasonably general. In this chapter, we'll start to make the sample more specific by defining document and view classes that are tailored to the way we want the application to behave overall. We'll continue to develop the *CDIB* and *COSBView* classes, adding new functions as we need them. **Figure 8-1** shows the class structure of this chapter's sample (in the Bkgnd directory) so that we can see how all the classes fit together. The Microsoft Foundation Class Library (MFC) classes are shown with a dark background.

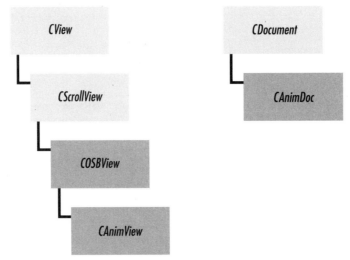

Figure 8-1 *The class structure of the Bkgnd sample.*

The *CAnimDoc* class will be the container for all the data needed to define an animated scene. So far as we are concerned now, it will hold the device-independent bitmap (DIB) for the background image. *CAnimView* is going to be responsible for painting the scene to the view window. Things are going to get a bit more interesting with this class because *CAnimView* won't be drawing to a regular Windows device context (DC); instead, it's going to be drawing to the buffer created in the *COSBView* class.

Document-View Communication

In a normal document-view application created by means of MFC, the view class gets access to the document through its *GetDocument* member function. The document potentially has many view classes to communicate with, and its primary means of doing this is through calls to the *UpdateAllViews* function. *UpdateAllViews* is a do-all function that has a provision for passing a 32-bit message parameter known as a *hint* to each of the views. In an earlier design, I used hints to communicate with the view class, defining hints for each function I required. So, for example, to tell the view that the document had a new background image, I defined a hint that passed a pointer to the new image to the view. As I reviewed this code, I found it to be rather cumbersome and felt that it cluttered up what I wanted to do with the details of the implementation. In addition, I felt it was extremely unlikely that anyone would want to create an animation that had more than one view. We hardly have the processor power for one animation, let alone several. Consequently, I have altered the design so that the document works with only the first view attached to the document and calls public member functions in the view rather than passing the view hints through *UpdateAllViews*. If you're an MFC purist, you can easily modify what I've done so that it uses hints instead of direct calls to the view class.

The Objective

We want to add a *CDIB* object to the document and have it made visible in the view. In order to achieve this seemingly simple objective, we must take many small steps. Some of the steps may seem pointless to you at this stage, but bear with me—we'll make more pointed use of them later, when we add sprites to the scene. I have chosen to handle menu events in the document class rather than in the view class since handling them in the document class makes more sense and allows me to reuse code more often. In particular, an event such as loading the background image in response to a user selection is very similar to loading a background image from a file containing an entire scene, and although we won't deal with saving and restoring scenes until later, having the code already present in the document class will reduce the work we need to do later.

The Bkgnd Application

I created the sample application in the Bkgnd directory by copying the source files for the OSBView sample and modifying them to include the new functionality. Let's go through the process step by step, looking at the code to see what each bit of it does.

\anim32\bkgnd

The first step is to add a *CDIB* object to the document class to contain the background image DIB. As usual, we also add a function to return a pointer to the object so that the view can access the object when it needs to be drawn. Here are the bits of ANIMDOC.H that are of interest:

```
class CAnimDoc : public CDocument
{
     :
     :
// Attributes
public:
    CDIB* GetBackground() {return m_pBkgndDIB;}
     :
     :
private:
    CDIB* m_pBkgndDIB;             // Pointer to background DIB
};
```

The *CAnimDoc* constructor and destructor functions in ANIMDOC.CPP are implemented in a way that should be getting very familiar to you by now:

```
CAnimDoc::CAnimDoc()
{
    m_pBkgndDIB = NULL;
}

CAnimDoc::~CAnimDoc()
{
    if (m_pBkgndDIB) {
        delete m_pBkgndDIB;
    }
}
```

The document now contains an object that we can use to hold the background image.

Let's leave the document for a moment and look at the view class. The biggest change from the previous sample (OSBView) is that the application's view class is now derived from *COSBView*. Because Visual C++ version 1.1 doesn't provide a way to create an application's view class based on a user-supplied class, we first create the skeleton of the application with the view class, *CAnimView*, based simply on *CView*, and then go into the code and manually change it so that the *CAnimView* class is derived from *COSBView*. Forcing this derivation involves changing all the occurrences of *CView* to *COSBView* in the ANIMVIEW.H and ANIMVIEW.CPP files. And that's not quite the end of the changes we need to make because *COSBView* is derived from *CScrollView*, not *CView*, so the *CAnimView* class needs to include an *OnInitialUpdate* function so that the scroll ranges can be set when the class is first created. Conveniently for now, we can let the *COSBView* base class handle this:

```
void CAnimView::OnInitialUpdate()
{
    COSBView::OnInitialUpdate();
}
```

The *OnDraw* function created by AppWizard can also be handled entirely by the *COSBView* base class:

```
void CAnimView::OnDraw(CDC* pDC)
{
    COSBView::OnDraw(pDC);
}
```

Now that this trivial piece of work is finished, the view class is capable of drawing the off-screen buffer contents created by the *COSBView* base class.

Let's return now to the document class and see what we need to do to create a new document. The *CAnimDoc::OnNewDocument* function is called whenever a new document is created. For single-document interface (SDI) applications, the document object is reused, so a part of the job of *OnNew-Document* is to reinitialize the document's member variables, being careful not to cause any memory leaks by forgetting to delete any objects we might have pointers to. After you first write the code, you may find the same few lines repeated in different places and can tidy up later on by using a few simple helper functions. We'll start out with the benefit of 20/20 hindsight and incorporate the helper functions right from the start. This will also allow me to write a few lines of code and reveal the workings in simple stages. Here's the *OnNewDocument* code:

```
BOOL CAnimDoc::OnNewDocument()
{
    if (!CDocument::OnNewDocument())
        return FALSE;
    // Create a new default background DIB just so that
    // there will be something to look at.
    CDIB* pDIB = new CDIB;
    pDIB->Create(320, 240);
    SetBackground(pDIB);
    SetModifiedFlag(FALSE);
    return TRUE;
}
```

A new 320-by-240-pixel *CDIB* object is created. Remember that the *CDIB* class will create an 8-bits-per-pixel (bpp) DIB by default and fill all the pixels with black. The new DIB is selected as the current background image by a call to the *SetBackground* helper function. The modification flag for the document is reset to indicate that no changes have occurred yet. We'll look at what *SetBackground* does in just a moment, but before we do that, we need to consider the issue of object ownership.

Object Ownership

One of the most hideous problems involved in passing pointers to objects as parameters is that it can be very hard to determine which bits of code can safely delete the object. Microsoft's component object model (COM), on which OLE is built, solves this problem by making it the responsibility of the object to delete itself when it is no longer in use by any other object. The object does this by effectively keeping track of how many times a pointer to the object has been created and how many times it has been told that one of those pointers is no longer in use. All COM objects support two functions, *AddRef* and *Release*, which are used to increment and decrement the object's usage count, respectively. For the COM system to work, code using COM objects has to be religious about calling *AddRef* and *Release* correctly, especially if the code ever copies pointers to COM objects. Given that the code is written correctly (that's a pretty big given!), there is no requirement for any user of a COM object to worry about whether it's safe to delete it because the object takes care of that by deleting itself when its own usage count falls to 0. You might say it's an "I have no more friends, so I'll shoot myself" system.

In implementing the code for the samples in this book, I was tempted to use the COM system for each of the objects. This is, after all, the up-and-coming way of doing things. I decided, though, that you probably had enough to do just learning about animation and that adding the requirement that you understand COM was too much, so no COM for you today.

Given that I haven't used the COM system for the objects, we need to be careful about object ownership in the code. If we aren't careful, the result will be memory leaks and access violations. The Visual C++ debug environment is very good at helping to track down both of these situations, so debugging for them is actually pretty easy, but it's still better to avoid a problem than to build one in and remove it later.

Setting the Background

The *SetBackground* function is called with a pointer to the new DIB that is to be used as the background image. The DIB becomes owned by the document as a result of this call and will be deleted by the document when the document is destroyed or when the background DIB is replaced by a new one. Changing the background image is obviously going to involve some redrawing operations, but we'll come to those shortly. Here's the code for the *SetBackground* function:

```
BOOL CAnimDoc::SetBackground(CDIB* pDIB)
{
    // Delete any existing background DIB and set the new one.
    if (m_pBkgndDIB) delete m_pBkgndDIB;
    m_pBkgndDIB = pDIB;

    // Note that the document has changed.
    SetModifiedFlag(TRUE);

    // Tell the view that it needs to create a new buffer
    // and palette.
    CAnimView* pView = GetAnimView();
    ASSERT(pView);
    return pView->NewBackground(m_pBkgndDIB);
}
```

Any existing background image is deleted and replaced by the new one. Note that passing a NULL pointer to *SetBackground* results in there being no background image at all. The document is then marked as having changed.

We'll come back to the *CAnimView::NewBackground* function in just a minute, but first let's add a menu item to load a new background image. I used App Studio to add a Load Background item to the File menu and then used ClassWizard to create a handler function for this command in the *CAnimDoc* class. Here's the handler code:

```
void CAnimDoc::OnFileLoadBkgnd()
{
    // Create a DIB to hold the image.
    CDIB* pDIB = new CDIB;
    // Show the File Open dialog for a DIB.
    if (!pDIB->Load()) {
        delete pDIB;
        return;
    }
    // Replace any existing background DIB with the new one.
    if (!SetBackground(pDIB)) {
        delete pDIB;
    }
}
```

OnFileLoadBkgnd uses a new *Load* function in the *CDIB* class to show a dialog box that allows the user to choose and load a DIB for the background image. If that's successful, the *SetBackground* function makes the newly loaded DIB the current background image. The *CDIB::Load* function shown on the next page is yet another overloading of the existing *CDIB::Load* function, which simply takes a file name or NULL.

```
BOOL CDIB::Load(LPSTR pszFileName)
{
    CString strFile;

    if ((pszFileName == NULL) ||
        (strlen(pszFileName) == 0)) {

        // Show an Open File dialog to get the name.
        CFileDialog dlg    (TRUE,      // Open
                            NULL,      // No default extension
                            NULL,      // No initial file name
                            OFN_FILEMUSTEXIST |
                            OFN_HIDEREADONLY,
                            "Image files (*.DIB, *.BMP)|*.DIB;*.BMP|\
All files (*.*)|*.*||");
        if (dlg.DoModal() == IDOK) {
            strFile = dlg.GetPathName();
        } else {
            return FALSE;
        }
    } else {
        // Copy the supplied file path.
        strFile = pszFileName;
    }

    // Try to open the file for read access.
    CFile file;
    if (!file.Open(strFile,
                   CFile::modeRead | CFile::shareDenyWrite)) {
        AfxMessageBox("Failed to open file");
        return FALSE;
    }

    BOOL bResult = Load(&file);
    file.Close();
    if (!bResult) AfxMessageBox("Failed to load file");
    return bResult;
}
```

Now we have a menu item for loading a new DIB image for the background and code for attaching the image to the document.

Next we need to do two things: create a new off-screen buffer and redraw the view. You'll recall that creating an off-screen buffer also involves creating a new palette to be used when the buffer is drawn to the view window's device context (DC). The palette is created from the color table of a DIB supplied to the *COSBView::Create* function. In the architecture of our sample application, the palette used for the scene is defined by the color table used in the background DIB. The palette could just as easily have come from somewhere else, but I found it convenient to base the palette on the background image because it already has a color table and this reduces the code. Some way has to be found to tell the view to create a new buffer based on the background image DIB passed to *SetBackground*. This is done by a call to the *NewBackground* function in the *CAnimView* class, which passes a pointer to the background DIB as an argument. Before we can call *CAnimView::NewBackground*, we need to get a pointer to the view; this is obtained by a call to the *CAnimDoc::GetAnimView* helper function:

```
CAnimView* CAnimDoc::GetAnimView()
{
    POSITION pos;
    pos = GetFirstViewPosition();
    ASSERT(pos);
    CAnimView* pView = (CAnimView*)GetNextView(pos);
    ASSERT(pView);
    ASSERT(pView->IsKindOf(RUNTIME_CLASS(CAnimView)));
    return pView;
}
```

The function gets a pointer to the first view associated with the document and verifies that it is a pointer to a *CAnimView* object before returning it. Remember, this works only for the first view. If you plan to have more than one view attached to the document, you'll need to look at using *UpdateAllViews* with hints.

Having obtained a pointer to the view, we can call the view's public member functions. Now we can see what *CAnimView::NewBackground* does:

```
BOOL CAnimView::NewBackground(CDIB* pDIB)
{
    // Create a new buffer and palette.
    if (!Create(pDIB)) {
        return FALSE;
    }

    // Map the colors of the background DIB to
    // the identity palette we just created for the background.
    pDIB->MapColorsToPalette(GetPalette());

    // Resize the main frame window to fit the background image.
    GetParentFrame()->RecalcLayout();
    ResizeParentToFit(FALSE); // Try shrinking first.
    ResizeParentToFit(TRUE);  // Let's be daring.

    // Render the entire scene to the off-screen buffer.
    Render();

    // Paint the off-screen buffer to the window.
    Draw();

    return TRUE;
}
```

The *COSBView::Create* base class function is called to create a new buffer the same size as the DIB and with a palette created from the DIB's color table. OK so far? Do you remember that in order to do fast screen updates, the palette we use must be an identity palette? Well, *COSBView* creates an identity palette from the color table we supplied in the DIB. That's all well and good, but we now need to modify the DIB so that its colors map exactly to the palette. If we don't do this, when we copy pixels (which are palette indices) from the DIB to the off-screen buffer, the colors will come out wrong. The call to *CDIB::MapColorsToPalette* remaps the DIB's pixel values so that they correctly index into the identity palette used by the off-screen view *and* alters the DIB's color table just in case we feel the need to use it later. In practice, we will constrain ourselves to using only the palette index values in the DIB and never again refer to the DIB color table, so altering the color table in the DIB to match the palette is redundant here.

To make things look pretty, we adjust the size of the parent frame so that the view window exactly fits the background image. The code here was taken from a Microsoft Foundation Class Library (MFC) *KnowledgeBase* article ("Using CFormView in SDI and MDI Applications," Q98598) and is a little bit obscure (to say the least).

Now that we have a new buffer and palette ready, we need to render the background DIB to the buffer and then update the screen. The *Render* function copies the background DIB to the off-screen buffer. The *Draw* function copies the off-screen buffer to the view window. Remember that *Draw* is implemented in the *COSBView* base class so we don't need to add any code here but that the *Render* function is new:

```
void CAnimView::Render(CRect* pClipRect)
{
    CAnimDoc* pDoc = GetDocument();
    CRect rcDraw;

    // Get the background DIB and render it.
    CDIB* pDIB = pDoc->GetBackground();
    if (pDIB) {
        pDIB->GetRect(&rcDraw);
        // If a clipping rectangle was supplied, use it.
        if (pClipRect) {
            rcDraw.IntersectRect(pClipRect, &rcDraw);
        }

        // Draw the image of the DIB to the off-screen buffer.
        ASSERT(m_pDIB);
        pDIB->CopyBits(m_pDIB,
                    rcDraw.left,
                    rcDraw.top,
                    rcDraw.right - rcDraw.left,
                    rcDraw.bottom - rcDraw.top,
```

```
                rcDraw.left,
                rcDraw.top);
    }
}
```

It might look a bit silly to have a separate function just for this, but
when we add some sprites to the scene later, the function will take on a whole
new role. The *pClipRect* parameter is optional and defaults to NULL, meaning
that the function should be clipped to the entire buffer area.

In rendering and drawing an image to the screen, it is most important to
the performance to always move as little data as possible, so clipping the area
to be modified down to the smallest rectangle possible is well worth the small
amount of code involved. In this case, the default action is to clip the area to
the size of the background image DIB. If a clipping rectangle is specified by
pClipRect, this rectangle is intersected by the background DIB rectangle, and
the area to be modified is thus defined.

The background DIB pixels are copied to the off-screen buffer DIB by a
call to another new function, *CDIB::CopyBits*:

```
void CDIB::CopyBits(CDIB* pdibDest,
                    int xd, int yd,
                    int w, int h,
                    int xs, int ys)
{
    ASSERT(m_pBMI->bmiHeader.biBitCount == 8);
    ASSERT(pdibDest);
    // Test for silly cases.
    if (w == 0 || h == 0) return;

    // Get pointers to the start points in the source and
    // destination DIBs. Note that these will be the bottom-left corners
    // of the DIBs because the scan lines are reversed in memory.
    BYTE* pSrc = (BYTE*)GetPixelAddress(xs, ys + h - 1);
    ASSERT(pSrc);
    BYTE* pDest = (BYTE*)pdibDest->GetPixelAddress(xd, yd + h - 1);
    ASSERT(pDest);

    // Get the scan line widths of each DIB.
    int iScanS = StorageWidth();
    int iScanD = pdibDest->StorageWidth();

    // Copy the lines.
    while (h--) {
        memcpy(pDest, pSrc, w);
        pSrc += iScanS;
        pDest += iScanD;
    }
}
```

Note that this version of *CopyBits* supports copying to and from 8-bpp DIBs only. Copying is performed by computing the width of the scan line segment affected and then using *memcpy* to move the bits from one DIB to the other. Note that all DIBs must have *DWORD*-aligned scan lines, so the line start pointers are incremented by the storage width, not by the logical width, of the DIB image. We'll be coming back to this function later to implement a version that copies only nontransparent pixels when a sprite is rendered.

Now that we have a background image, we can move on and look at what it takes to create a sprite or two and add them to the scene.

CHAPTER

Sprites, Transparency, Hit Testing, and Sharing the Palette

n this chapter, we will create a new class called *CSprite*, based on the *CDIB* class, to handle sprites. Since sprites are typically irregular in shape, we will need to be able to draw the images of the sprites with some areas transparent, and since all the sprites will be displayed over a common background, we will need to share a palette between the sprites and the background in order to get the performance we want. We will also add code to detect when a mouse click occurs on the nontransparent area of a sprite. Such detection is usually referred to as *hit testing*. We'll add some more code to allow a sprite to be dragged by the mouse to any position on the screen. Sound like a tall order to you? Actually it's not that bad, and as usual, we'll go through it step by step. To simplify things a little, the sample we'll create for this chapter will handle only one sprite, and when the sprite gets moved, we'll simply repaint the entire scene. We'll add more sprites and a better repaint algorithm in later chapters.

The *CSprite* Class

Let's begin with a look at the new *CSprite* class. Since sprites are images of a sort, it makes sense to derive the *CSprite* class from *CDIB*. If we do this the right way, we can use a lot of the functions in *CDIB* directly, and for those functions that do the same sort of thing as the ones in *CDIB* but are different for sprites (the *Load* functions, for example), we can implement the variant function in the *CSprite* class. *Figure 9-1* shows how *CSprite* fits into the class hierarchy. Again, the Microsoft Foundation Class Library (MFC) classes are shown with a dark background.

A sprite differs from a simple image by having an irregular shape and having a position in the overall scene that can be described by *x*, *y*, and *z* screen coordinates. The irregular shape is achieved by defining one color in the image as transparent. I chose to use the color of the top-left pixel of the sprite image to define the transparency color of my sprites. When authoring a sprite, you simply reserve one color for the transparent areas and fill the out-

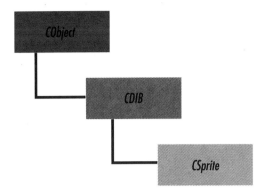

Figure 9-1 *The line of derivation for* CSprite.

side (and any holes) with that color, being sure to include the top-left pixel in the outside fill. The *x* and *y* coordinates control where the sprite will appear in the scene, and the *z* coordinate controls the sprite's depth in the picture.

Our *CSprite* class needs some variables in which to store its coordinates and its transparency information. Let's look at the header file to see how the variables are defined. For the coordinates, we will also include member functions to retrieve them from the object as usual. Here are the bits of SPRITE.H that are of interest:

\anim32\sprite

```
class CSprite : public CDIB
{
public:
    virtual int GetX() {return m_x;}    // Get x.
    virtual int GetY() {return m_y;}    // Get y.
    virtual int GetZ() {return m_z;}    // Get z-order.
    .
    .
    .
protected:
    int m_x;                    // x coordinate of top-left corner
    int m_y;                    // y coordinate of top-left corner
    int m_z;                    // z-order for sprite
    BYTE m_bTransIndex;         // Transparency index value
    .
    .
    .
};
```

Note that the transparency information is stored as the palette index of the transparency color. This is done to improve performance. We could have omitted this variable and simply looked at the top-left pixel color of the image every time the sprite was drawn, but by caching the data here, we avoid a huge number of calls to the same piece of code. Note, too, that I am assuming the sprite is based on an 8-bit-per-pixel (bpp) DIB. If you wanted to make this more general, you could define the transparency information as a COLORREF item that could be either a palette index or an RGB value. I chose to simply use the palette index, as it makes the code a little simpler and easier to follow.

As with the other classes we have created, the constructor and destructor functions are kept as simple as possible:

```
CSprite::CSprite()
{
    m_x = 0;
    m_y = 0;
    m_z = 50;
    m_bTransIndex = 0;
}


CSprite::~CSprite()
{
}
```

The z-order is set to 50, which is (in this design) halfway between the back and the front of the scene.

Adding a Sprite to the Document

Now we need to add some code and data to the application's document class so that we can load a sprite into the scene. To simplify things for now, we'll have only one sprite. That will allow us to implement all the sprite code and test it without having to worry about lists, z-order, and so on. The ANIMDOC.H file now has a single *CSprite* object pointer and a function to return the pointer:

```
class CAnimDoc : public CDocument
{
public:
    CDIB* GetBackground() {return m_pBkgndDIB;}
    CSprite* GetSprite() {return m_pSprite;}
      .
      .
private:
    CDIB* m_pBkgndDIB;          // Pointer to background DIB
    CSprite* m_pSprite;         // Pointer to a single sprite
      .
      .
};
```

So now our document can have a background image and a single sprite. The *CAnimDoc* constructor and destructor need to have code added to handle the new sprite object:

```
CAnimDoc::CAnimDoc()
{
    m_pBkgndDIB = NULL;
    m_pSprite = NULL;
}
```

```
CAnimDoc::~CAnimDoc()
{
    if (m_pBkgndDIB) {
        delete m_pBkgndDIB;
    }
    if (m_pSprite) {
        delete m_pSprite;
    }
}
```

Since the background image is used to define the common palette used for a scene and all sprites must be mapped to this palette if their colors are to come out right when they are drawn, I chose to make the action of loading a new background image destroy any existing sprite in a scene. This might not be what you want, but it helps to keep things simple in the sample in this chapter. Since changing a scene usually involves at least repositioning its sprites, I didn't consider this too restrictive to the design.

Another convenience of using a new background to reset the entire scene is that it helps keep all the tidy-up code in one place—all the cleanup is done in the *CAnimDoc::SetBackground* function. So the code for this version of the application simply destroys any existing sprite:

```
BOOL CAnimDoc::SetBackground(CDIB* pDIB)
{
    // Delete any existing sprite.
    if (m_pSprite) {
        delete m_pSprite;
        m_pSprite = NULL;
    }

    // Delete any existing background DIB and set the new one.
    if (m_pBkgndDIB) delete m_pBkgndDIB;
    m_pBkgndDIB = pDIB;

    // Note that the document has changed.
    SetModifiedFlag(TRUE);

    // Tell the view that it needs to create a new buffer
    // and palette.
    CAnimView* pView = GetAnimView();
    ASSERT(pView);
    return pView->NewBackground(m_pBkgndDIB);
}
```

Now we can add a menu item for loading a sprite. I used AppWizard to add a Load Sprite menu item to the File menu and ClassWizard to add a handler function for the new menu item to the *CAnimDoc* class.

```
void CAnimDoc::OnFileLoadSprite()
{
    // Create a sprite to hold the image.
    CSprite* pSprite = new CSprite;
    // Show the File Open dialog for a sprite.
    if (!pSprite->Load()) {
        delete pSprite;
        return;
    }
    // Replace any existing sprite with the new one.
    if (m_pSprite) {
        delete m_pSprite;
    }
    m_pSprite = pSprite;
    // Tell the view about the new sprite.
    GetAnimView()->NewSprite(pSprite);
}
```

A new *CSprite* object is created, and its *Load* function is invoked to show the dialog box that enables the user to select the image file. Note that the *Load* function is the one defined in the *CDIB* class from which *CSprite* is derived. Using *CDIB*'s *Load* will work very nicely for now since all we care about is getting the DIB image loaded. Once the image is loaded, a call is made to *NewSprite*, a new function in the view class, to tell it about the new sprite so that the sprite can be drawn.

Drawing a New Sprite in the View

There are two reasons for notifying the view that a new sprite has been added to the scene. First (and rather obviously), the sprite needs to be made visible by drawing, and second, the colors in the sprite must be mapped to the palette being used by the off-screen view buffer.

Note that even if the background and sprites are all authored with the same palette, there is still a need to map the sprite to the off-screen buffer palette because of the way in which the system colors affect the logical-to-physical mapping of palette entries. The palette in the off-screen buffer is created from the color table in the background DIB. When the palette is made into an identity palette (for maximum performance), the colors can potentially be reordered, so the pixels in the background DIB and any sprites must be altered to correctly index into the new (identity) palette. If you don't map the sprite's colors to the off-screen palette, the sprite's colors will come out all wrong. Still not sure? That's OK—you're not alone. Go back and review Chapter 3, "Palettes and the Palette Manager," if you want to get the details straight, or just accept this as one of those things you need to do and press on.

This all sounds like a lot of work, so before panic sets in let's look at the simple *CAnimView::NewSprite* function:

```
void CAnimView::NewSprite(CSprite* pSprite)
{
    // Map the colors in the sprite DIB to the
    // palette in the off-screen buffered view.
    if (m_pPal) {
        pSprite->MapColorsToPalette(m_pPal);
    }

    // Render the scene with the new sprite.
    Render();

    // Draw the result.
    Draw();
}
```

Nothing to it, eh? The DIB's colors are mapped to the palette by a call to the *MapColorsToPalette* function. The *Render* function is called to render the image of the sprite to the off-screen buffer, and the *Draw* function copies the buffer to the screen, making the sprite visible in the scene. The *MapColorsToPalette* function is almost identical to the one we developed for the *CDIB* class:

```
BOOL CSprite::MapColorsToPalette(CPalette* pPal)
{
    BOOL bResult = CDIB::MapColorsToPalette(pPal);
    // Get the transparency info again.
    Initialize();
    return bResult;
}
```

NOTE

We are currently ignoring the sprite's position and simply rendering and drawing the entire scene. We'll look at optimizing these operations in the next chapter.

In fact, you can see that *CDIB::MapColorsToPalette* is called to do the actual mapping, and the only work specific to the *CSprite* class that we need to do is to get the transparency information again. We need to do this because we are using a palette index to define which color in the sprite image is transparent and that color may get remapped when *MapColorsToPalette* is called.

The *Render* function needs a small addition to handle rendering the sprite in addition to rendering the background image:

```
void CAnimView::Render(CRect* pClipRect)
{
    CAnimDoc* pDoc = GetDocument();
    CRect rcDraw;

    // Get the background DIB and render it.
    CDIB* pDIB = pDoc->GetBackground();
    if (pDIB) {
        pDIB->GetRect(&rcDraw);
```

(continued)

```
    // If a clipping rectangle was supplied, use it.
    if (pClipRect) {
        rcDraw.IntersectRect(pClipRect, &rcDraw);
    }

    // Draw the image of the DIB to the off-screen buffer.
    ASSERT(m_pDIB);
    pDIB->CopyBits(m_pDIB,
                   rcDraw.left,
                   rcDraw.top,
                   rcDraw.right - rcDraw.left,
                   rcDraw.bottom - rcDraw.top,
                   rcDraw.left,
                   rcDraw.top);
}

// Get the sprite and render it.
CSprite* pSprite = pDoc->GetSprite();
if (pSprite) {
    pSprite->Render(m_pDIB, &rcDraw);
}
}
```

The background image is rendered to the buffer first. If a sprite exists, it's rendered to the off-screen buffer on top of the background. This is what I call "object-oriented cheating." Instead of writing a lot of code to render the image of the sprite to the off-screen buffer, we just ask the sprite to do the job itself. Joking aside, this makes a lot of sense since it keeps the sprite-specific code in the sprite object and allows us to focus on functionality rather than implementation details here.

Of course, we still have to write the rendering code for the sprite, so let's see that next:

```
void CSprite::Render(CDIB* pDIB, CRect* pClipRect)
{
    ASSERT(pDIB);

    // Get the sprite rectangle.
    CRect rcDraw;
    GetRect(&rcDraw);

    // If a clipping rectangle was supplied, see if the sprite
    // is visible inside the rectangle.
    if (pClipRect) {
        if (!rcDraw.IntersectRect(pClipRect, &rcDraw)) {
            return; // Not visible
        }
    }
```

```
    // Copy the image of the sprite.
    CopyBits(pDIB,                            // Destination DIB
            rcDraw.left,                      // Destination x
            rcDraw.top,                       // Destination y
            rcDraw.right - rcDraw.left,       // Width
            rcDraw.bottom - rcDraw.top,       // Height
            rcDraw.left - m_x,                // Source x
            rcDraw.top - m_y,                 // Source y
            PALETTEINDEX(m_bTransIndex));     // Transparent color index
}
```

We first need to test whether the sprite is visible inside the clipping rectangle (if one was supplied). There's no point in wasting time drawing something that's not visible. Once the actual drawing rectangle has been computed, the *CDIB::CopyBits* function is used to copy the nontransparent parts of the sprite image to the off-screen buffer. The transparency feature of *CDIB::CopyBits* is new, and we'll look at that next.

Transparency

It would have been possible to add a *CopyBits* function to the *CSprite* class that handles transparency, but because much of the function would have been common to what *CDIB::CopyBits* already does, I decided that all I had to do was to expand the *CDIB::CopyBits* function to make it do what I wanted.

The new version of *CDIB::CopyBits* takes a COLORREF value to define the transparency color. You'll recall that a COLORREF value can be created from a palette index value or an RGB value. My sprites currently work only with 8-bpp DIBs. All manipulation of the pixels is done by effectively playing with palette index values, so the expanded *CDIB::CopyBits* function was written to handle only COLORREF values created with the PALETTEINDEX macro. You could expand the function to handle RGB values if that's what you needed. Here's the new version of *CDIB::CopyBits* from DIB.CPP:

```
void CDIB::CopyBits(CDIB* pdibDest,
                    int xd, int yd,
                    int w, int h,
                    int xs, int ys,
                    COLORREF clrTrans)
{
    ASSERT(m_pBMI->bmiHeader.biBitCount == 8);
    ASSERT(pdibDest);
    // Test for silly cases.
    if (w == 0 || h == 0) return;

    // Get pointers to the start points in the source and destination
    // DIBs. Note that the start points will be in the bottom-left
```

(continued)

```
// corner of the DIBs because the scan lines are reversed in memory.
BYTE* pSrc = (BYTE*)GetPixelAddress(xs, ys + h - 1);
ASSERT(pSrc);
BYTE* pDest = (BYTE*)pdibDest->GetPixelAddress(xd, yd + h - 1);
ASSERT(pDest);

// Get the scan line widths of each DIB.
int iScanS = StorageWidth();
int iScanD = pdibDest->StorageWidth();

if (clrTrans == 0xFFFFFFFF) {
    // Copy the lines.
    while (h--) {
        memcpy(pDest, pSrc, w);
        pSrc += iScanS;
        pDest += iScanD;
    }
} else {
    // Copy lines with transparency.
    // We accept only a PALETTEINDEX description
    // for the color definition.
    ASSERT((clrTrans & 0xFF000000) == 0x01000000);
    BYTE bTransClr = LOBYTE(LOWORD(clrTrans));
    int iSinc = iScanS - w; // Source increment value
    int iDinc = iScanD - w; // Destination increment value
    int iCount;
    BYTE pixel;
    while (h--) {
        iCount = w;     // Number of pixels to scan
        while (iCount--) {
            pixel = *pSrc++;
            // Copy pixel only if it isn't transparent.
            if (pixel != bTransClr) {
                *pDest++ = pixel;
            } else {
                pDest++;
            }
        }
        // Move on to the next line.
        pSrc += iSinc;
        pDest += iDinc;
    }
}
}
```

The exciting bit starts when we find that a transparency color has been supplied. The only clever stuff here is in dealing with the fact that DIB scan lines are *DWORD*-aligned, so the pointer arithmetic uses the storage width, not the logical image width, of the DIB image.

A closer look at the code shows two nested loops. The outer loop handles the scan lines, and the inner loop takes care of the pixels on that scan line. This is obviously not what we might call optimized code! Even so, it performs quite adequately. The results of testing the time this function takes to render a sprite compared to the time it takes to copy the rendered part of the off-screen buffer to the screen device context (DC) show that the rendering time is almost insignificant. This becomes less true when the *CreateDIBSection* function (rather than *StretchDIBits*) is used for the screen update, but the execution time of this simple piece of code is still much less than the blt time. In any case, if you want to, you can get out the assembler at this point and optimize to your heart's content. My point is that this piece of code does what we need and doesn't get in the way of the overall performance.

The Small Stuff

In trying to show you the code in a reasonably logical way, I have skipped over a couple of small but important details. Earlier on, I mentioned that we could use the *CDIB::Load* function to load the sprite image. Well, we can, but if we do that, the transparency data won't get set and the sprite will come out with random bits missing. To fix this problem, we need to ensure that whenever a sprite is created from a DIB image, the transparency color information is captured. This kind of situation can occur in several places, so I created a single simple function to keep the code in one place and make it easy to expand on if we alter the *CSprite* class later:

```
void CSprite::Initialize()
{
    // Get the address of the top-left pixel.
    BYTE* p = (BYTE*)GetPixelAddress(0, 0);
    ASSERT(p);
    // Get the pixel value and save it.
    m_bTransIndex = *p;
}
```

This function gets the value of the top-left pixel and stores it in the *m_bTransIndex* variable so that the *Render* function can use the value later.

The *CDIB* class has two versions of the *Load* function, and we need to overload both of those to ensure that, when a sprite image is loaded, the transparency data is set:

```
BOOL CSprite::Load(char* pszFileName)
{
    if (!CDIB::Load(pszFileName)) {
        return FALSE;
    }
    Initialize();
    return TRUE;
}
```

(continued)

```
BOOL CSprite::Load(CFile* fp)
{
    if (!CDIB::Load(fp)) {
        return FALSE;
    }
    Initialize();
    return TRUE;
}
```

This piece of code is no big deal. It just calls the base class *Load* function to do most of the work and then calls the *CSprite::Initialize* function to set the transparency information.

The last minor point is that the *CDIB::GetRect* function needs to be altered for a sprite so that it correctly reflects the sprite's position as well as its size.

```
void CSprite::GetRect(CRect* pRect)
{
    ASSERT(pRect);
    pRect->left = m_x;
    pRect->top = m_y;
    pRect->right = m_x + GetWidth();
    pRect->bottom = m_y + GetHeight();
}
```

You can build the application and test it at this point. If you load a sprite, you should see it drawn at the top-left of the window. If you load a background first and then load a sprite, the sprite should show correctly on top of the background with its colors correctly rendered. The next step is to add support for moving the sprite by dragging it with the mouse.

Adding Hit Detection and Mouse Drag

In order to be able to drag a sprite with the mouse, we need to do several things. First, we must add a function that tests whether a mouse click has occurred on a visible part of the sprite. Note that I say *visible part*, not just in the area of the sprite. If a sprite has a hole in it and you click through the hole onto a sprite behind it, you would expect to select the sprite you clicked, not the one with the hole in it. In *Figure 9-2*, for instance, the mouse pointer selects the gray circle sprite through the hole in the red rectangle sprite.

Once the sprite has been selected and the mouse has moved, there needs to be a way to tell the sprite object that its position has changed and a way to redraw the scene with the sprite in the new position. Let's begin by looking at the view and how it deals with the mouse events.

Figure 9-2 *Mouse-click selection affected by the irregular shapes of sprites.*

I used ClassWizard to add message handlers to the *CAnimView* class for the WM_LBUTTONDOWN, WM_MOUSEMOVE, and WM_LBUTTONUP messages. Here are the handler functions that process these mouse events in the view class:

```
void CAnimView::OnLButtonDown(UINT nFlags, CPoint point)
{
    if (!m_bMouseCaptured) {
        CAnimDoc* pDoc = GetDocument();
        // See if the mouse clicked on a sprite.
        CSprite* pSprite = pDoc->GetSprite();
        if (pSprite && pSprite->HitTest(point)) {
            m_bMouseCaptured = TRUE;
            m_pCapturedSprite = pSprite;
            SetCapture();
            m_ptOffset.x = point.x - m_pCapturedSprite->GetX();
            m_ptOffset.y = point.y - m_pCapturedSprite->GetY();
        }
    }
}
```

A number of variables were added to the *CAnimView* class to support the mouse events. The first of these is *m_bMouseCaptured*, which keeps track of the capture state of the mouse. Drag operations occur during mouse movement only when the capture flag is set. The *OnLButtonDown* function captures the mouse and sets the capture flag. A test is made to see if the mouse click occurred on a visible part of the sprite by a call to *CSprite::HitTest*. If a hit is detected, the *m_pCapturedSprite* variable is used to store a pointer to the captured sprite.

The *m_ptOffset* variable is used to store a vector that represents exactly where inside the sprite rectangle the mouse hit occurred. This is required so that, as the mouse drags the sprite, the correct relative positions of the sprite can be maintained with respect to the positions of the mouse cursor.

> **NOTE**
>
> Yes, I know we have only one sprite right now, so this is a bit redundant, but bear with me—there will be lots of sprites coming in the following chapters.

Let's look at the mouse movement handler next:

```
void CAnimView::OnMouseMove(UINT nFlags, CPoint point)
{
    if (m_bMouseCaptured) {
        ASSERT(m_pCapturedSprite);
        m_pCapturedSprite->SetPosition(point.x - m_ptOffset.x,
                                        point.y - m_ptOffset.y);
        // Render and draw the whole scene.
        Render();
        Draw();
    }
}
```

As the mouse moves, a test is made to see if we currently have it captured, and if we do, the currently captured sprite is moved to a new position under the mouse cursor and the scene is redrawn to show the change.

Finally, let's see what happens when the mouse button is released:

```
void CAnimView::OnLButtonUp(UINT nFlags, CPoint point)
{
    if (m_bMouseCaptured) {
        ::ReleaseCapture();
        m_bMouseCaptured = FALSE;
        m_pCapturedSprite = NULL;
    }
}
```

If the mouse was captured, it is released and the capture variables are reset.

The *CSprite::SetPosition* function is trivial:

```
void CSprite::SetPosition(int x, int y)
{
    // Set the new position values.
    m_x = x;
    m_y = y;
}
```

A point to note here is that the code that moved the sprite has the responsibility for making the view show the changes. It doesn't have to be done this way. It would be possible for the sprite to include a callback pointer to, say, the view class, so that when *CSprite::SetPosition* was called, the sprite object could notify the view that it had moved and supply the information about which areas of the view needed to be redrawn. In a later chapter, we'll implement a version of this code using callback objects. For this example, I decided that simply having the view redraw the sprite requires less code and is much easier to debug. Sure, call me a wimp, but if it's simple, I like it.

Build and Test Again

Time once more to build and test. In this chapter, we've altered several files from the Bkgnd sample and added SPRITE.H and SPRITE.CPP, which implement the *CSprite* class. When you run the application, load a background and then a sprite—it doesn't really matter which background and which sprite. Try dragging the sprite with the mouse. You'll notice that it moves somewhat jerkily but that at least it doesn't flicker. It doesn't flicker because we use the off-screen buffer for the rendering. The awful, jerky, performance comes from the fact that every time the sprite moves, the entire scene is rendered and copied to the screen. Next up on our list of tasks is to improve the performance by being a lot more intelligent about which bits of a scene are rendered and drawn to the screen.

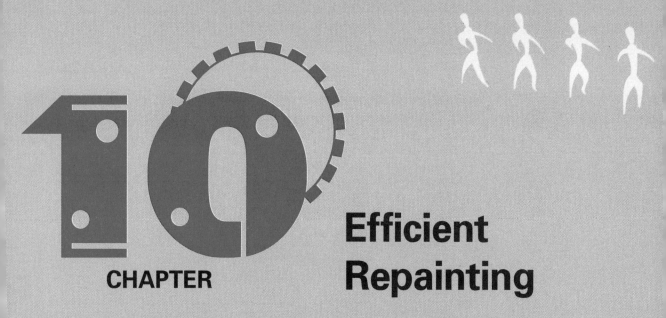

10

CHAPTER

Efficient
Repainting

Repainting Moving Sprites

Implementing Dirty Regions

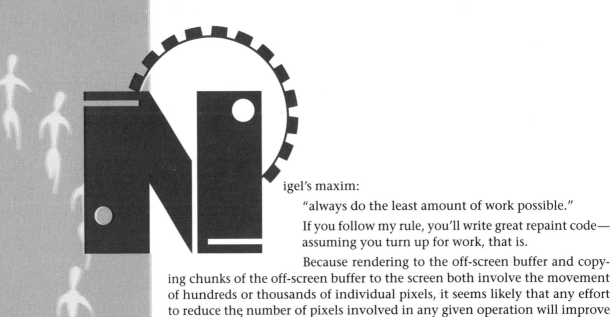

igel's maxim:

"always do the least amount of work possible."

If you follow my rule, you'll write great repaint code—assuming you turn up for work, that is.

Because rendering to the off-screen buffer and copying chunks of the off-screen buffer to the screen both involve the movement of hundreds or thousands of individual pixels, it seems likely that any effort to reduce the number of pixels involved in any given operation will improve the overall performance of our application. In this chapter, we'll look at some ideas for handling the rendering and painting of dirty regions and the code required to implement the operations.

Repainting Moving Sprites

Let's begin by looking in *Figure 10-1* at a simple animation in which there are two dolphin sprites in motion.

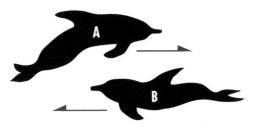

Figure 10-1   Two sprites in motion.

Now let's look at *Figure 10-2* to see what the states of the dolphin sprites are after one update cycle.

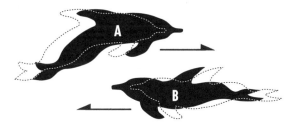

Figure 10-2 *After one update cycle, the dolphin sprites shown as having moved.*

In order to draw the scene with the sprites in their new positions, we must erase the sprites from their old positions (shown in dotted outline in Figure 10-2) and redraw them in their new positions. Let's look at one of the sprites in more detail in **Figure 10-3** and observe the bounding rectangles for the old and the new sprite positions.

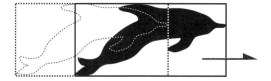

Figure 10-3 *The bounding rectangles of the old and the new sprite positions.*

Notice that there is quite a large overlap between the old (dotted-line) position and the new (solid-line) position. This is a fairly typical situation for a sprite moving at a reasonable velocity. It should be obvious that we don't want to render and paint the overlapping region twice. That would simply be a waste of time, so we need to find a technique for rendering and painting that avoids this redundancy. One solution is to break the regions down further, as shown in **Figure 10-4**.

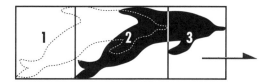

Figure 10-4 *The overlapping regions broken into three separate regions.*

Now we have three small regions to render and paint with no redundancy. But let's consider a second solution—combining the regions, as shown in **Figure 10-5**.

Figure 10-5 *The overlapping regions merged into one large region.*

In this case, there is just one rectangle to render and paint to the screen. Which solution is better? On the face of it, the second solution seems the better because it moves the same number of pixels but does so with one set of calls instead of three. That's probably a small saving but is a saving nonetheless. Before we get too keen on it and run to the keyboard to code the solution, though, let's consider another situation, shown in *Figure 10-6*.

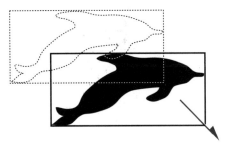

Figure 10-6   *Movement resulting in less overlap.*

In the case shown in Figure 10-6, the sprite has moved in both the *x* and *y* axes and the overlap is significantly less. Now let's see what regions we get if we split the two overlapping regions into three nonoverlapping regions, as shown in *Figure 10-7*.

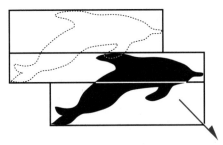

Figure 10-7   *The two regions split into three nonoverlapping regions.*

Now compare Figure 10-7 with the region obtained by combining the old and new rectangles into a single rectangle, as shown in *Figure 10-8*.

Figure 10-8   *The update regions combined into one region.*

Notice that the area of the single combined region is much greater than the combined area of the three separate regions in Figure 10-7. So which solution is better now? My guess is that the three smaller regions will be rendered and drawn faster than the single, large region simply because there is less data to manipulate and the call overhead is small by comparison. But the argument is actually a little more complex than that.

I have been using the terms *region* and *rectangle* somewhat interchangeably, which is a bit naughty since a region can be an arbitrary shape—not necessarily a rectangle. Microsoft Windows supports what it calls *complex regions,* and these can be constructed by combining rectangles, polygons, ellipses, and so on. Having created a region, we can constrain Windows graphics device interface (GDI) operations to be clipped to the inside of the region. So if we were to use Windows regions to define our dirty areas, perhaps we could get Windows to do the work for us and arrive at the optimal solution.

Those of you with experience in using regions in older versions of Windows will be laughing now. Certainly drawing performance using regions in the past could not have been called fast by any stretch of the imagination. But that isn't true today. Windows 95 and Windows NT version 3.5 support substantially faster region drawing than region drawing in earlier versions of Windows. This leads us to an interesting dilemma: should we use our own rectangular regions or use Windows complex regions?

Obviously, we could consider other questions to help us decide which software technique performs the best, but the result would simply be more speculation. What we need is a controlled experiment that determines the best way to go. But on which platform should we perform the experiment? Windows 3.1, Windows NT 3.1, Windows 95, or Windows NT 3.5? Each might produce a different result.

Perhaps we should use different systems at run time to get the best performance possible on any given platform. But this sort of dynamic solution would obviously involve a lot of code, both in implementing the various solutions and in testing which works best under any given situation. Let's apply Nigel's maxim at this point—"do the least work possible"—and see what happens. If we do the design right, we can try different solutions later and then come to a decision about which ones are best.

What it really comes down to right now is, which solution is simplest to code? The solution I implemented uses rectangles to define the dirty regions and simply combines overlapping rectangles into a single rectangle, as in Figure 10-8. But in fact, the solution doesn't necessarily involve combining all overlapping rectangles. When a rectangle is added to the dirty list, a simple test is made to see if this rectangle overlaps the one added immediately before it. If the two consecutive rectangles overlap, they are combined into one rectangle. This expedient handles the common case in which a sprite moves a small distance and creates two overlapping dirty regions, as in Figure 10-3. This solution doesn't always detect the case in which two sprites cross while several sprites are in motion, but it avoids either having to walk the dirty list looking for overlaps when any new region is added or having to create a piece of code to walk the dirty list at render and draw time to merge any overlapping regions, which is potentially recursive and therefore slow.

Implementing Dirty Regions

\anim32\repaint

In order to implement dirty regions, we need to keep a list of the regions somewhere, a means to add items to the list, and a way of walking the list when we need to perform a render and draw cycle. Since the rendering and drawing are mainly concerned with the off-screen buffer in the *COSBView* class, I decided to add the dirty list and its management functions to *COSBView*.

Let's begin by seeing how the dirty list is used by the rest of the application and then go on to see how its functions are implemented. We'll start by looking at a variant of the code we saw in Chapter 9 for implementing the mouse dragging a sprite in ANIMVIEW.CPP:

```
void CAnimView::OnMouseMove(UINT nFlags, CPoint point)
{
    if (m_bMouseCaptured) {
        ASSERT(m_pCapturedSprite);
        CRect rcOld, rcNew;
        m_pCapturedSprite->GetRect(&rcOld);
        m_pCapturedSprite->SetPosition(point.x - m_ptOffset.x,
                                       point.y - m_ptOffset.y);
        m_pCapturedSprite->GetRect(&rcNew);
        // Add the changed regions to the view's dirty list.
        AddDirtyRegion(&rcOld);
        AddDirtyRegion(&rcNew);
        // Render and draw the changes.
        RenderAndDrawDirtyList();
    }
}
```

The sprite's position is saved in a *CRect* object. The sprite is moved, and its new position is obtained. The old and new rectangles are added to the dirty list by a call to *AddDirtyRegion*. Once the regions have been added, a call is made to *RenderAndDrawDirtyList* to draw the changed areas. *AddDirtyRegion* and *RenderAndDrawDirtyList* are new functions in *COSBView*.

The *COSBView* class has a new object to hold the dirty list and several new member functions. Here are the new parts of OSBVIEW.H:

```
class COSBView : public CScrollView
{
    :
    :
public:
virtual void Render(CRect* pClipRect = NULL) {return;}
    void AddDirtyRegion(CRect* pRect);
```

```
    void RenderAndDrawDirtyList();
    :
    :
private:
    CObList m_DirtyList;              // Dirty regions

    void EmptyDirtyList();
    :
    :
};
```

Note that the dirty list is implemented as a *CObList* object that is supplied by the Microsoft Foundation Class Library (MFC). The *CObList* class maintains a list of pointers to objects, each object being derived from the *CObject* class. The list is used here to hold pointers to *CRect* objects (in this implementation of dirty regions), and I could have been a little bit more type-safe by creating a class derived from *CObList,* which would have manipulated only *CRect* objects. Doing it the way I've done it here requires type casting and is a little more dangerous for the novice, but in the words of *Star Trek*'s Dr. McCoy, "I choose the danger." Let's look at the *AddDirtyRegion* function so that we can see how the list is used:

```
void COSBView::AddDirtyRegion(CRect* prcNew)
{
    // Get the rectangle currently at the top of the list.
    POSITION pos = m_DirtyList.GetHeadPosition();
    if (pos) {
        CRect* prcTop = (CRect*)m_DirtyList.GetNext(pos);
        CRect rcTest;
        // If the new rectangle intersects the rectangle
        // at the top of the list, merge them.
        if (rcTest.IntersectRect(prcTop, prcNew)) {
            prcTop->UnionRect(prcTop, prcNew);
            return;
        }
    }
    // List is empty, or there was no intersection.
    CRect *prc = new CRect;
    *prc = *prcNew; // Copy the data.
    // Add a new rectangle to the list.
    m_DirtyList.AddHead((CObject*)prc);
}
```

Remember that the only optimization in use here is the combining of a new rectangle with the one on the top of the dirty list if they overlap. The code first gets the rectangle at the top of the list—notice the *CRect** cast. If the list is empty, the new rectangle is simply added to the top of the list. If a rectangle already exists at the top of the list, a test is made to see if it intersects the new rectangle. If it does, it is simply enlarged to include the new rectangle. If no intersection is found, the new rectangle is added to the top of the list.

Now let's look at the *RenderAndDrawDirtyList* function:

```
void COSBView::RenderAndDrawDirtyList()
{
    POSITION pos = m_DirtyList.GetHeadPosition();
    // Render all the dirty regions.
    while (pos) {
        // Get the next region.
        CRect* pRect = (CRect*)m_DirtyList.GetNext(pos);
        // Render it.
        Render(pRect);
    }
    // Draw all the dirty regions to the screen.
    while (!m_DirtyList.IsEmpty()) {
        // Get the next region.
        CRect* pRect = (CRect*)m_DirtyList.RemoveHead();
        Draw(NULL, pRect);
        // Done with it.
        delete pRect;
    }
}
```

For each rectangle in the dirty list, a call that passes the rectangle as a clipping region is made to the *Render* function. The list is then walked again, this time to copy the rendered buffer areas to the screen by means of a call to the *Draw* function.

In order to be able to include this function in the *COSBView* class, I had to add a dummy *Render* function as well. This is a virtual function that gets overridden by the implementation you provide. Here's the dummy that is actually defined in the header file:

```
virtual void Render(CRect* pClipRect = NULL) {return;}
```

Let's look now at the real *Render* function in *CAnimView*:

```
void CAnimView::Render(CRect* pClipRect)
{
    CAnimDoc* pDoc = GetDocument();
    CRect rcDraw;

    // Get the background DIB and render it.
    CDIB* pDIB = pDoc->GetBackground();
    if (pDIB) {
        pDIB->GetRect(&rcDraw);
        // If a clipping rectangle was supplied, use it.
        if (pClipRect) {
            rcDraw.IntersectRect(pClipRect, &rcDraw);
        }
```

```
        // Draw the image of the DIB to the off-screen buffer.
        ASSERT(m_pDIB);
        pDIB->CopyBits(m_pDIB,
                       rcDraw.left,
                       rcDraw.top,
                       rcDraw.right - rcDraw.left,
                       rcDraw.bottom - rcDraw.top,
                       rcDraw.left,
                       rcDraw.top);
    }


    // Get the sprite and render it.
    CSprite* pSprite = pDoc->GetSprite();
    if (pSprite) {
        pSprite->Render(m_pDIB, &rcDraw);
    }
}
```

There isn't anything new here, but I wanted to show *Render* again so that you can see how the clipping rectangle is used to constrain the affected area of the buffer.

The Proof of the Pudding

If you compile and run the Repaint sample and compare its performance with the Sprite sample's performance, you'll find that Repaint is substantially faster at moving small sprites around the scene.

Now that we have reasonable performance for moving a single sprite, we can go on and add some more sprites to the scene to make it a bit more interesting.

Adding a Third Dimension and Notification Objects

CHAPTER

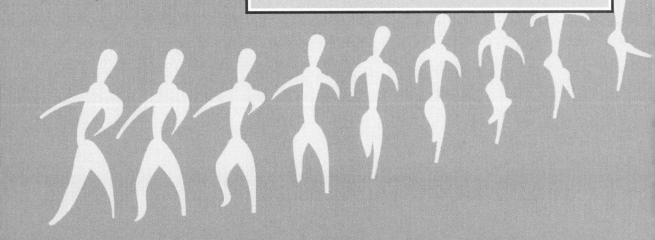

n this chapter, we'll look at what's involved in having multiple sprites in a single scene. Two issues arise from this apparently simple requirement: the first is that we need a way to define which sprites are in front of the others—z-order—and the second is that, when we ask a sprite to move to a new position or to a new z-order position, we need a simple way to render and draw the regions of the scene that have been affected by the change.

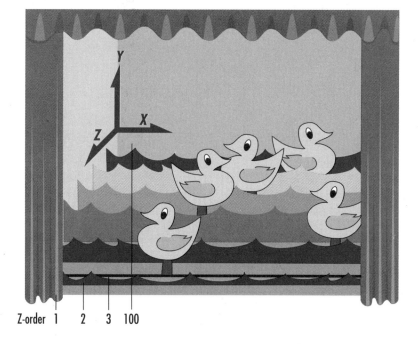

Z-order 1   2   3   100

Z-Order Problems

The red circle and the gray rectangle in *Figure 11-1* show you what z-order is all about.

Figure 11-1 *A red circle in front of a gray rectangle.*

How do we know the red circle is in front of the gray rectangle? Because the image of the circle is shown whole and the image of the rectangle is clipped to the boundary of the circle, creating the illusion that part of the rectangle is obscured by the circle. OK, no big deal really. All we need to do to make one object appear to be in front of another is to be sure to draw the front object later than we draw the one behind it. (Remember all the discussion of sprite rendering in Chapter 5?) So that the sprites will appear in correct z-order, it would be most convenient to hold them in a list sorted by z-order. Then, when we needed to render them, we could simply walk down the list rendering each one in turn. *Figure 11-2* shows the idea.

\anim32\zorder

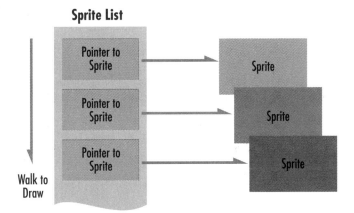

Figure 11-2 *Sprites redrawn in z-order according to a walk down the list.*

Listing the sprites in z-order is very helpful for the repaint code but not so convenient elsewhere. How, for example, do we change the z-order of a sprite? It would be nice if we could simply write code like this:

```
pSprite->SetZ(10);
```

Unfortunately, the result of this call would be to simply alter the m_z variable in the sprite—it would have no effect at all on the position of the sprite in the list. So to correctly set the z value of a sprite, we need to do something more like this, where the *InsertSprite* function uses the sprite z value to determine where to add the sprite to the list:

```
pList = pDoc->GetSpriteList();
pList->RemoveSprite(pSprite);
pSprite->SetZ(10);
pList->InsertSprite(pSprite);
```

Obviously, we could write a list function to do most of the work in one call—something like this:

```
pList->SetSpriteZOrder(pSprite, 10);
```

But this would get us further and further away from the object-oriented idea. Not only that—it would also fail to deal with the issue of redrawing the changes to the scene caused by the alteration of the z-order. What we need is some way to tell the sprite what we want it to do and have the sprite itself deal with the rest of the problem.

Position Changes Posing the Same Problem

The same arguments apply to setting the x and y position of a sprite. To move a sprite to a new position, for example, we would like to be able to simply call *CSprite::SetPosition*. Unfortunately, all this would do is alter some internal variables in the sprite object; it would have no effect on the view of the object in the scene. In order to have the scene reflect the change in the sprite's position, we must create a piece of code like this:

```
Crect rc;
pSprite->GetRect(&rc);
pView->AddDirtyRegion(&rc);
pSprite->SetPosition(x, y);
pSprite->GetRect(&rc);
pView->AddDirtyRegion(&rc);
pView->Render(&rc);
pView->Draw(NULL, &rc);
```

The code would get repetitious if there were many calls to the *CSprite::SetPosition* or to any other sprite function that would affect the image of the sprite.

Some Possible Solutions

We could give each sprite a pointer to the view object when the sprite was created and have the sprite call the view directly to update the dirty regions and draw itself. The problem with this approach is that there would be no coordination among sprites to signal when a rendering or draw operation should be done. Ideally, we want to do all the rendering operations together and then all the draw operations together because that would give us the best screen update appearance.

A better approach might be to give each sprite a pointer to the list object in which the sprite is held and simply notify the list object of the changes, leaving it up to the list object to determine when a render and draw cycle should be performed. That would work, but it would involve putting some very specific code into the sprite class to deal with the list, which would rather spoil the generality of the sprite class.

A third approach would be to define another object—a notification object—that the sprite class understands. Such an object could be used to make notifications of dirty regions, z-order changes, and so on, and a list or view object could use the notification object to receive these notifications. In fact, this notification object wouldn't need to have any data or code associated with it. It would simply be a specification for a set of member functions. This is exactly how interfaces in the component object model (COM) used by OLE are defined.

Notification Objects

We can define an interface for notification events that an object such as our sprite list can support and have each sprite created with a pointer to the notification interface so that, as the sprite moves or changes its appearance, it has a way to communicate back to the list object what has happened to it. *Figure 11-3* shows how these notification objects might be used.

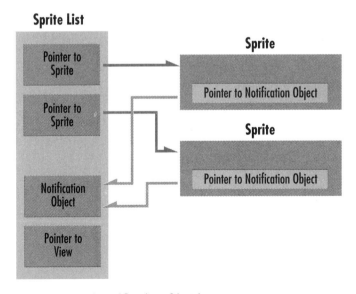

Figure 11-3 *A notification object in use.*

Let's see what happens when we want to move a sprite that is using a notification object:

1. *CSprite::SetPosition* is called to change the sprite's position parameters.

2. The sprite updates its internal *m_x* and *m_y* variables and then tests to see if it has a valid notification object pointer.

3. If a notification object pointer has been set, the sprite calls through the pointer to the notification object to report both the area previously occupied by the sprite and the new area occupied by the sprite as dirty.

4. The sprite list, which contains the notification object, receives the dirty area information and adds the information to the view's dirty area list.

5. The sprite list decides whether to render and redraw now or defer the operation until later.

The last step, in which the sprite list decides whether to redraw now or not, may seem a bit vague, but consider how the sprite is generally going to be getting calls to its *SetPosition* function. The most general case would be for the application to be using a *PeekMessage* loop or some other idle time processing technique to determine which sprites needed to be moved. The application may simply walk the sprite list asking each sprite to update its position. If that were the case, it would be a simple matter to set a flag at the start of the list walk to prevent render and draw operations and then clear the flag at the end of the cycle. Once the entire list had been traversed, any dirty areas would be rendered and redrawn. Here's the sort of code fragment that might accomplish such a deferral:

```
bDeferRedraw = TRUE;
pos = GetFirstSpritePos();
while (pos) {
    pSprite = GetNextSprite(pos);
    pSprite->UpdatePosition();
}
bDeferRedraw = FALSE;
RenderAndDrawDirtyRegions();
```

The notification object code would look something like this:

```
void NotifyDirty(CRect* prc)
{
    AddDirtyRegion(prc);
    if (!bDeferRedraw) {
        Render(prc);
        Draw(prc);
    }
}
```

Any other time that *CSprite::SetPosition* were called—for example, when a sprite was first made visible in a scene—the sprite would be automatically rendered and drawn.

Although using notification objects may seem somewhat complex, in practice it greatly reduces the number of lines of code involved in dealing with the sprites, and more important it helps keep all the render and draw code in one place, making code maintenance much easier.

Types of Notification

The sprite could send a notification in any of three situations:

- The z-order of the sprite changes, and the notification is the rectangle describing the position of the sprite. The rectangle information is used to redraw the affected area.

- The position of the sprite changes, and the notification consists of two rectangles—one describing the old position of the sprite; the other, the new position. This rectangle information is used to update the dirty region list and possibly redraw the area around the changes.

- The image of the sprite changes, and the notification is the rectangle describing the position of the sprite. The information is used to redraw the affected area.

The Notification Object Class

A notification class with a single member function and some flags will do all we want, and we can define the entire thing in just a few lines (from SPRITENO.H):

```
class CSpriteNotifyObj : public CObject
{
public:
    enum CHANGETYPE {
        ZORDER      = 0x0001,
        POSITION    = 0x0002,
        IMAGE       = 0x0004
    };

public:
    virtual void Change(CSprite* pSprite,
                        CHANGETYPE change,
                        CRect* pRect1 = NULL,
                        CRect* pRect2 = NULL) = 0;
};
```

This code defines the *CSpriteNotifyObj* class as having a single pure virtual *Change* function. This means that in order to use the class, you must derive your own class from it that contains a real implementation of the *Change* function. In this sense, the *CSpriteNotifyObj* class is really just a specification for the interface rather than an implementation of it.

Changes to *CSprite* to Use *CSpriteNotifyObj*

Before we see how we use the *CSpriteNotifyObj* class to process notification events, let's look at how the notification object is used within the *CSprite* class. Each sprite now includes a pointer to a *CSpriteNotifyObj*, which is initially set to NULL in the *CSprite* constructor code.

```
class CSprite : public CDIB
{
public:
virtual void SetNotificationObject(CSpriteNotifyObj* pNO)
        {m_pNotifyObj = pNO;}
    .
    .
    .
protected:
CSpriteNotifyObj* m_pNotifyObj; // Pointer to a notification object
    .
    .
    .
};

CSprite::CSprite()
{
    m_x = 0;
    m_y = 0;
    m_z = 50;
    m_bTransIndex = 0;
    m_pNotifyObj = NULL;
}
```

The other changes to *CSprite* are in the *SetPosition* and *SetZ* functions, which now need to make a notification call if the sprite has a notification object attached.

```
void CSprite::SetPosition(int x, int y)
{
    // Save the current position.
    CRect rcOld;
    GetRect(&rcOld);
    // Move to new position.
    m_x = x;
    m_y = y;
    CRect rcNew;
    GetRect(&rcNew);
    // Notify that we have moved.
    if (m_pNotifyObj) {
        m_pNotifyObj->Change(this,
```

```
                                 CSpriteNotifyObj::POSITION,
                                 &rcOld,
                                 &rcNew);
    }
}


void CSprite::SetZ(int z)
{
    if (m_z != z) {
        m_z = z;
        // See if we have to notify anyone.
        if (m_pNotifyObj) {
            m_pNotifyObj->Change(this, CSpriteNotifyObj::ZORDER);
        }
    }
}
```

Now that *CSprite* supports notification objects, let's see how we make use of them in the application. The sprite list is the central piece of code used to manage the sprites in a scene, so it's to this list that we will add a notification object. Remember that the *CSpriteNotifyObj* class does not actually contain an implementation—it is simply a design for a class—so the first thing we must do is derive a class from *CSpriteNotifyObj* and fill in the implementation of the *Change* function, having it do whatever we need in terms of our sprite list. Not clear? Let's look at the code for the implementation of the derived notification class *CSpriteListNotifyObj*, which should at least clear up what we are going to have such an object do, and then look at how the notification object works in the sprite list after that. Remember that the implementation of the notification object is specific to the application—we can make it do whatever we want. Here's the header file SPLSTNO.H:

```
class CSpriteListNotifyObj : public CSpriteNotifyObj
{
public:
    CSpriteListNotifyObj();
    ~CSpriteListNotifyObj();
    void SetList(CSpriteList* pSpriteList)
        {m_pSpriteList = pSpriteList;}
    void SetView(CAnimView* pAnimView)
        {m_pAnimView = pAnimView;}
    void Change(CSprite* pSprite,
                CHANGETYPE change,
                CRect* pRect1 = NULL,
                CRect* pRect2 = NULL);

protected:
    CSpriteList* m_pSpriteList;
    CAnimView* m_pAnimView;
};
```

Notice that the *Change* function is there but that two other functions are used to set the *m_pSpriteList* and *m_pAnimView* variables. These two variables are used in the *Change* function shown here from SPLSTNO.CPP:

```
void CSpriteListNotifyObj::Change(CSprite* pSprite,
                                  CHANGETYPE change,
                                  CRect* pRect1,
                                  CRect* pRect2)
{
    if (change & CSpriteNotifyObj::ZORDER) {
        // Reposition the sprite in the z-order list.
        ASSERT(m_pSpriteList);
        m_pSpriteList->Reorder(pSprite);
        // Add the sprite position to the dirty list.
        ASSERT(m_pAnimView);
        m_pAnimView->AddDirtyRegion(pRect1);
    }
    if (change & CSpriteNotifyObj::POSITION) {
        // pRect1 and pRect2 point to old and new rect positions.
        // Add these rects to the dirty list.
        ASSERT(m_pAnimView);
        m_pAnimView->AddDirtyRegion(pRect1);
        m_pAnimView->AddDirtyRegion(pRect2);
    }
}
```

Note here that when a sprite changes its *z* value the sprite rectangle is added to the dirty list, and the sprite is repositioned correctly in the sprite list so that the next time a render and draw cycle takes place, the sprite will be drawn in its new position. Similarly for a position change, the sprite's old and new positions are added to the dirty list for a later render and draw operation.

The sprite list includes a *CSpriteListNotifyObj*, and each time a sprite is added to the list by the *Insert* function, the sprite's notification object pointer is set:

```
BOOL CSpriteList::Insert(CSprite* pNewSprite)
{
    // Set the notification object pointer in the sprite
    // to the sprite list's notification object.
    pNewSprite->SetNotificationObject(&m_NotifyObj);

    // Walk down the list until we either get to the end or
    // find a sprite with the same or higher z-order, in which
    // case we insert the new sprite just before that one.

    POSITION pos, posThis;
    CSprite* pSprite;
    for (pos = GetHeadPosition(); pos != NULL;) {
        posThis = pos;
```

```
        pSprite = GetNext(pos); // Increment position.
        if (pSprite->GetZ() >= pNewSprite->GetZ()) {
            InsertBefore(posThis, pNewSprite);
            return TRUE;
        }
    }
    // Nothing with the same or a higher z-order, so add the sprite to
    // the end.
    AddTail(pNewSprite);
    return TRUE;
}
```

That's all we need to be able to move a sprite by calling its *SetPosition* function and have it automatically add its dirty areas to the dirty list in the view.

Having done all this, let's see how these changes affect something like the *OnMouseMove* function in ANIMVIEW.CPP:

```
void CAnimView::OnMouseMove(UINT nFlags, CPoint point)
{
    if (m_bMouseCaptured) {
        ASSERT(m_pCapturedSprite);
        m_pCapturedSprite->SetPosition(point.x - m_ptOffset.x,
                                       point.y - m_ptOffset.y);
        // Render and draw the changes.
        RenderAndDrawDirtyList();
    }
}
```

This is much simpler and rather more object oriented in its looks if not in the underlying implementation.

A Return to the Z-Order Problem

Now that we have a system for notifying the sprite list of changes to the sprites, we can take a look at the few remaining details of the sprite list itself and at some small additions to the user interface that will allow the manipulation of the sprites in the scene.

Let's begin with a look at the changes to the document required to support a list of sprites rather than the single sprite we've had up to now. So far as the header is concerned, we simply replace the *CSprite* object with a *CSprite-List* object and provide a different access function:

```
class CAnimDoc : public CDocument
{
public:
    CSpriteList* GetSpriteList() {return &m_SpriteList;}
    :
    :
```

(continued)

```
private:
    CSpriteList m_SpriteList;    // Sprite list
        .
        .
        .
};
```

The sprite list notification object needs to know about the view so that it can communicate with the view, and I found the easiest place to give the notification object a pointer to the view was in *CAnimDoc::OnNewDocument* because it is always called before we need to use the list:

```
BOOL CAnimDoc::OnNewDocument()
{
    if (!CDocument::OnNewDocument())
        return FALSE;

    // Tell the sprite list notification object where the view is
    // so that when we add sprites, the dirty list can be
    // maintained automatically.
    CAnimView* pView = GetAnimView();
    ASSERT(pView);
    m_SpriteList.m_NotifyObj.SetView(pView);

    // Create a new default background DIB just so
    // that there will be something to look at.
    CDIB* pDIB = new CDIB;
    pDIB->Create(320, 240);
    SetBackground(pDIB);
    SetModifiedFlag(FALSE);

    return TRUE;
}
```

Note that I have cheated a little bit here by making the *m_NotifyObj* member in the sprite list public. The *CAnimDoc::SetBackground* function has been slightly changed to delete all the sprites in the list before a new background is loaded:

```
BOOL CAnimDoc::SetBackground(CDIB* pDIB)
{
    // Delete any existing sprites.
    m_SpriteList.RemoveAll();
        .
        .
        .
}
```

The last change to the document file is in *CAnimDoc::OnFileLoadSprite*, which adds the new sprite to the list:

```
void CAnimDoc::OnFileLoadSprite()
{
    // Create a sprite to hold the image.
    CSprite* pSprite = new CSprite;
    // Show the File Open dialog for a sprite.
    if (!pSprite->Load()) {
        delete pSprite;
        return;
    }
    // Add the new sprite to the sprite list.
    m_SpriteList.Insert(pSprite);
    SetModifiedFlag(TRUE);
    // Tell the view about the new sprite.
    GetAnimView()->NewSprite(pSprite);
}
```

The *CSpriteList::Insert* function inserts the sprite in the list in a position determined by its z-order value. For a new sprite, the z-order is set to 50. Here's the function:

```
BOOL CSpriteList::Insert(CSprite* pNewSprite)
{
    // Set the notification object pointer in the sprite
    // to the list's notification object.
    pNewSprite->SetNotificationObject(&m_NotifyObj);

    // Walk down the list until we either get to the end or
    // find a sprite with the same or higher z-order, in which
    // case we insert the new sprite just before that one.

    POSITION pos, posThis;
    CSprite* pSprite;
    for (pos = GetHeadPosition(); pos != NULL;) {
        posThis = pos;
        pSprite = GetNext(pos); // Increment position.
        if (pSprite->GetZ() >= pNewSprite->GetZ()) {
            InsertBefore(posThis, pNewSprite);
            return TRUE;
        }
    }
    // Nothing with the same or a higher z-order, so add the sprite to
    // the end.
    AddTail(pNewSprite);
    return TRUE;
}
```

Note that if two sprites have the same z-order position, the more recently added sprite will appear on top. This makes sense visually because, if you add multiple sprites with the default z-order, the most recent one appears on the top of the pile.

Setting the Z-Order and Deleting Sprites

Now that we have more than one sprite in a scene, it would be nice if there were an easy way to set the z-order of a sprite and also to remove a sprite from the scene. In a previous life, I created a dialog box that allowed direct entry of a sprite's parameters, and this dialog box was invoked by double-clicking the sprite. In designing this version of the code, I thought it would be nice to have a more direct way to set things like z-order, so I have provided for using the right mouse button to bring up a pop-up menu that has a set of predefined z-order values to choose from. This pop-up menu also includes an item for deleting a sprite.

Creating the Sprite Pop-Up Menu

I used App Studio to create a new menu item, and then I gave it the ID IDR_SPRITEPOPUP. I added the items I wanted for z-order values and an item for deleting a sprite. The z-order list was added as a cascaded pop-up menu to keep the main pop-up list uncluttered.

Having created the resource for the menu, I used ClassWizard to add a handler for the WM_RBUTTONDOWN message to the *CAnimView* class. I then used ClassWizard to add individual handlers for each menu item to the *CAnimView* class too.

The *CAnimView::OnRButtonDown* function, which invokes the pop-up menu, looks like this:

```
void CAnimView::OnRButtonDown(UINT nFlags, CPoint point)
{
    CAnimDoc* pDoc = GetDocument();
    // See if the mouse hit a sprite.
    CSpriteList* pList = pDoc->GetSpriteList();
    CSprite* pSprite = pList->HitTest(point);
    if (pSprite) {
        m_pMenuSprite = pSprite;
        // Show the sprite pop-up menu.
        CMenu Menu;
        Menu.LoadMenu(IDR_SPRITEPOPUP);
        CMenu* pPopup = Menu.GetSubMenu(0);
        ClientToScreen(&point);
        pPopup->TrackPopupMenu(TPM_LEFTALIGN | TPM_RIGHTBUTTON,
                            point.x, point.y,
                            this);
```

```
    } else {
        m_pMenuSprite = NULL;
    }
}
```

A test is made to see if the click occurred on a sprite. If it did, the sprite pop-up menu is loaded and shown. Note that the actual sprite hit is saved in the *m_pMenuSprite* variable so that the subsequent menu item handler can get access to the correct sprite. Kind of yucky code, but it's simple and it works.

I added quite a few z-order menu items and wanted to process them all in much the same way, so I created a simple helper function to do most of the work when a new z-order value is selected:

```
void CAnimView::SetSpriteZ(int z)
{
    if (!m_pMenuSprite) return;
    // Set the new z value in the currently selected sprite.
    m_pMenuSprite->SetZ(z);
    // Redraw the area around the sprite to show the change.
    RenderAndDrawDirtyList();
}
```

Remember that the sprite is using the notification object to add its own dirty area to the view's dirty list, so after having set the sprite's new z value, we can simply call *RenderAndDrawDirtyList* to get it redrawn in its new position.

Having created the helper function, I tidied up the many z-order menu item handlers and had them simply call the helper function:

```
void CAnimView::OnSpritez0()    {SetSpriteZ(0);}
void CAnimView::OnSpritez10()   {SetSpriteZ(10);}
void CAnimView::OnSpritez20()   {SetSpriteZ(20);}
void CAnimView::OnSpritez30()   {SetSpriteZ(30);}
void CAnimView::OnSpritez40()   {SetSpriteZ(40);}
void CAnimView::OnSpritez50()   {SetSpriteZ(50);}
void CAnimView::OnSpritez60()   {SetSpriteZ(60);}
void CAnimView::OnSpritez70()   {SetSpriteZ(70);}
void CAnimView::OnSpritez80()   {SetSpriteZ(80);}
void CAnimView::OnSpritez90()   {SetSpriteZ(90);}
```

In days of old when knights were bold and MFC wasn't invented, we would have had a case for each menu item here in a common WM_COMMAND switch statement, and life would have been very simple. I could have hacked away at the code generated by ClassWizard, I suppose, so that it resulted in my calling only one function to handle any of the z-order items, but that would have been much harder to follow. So excuse the redundancy here. If you want to be clever and optimize it, be my guest—but don't complain if it breaks when the next version of Visual C++ is released.

The final menu item to deal with is the one that deletes a sprite. Here's the handler:

```
void CAnimView::OnSpritedelete()
{
    // Get the area occupied by the sprite.
    CRect rc;
    m_pMenuSprite->GetRect(&rc);
    // Remove the sprite from the list.
    CAnimDoc* pDoc = GetDocument();
    CSpriteList* pList = pDoc->GetSpriteList();
    CSprite* pSprite = pList->Remove(m_pMenuSprite);
    ASSERT(pSprite);
    // Delete the sprite.
    delete pSprite;
    // Redraw the area around the sprite to show the change.
    Render(&rc);
    Draw(NULL, &rc);
}
```

Notice here that we have to do the work ourselves to add the sprite area to the dirty list and redraw to show the change. I could have added a notification to *CSprite* to handle the destroy case, but I'll leave that as an exercise for the student.

Onward....

So now we can have a nice scene with a background and several sprites. I'm sure you're getting frustrated with manually loading the background and then loading the sprites one by one, though. It's about time we took a look at what's required to serialize a scene into a single file so that we can reload the whole thing from one place. We'll do that next.

12
CHAPTER

Saving and Loading Scenes

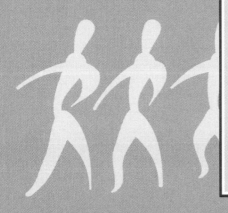

n this short chapter, we'll add serialization code to each of the object classes we have created so far so that an entire scene can be saved to a single file and subsequently reloaded. The basic *CObject* class that the Microsoft Foundation Class Library (MFC) provides includes a *Serialize* function, which is called to save or load the object. It's to this function, in each of our derived object classes, that we add code dealing with the specifics of how an object of that class is saved in a file.

In cases such as the *CDIB* class, we have already written code to create the object from a published file format. In serializing such an object, we are not required to save it in the same format in which it might be saved in a stand-alone file, but it is often simpler to do this because we can then reuse the existing code. You'll see what I mean when we look at how each of the object classes we have created is serialized.

To save a scene to a disk file, we need to add serialization code to *CDIB*, *CSprite*, *CSpriteList*, and *CAnimDoc*. We don't need to save a *CDIBPal* object because the palette for a scene is derived from the background device-independent bitmap (DIB), but I've included code in the *CDIBPal* class to load and save a palette from or to a .PAL file. As something of a bonus I've included a sample application that allows you to edit a palette.

Serializing *CDIB* Objects

The code for *CDIB* already contains two *Load* functions. One loads the DIB from a named file, and the other loads the DIB from an open *CFile* object. If we serialize a *CDIB* object to a file in the same way we would write out a native DIB file, we should be able to leverage the code in the *CDIB::Load* functions we already have when we want to reverse the process and serialize the *CDIB* object back from the archive.

Because we are primarily interested in 8-bit-per-pixel (bpp) DIBs, we'll write a *Save* function that handles only that case. You can easily expand the function to handle other DIB formats if you need to. The function will always write a 256-entry color table because the *CDIB* class always creates 256 entries. We'll write two *Save* functions—one that takes the name of the file and another that takes a pointer to an open *CFile* object. Let's look at the one that takes a pointer to an open *CFile* object first:

\anim32\fileio

```
BOOL CDIB::Save(CFile* fp)
{
    BITMAPFILEHEADER bfh;

    // Construct the file header.
    bfh.bfType = 0x4D42; // 'BM'
    bfh.bfSize =
        sizeof(BITMAPFILEHEADER) +
        sizeof(BITMAPINFOHEADER) +
        256 * sizeof(RGBQUAD) +
        StorageWidth() * DibHeight();
    bfh.bfReserved1 = 0;
    bfh.bfReserved2 = 0;
    bfh.bfOffBits =
        sizeof(BITMAPFILEHEADER) +
        sizeof(BITMAPINFOHEADER) +
        256 * sizeof(RGBQUAD);

    // Write the file header.
    int iSize = sizeof(bfh);
    TRY {
        fp->Write(&bfh, iSize);
    } CATCH(CFileException, e) {
        TRACE("Failed to write file header");
        return FALSE;
    } END_CATCH

    // Write the BITMAPINFO structure.
    // Note: we assume that there are always 256 colors in the
    // color table.
    ASSERT(m_pBMI);
    iSize =
        sizeof(BITMAPINFOHEADER) +
        256 * sizeof(RGBQUAD);
    TRY {
        fp->Write(m_pBMI, iSize);
    } CATCH(CFileException, e) {
        TRACE("Failed to write BITMAPINFO");
        return FALSE;
    } END_CATCH

    // Write the bits.
    iSize = StorageWidth() * DibHeight();
```

(continued)

```
    TRY {
        fp->Write(m_pBits, iSize);
    } CATCH(CFileException, e) {
        TRACE("Failed to write bits");
        return FALSE;
    } END_CATCH

    return TRUE;
}
```

A bitmap file header is constructed and written to the file first. Then the BIT-MAPINFO structure from the *CDIB* object is written to the file followed by the bits of the image itself. Not very complicated, but remember that this *Save* function is for an 8-bpp DIB with a 256-entry color table *only*. Any other case will call for altering this code.

Now let's see the other *Save* function—the one that saves a *CDIB* object to a named file:

```
BOOL CDIB::Save(LPSTR pszFileName)
{
    CString strFile;

    if ((pszFileName == NULL)
    !! (strlen(pszFileName) == 0)) {

        // Show a File Save dialog to get the name.
        CFileDialog dlg   (FALSE,    // Save
                           NULL,     // No default extension
                           NULL,     // No initial file name
                           OFN_OVERWRITEPROMPT
                             ! OFN_HIDEREADONLY,
                           "Image files (*.DIB, *.BMP)!*.DIB;*.BMP\
!All files (*.*)!*.*!!");
        if (dlg.DoModal() == IDOK) {
            strFile = dlg.GetPathName();
        } else {
            return FALSE;
        }
    } else {

        // Copy the supplied file path.
        strFile = pszFileName;
    }

    // Try to open the file for write access.
    CFile file;
    if (!file.Open(strFile,
                   CFile::modeReadWrite
                     ! CFile::modeCreate
                     ! CFile::shareExclusive)) {
```

```
        AfxMessageBox("Failed to open file");
        return FALSE;
    }

    BOOL bResult = Save(&file);
    file.Close();
    if (!bResult) AfxMessageBox("Failed to save file");
    return bResult;
}
```

If no file name is provided, the user can select one from a dialog box. Once we have a file name, a *CFile* object is created and opened in read/write mode. A pointer to the open *CFile* object is then passed as an argument to the other *Save* function, which completes the process.

Now that we have a function to save the *CDIB* object in the standard Windows bitmap file format, let's see how the serialization code can make use of the *Save* function to serialize a *CDIB* object to an archive file. Here's the *CDIB::Serialize* function:

```
void CDIB::Serialize(CArchive& ar)
{
    ar.Flush();
    CFile* fp = ar.GetFile();

    if (ar.IsStoring()) {
        Save(fp);
    } else {
        Load(fp);
    }
}
```

If the words "Wow, this is easy" didn't just leap from your lips, I suspect you're really too tired, so put the book down and start again tomorrow morning. Joking aside, the serialization process really is trivial if we already have code to read and write the object data to a regular file. *Serialize* receives a reference to a *CArchive* object as its only parameter. *CArchive* supports a *GetFile* function that returns a pointer to the *CFile* object in which the archive is being created or read back from. Before we can call *CArchive::GetFile*, the documentation says, we must flush the archive by calling *CArchive::flush*. Having obtained the *CFile* pointer, we can use *CDIB::Load* or *CDIB::Save* as required to complete the function.

I am reminded here of the scene in Monty Python's *Holy Grail* in which the knights have arrived at the Bridge of Death and (Brave) Sir Robin says, "That's *easy…*" and proceeds to get himself killed. Yes, this is pretty easy (especially when viewed with 20-20 hindsight), but be aware that some bits of this serializing process are not quite as obvious as they might seem at this point. Enough waffle—on with the task.

Serializing *CSprite* Objects

Since *CSprite* is derived from *CDIB*, most of the work for serializing *CSprite* is simply done by the base class *CDIB::Serialize* function. The *CSprite::Serialize* function is only a matter of adding read and write operations for the member variables of *CSprite*.

```
void CSprite::Serialize(CArchive& ar)
{
    CDIB::Serialize(ar);
    if (ar.IsStoring()) {
        ar << (DWORD) m_x;
        ar << (DWORD) m_y;
        ar << (DWORD) m_z;
    } else {
        DWORD dw;
        ar >> dw; m_x = (int) dw;
        ar >> dw; m_y = (int) dw;
        ar >> dw; m_z = (int) dw;
        // Now generate the other parameters from the DIB.
        Initialize();
    }
}
```

First we call the base class *Serialize* function. Note that we do this independently of whether *Serialize* is being called to save or to load the object. Another point to note here is that *CArchive* has **<<** operator support for only a few types—for *DWORD*, for example. This limitation helps keep the size of items in a file format well defined but it can be a bit irritating in the code. The various int members, for instance, have to be cast to *DWORD* before they can be written to the archive.

Loading from the archive requires extracting *DWORD* items again and then converting them to the different member variable types. In addition, we call the *Initialize* function to extract any data from the DIB that we might use, such as the transparency color information.

You might have noticed that *m_pNotifyObj* is not saved. There is no point in saving a pointer <grin> because it will be invalid the next time the object is reloaded. To see how this inconstancy is handled, we need to look at how the *CSpriteList* class is serialized.

Serializing the *CSpriteList* Object

The *CObList* class from which *CSpriteList* is derived provides most of the serialization functionality we need. If we are saving the list of sprites, *CObList* provides all of the functionality we need. If we are creating a list of sprites dynamically from the archive (loading), *CObList* will create the *CSprite* objects for us, but this is where we must be very careful. Let's look at the code, and then I'll explain the problem:

```cpp
void CSpriteList::Serialize(CArchive& ar)
{
    // Let the base class create the set of objects.
    CObList::Serialize(ar);

    // If we've just loaded, initialize each sprite.
    if (ar.IsLoading()) {
        for (POSITION pos = GetHeadPosition(); pos != NULL;) {
            CSprite* pSprite = GetNext(pos); // Increment position.
            pSprite->SetNotificationObject(&m_NotifyObj);
        }
    }
}
```

Remember that we didn't bother to save the *m_NotifyObj* member of *CSprite* when it was serialized because it holds a pointer to another object and the pointer would be invalid the next time the object was loaded. So when we create a new list of sprites, we'll have to give each member of the list its *m_NotifyObj* set of members. We'll accomplish this by means of a call to *CSprite::SetNotificationObject*.

If you forget to add the *Serialize* function to *CSpriteList*, you'll find that the application will load the sprites OK but that nothing will paint correctly since the sprites won't have anywhere to send notification messages about their changes of position.

Serializing *CAnimDoc*

Now that each of the classes can be serialized, let's add the serialization code to the document. I decided that it should be possible to save a scene that has only a list of sprites—keeping that background DIB optional. To this end, I added a flag to the archive structure that indicates whether a background DIB is present or not. I could have handled this problem in other ways, but this way is easy to implement and obvious in the way it works.

```cpp
void CAnimDoc::Serialize(CArchive& ar)
{
    CDocument::Serialize(ar);
    if (ar.IsStoring()) {
        if (m_pBkgndDIB) {
            ar << (DWORD) 1; // Say we have a background DIB.
            m_pBkgndDIB->Serialize(ar);
        } else {
            ar << (DWORD) 0; // Say we have no background DIB.
        }
        m_SpriteList.Serialize(ar);
```

(continued)

```
        } else {
            DWORD dw;
            // See if we have a background DIB to load.
            ar >> dw;
            if (dw != 0) {
                CDIB* pDIB = new CDIB;
                pDIB->Serialize(ar);
                // Attach the background DIB to the document.
                SetBackground(pDIB);
            }
            // Read the sprite list.
            m_SpriteList.Serialize(ar);
            SetModifiedFlag(FALSE);
            UpdateAllViews(NULL, 0, NULL);
        }
}
```

When the scene is saved, a test is made to see if a background DIB is present. If one is, a 1 is written to the archive, followed by the background DIB itself. If no background DIB is present, a 0 is written to the archive. Then the sprite list is written out.

At loading, the background DIB flag is read. If the flag is nonzero, the background DIB is loaded and a call is made to *SetBackground* to create the off-screen buffer, the palette, and so on. The sprite list is then created from the archive, and finally a call is made to *UpdateAllViews*, which calls the *OnUpdate* function in the view to redraw the entire thing.

We haven't had a use for the *OnUpdate* function until now because all the rendering and drawing has been done by direct calls to the view class. Let's add *OnUpdate* to the *OSBView* class now. First we add a definition to the header file:

```
class COSBView : public CScrollView
{
    :
    :
public:
virtual void OnUpdate(CView* pSender,
                      LPARAM lHint,
                      CObject* pHint);
    :
    :
};
```

And now the function itself:

```
void COSBView::OnUpdate(CView* pSender,
                        LPARAM lHint,
                        CObject* pHint)
```

```
{
    // Render and draw everything.
    Render();
    Draw();
}
```

Not quite in the rocket science league, but an important piece of code if we actually want to be able to see a scene once it's been loaded.

Testing Time

That's it for serialization of a scene. Compile and test the FileIO sample to see the results. Load a background image and some sprites, and then try saving the scene. Now you should be able to load what you've saved and see the scene exactly as it was. In the future when we create a new class, we'll add the serialization code too, assuming that it makes sense to do that for the particular object.

Serializing *CDIBPal*

Adding serialization support for the *CDIBPal* class isn't required in order to save an animation, but I thought it might be very useful if a *CDIBPal* object could be created from a file with a Palette file format (.PAL) and if one of these files could be created from a *CDIBPal* object. With this functionality added to *CDIBPal*, it will be possible to create some useful tools—a palette editor, for instance. And indeed the Palette sample uses the enhanced *CDIBPal* class to implement a very basic palette editor. With it you can create a palette, add, edit, and delete color entries, and save the result to a .PAL file.

We will add a number of *Load* and *Save* functions to *CDIBPal* in much the same way that we added functions to the *CDIB* class. The main difference between serializing *CDIBPal* objects and *CDIB* objects is that the file format for .PAL files is very different from the one for DIBs.

Windows Palette Files
and Other RIFF Forms

Windows palette files (.PAL) conform to the Resource Interchange File Format (RIFF) specification. RIFF is a file format loosely based on the Interchange File Format (IFF) developed by Electronic Arts. The RIFF format is documented in volume 2 of the *Microsoft Win32 Programmer's Reference*. A detailed discussion of RIFF files is outside the scope of this book, but since RIFF formats are used to describe palette files and sound files—two kinds of files that might be of interest to us as we create animations—I thought it would be useful to look at what's involved in reading and writing RIFF files.

A RIFF file consists essentially of a header identifying the file as a RIFF file followed by one or more chunks of data. Each data chunk consists of a 32-bit tag (name), a 32-bit length, a 32-bit tag that identifies the file type, and then the data bytes themselves. A data chunk can contain subchunks, which allows complex nested structures to be created. As an example, let's look at a Windows palette file that is in a very simple RIFF format. *Figure 12-1* shows the overall structure.

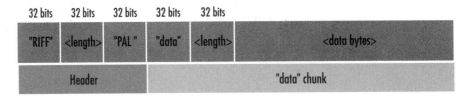

Figure 12-1   *The structure of a Windows palette file.*

Figure 12-2 shows a file dump of a palette file. You can use the FileDump sample application to dump out other palette files and see what they contain.

\anim32\filedump

```
000000   52 49 46 46 18 00 00 00 50 41 4C 20 64 61 74 61    RIFF....PAL data
000016   0C 00 00 00 00 03 02 00 FF FF FF 00 00 00 00 00    ................
```

Figure 12-2   *A file dump of a small palette file.*

As you can see, each of the file's 32-bit tag values is conveniently constructed from four ASCII characters. The header consists of the "RIFF" tag followed by the length of the remainder of the file, followed by a tag to identify the file type. The tag "PAL " (one trailing space) identifies the file as a palette file. The file contains only one chunk, and that is a data chunk. The length item in the data chunk is the number of bytes in the data section.

In the case of a palette file, the data chunk actually contains a LOG-PALETTE structure we can use to create a Windows palette from. As you can see, the file format is not very complex, and we could easily write some code to parse through it and extract the data chunk. Looking at the data in the example in Figure 12-2, we can see that the LOGPALETTE members are as shown in **Table 12-1**.

Table 12-1
Data from the File Dump in Figure 12-2

Field	Type	Value
palVersion	*WORD*	0x0300
palNumEntries	*WORD*	0x0002
palPalEntry[0]	*PALETTEENTRY*	255,255,255 (white)
palPalEntry[1]	*PALETTEENTRY*	0,0,0 (black)

Fortunately, as we deal with RIFF files, we won't need to be able to parse the format ourselves. Volume 2 of the *Microsoft Win32 Programmer's Reference* contains a series of functions with the prefix *mmio* (for multimedia i/o), which will do the job for us, and it's this series of functions that we will use to read and write in the RIFF file format used by the Windows palette files.

The *CDIBPal* Serialization Functions

Let's begin by looking at the functions that will allow us to create a *CDIBPal* object from a palette file. As we did for the *CDIB* object, we'll create four *Load* functions that will allow us to load a *CDIBPal* object from either a named file or a handle to an open file object. Because the *mmio* functions use their own file handle type (HMMIO), we'll also create a *Load* function that works with *mmio* handles. These functions are much easier to code than to describe, so let's take a look at the functions themselves, beginning with the version that loads a *CDIBPal* object from a named file.

```
BOOL CDIBPal::Load(char* pszFileName)
{
    CString strFile;

    if ((pszFileName == NULL)
    || (strlen(pszFileName) == 0)) {

        // Show a File Open dialog to get the name.
        CFileDialog dlg    (TRUE,     // Open
                           NULL,     // No default extension
                           NULL,     // No initial file name
                           OFN_FILEMUSTEXIST
                             | OFN_HIDEREADONLY,
                           "Palette files (*.PAL)|*.PAL|All files\
(*.*)|*.*||");
        if (dlg.DoModal() == IDOK) {
            strFile = dlg.GetPathName();
        } else {
            return FALSE;
        }
    } else {
        // Copy the supplied file path.
        strFile = pszFileName;
    }

    // Try to open the file for read access.
    CFile file;
```

(continued)

```
    if (!file.Open(strFile,
                CFile::modeRead | CFile::shareDenyWrite)) {
        AfxMessageBox("Failed to open file");
        return FALSE;
    }

    BOOL bResult = Load(&file);
    file.Close();
    if (!bResult) AfxMessageBox("Failed to load file");
    return bResult;
}
```

If no file name is supplied, the user can choose a file name from a dialog box and open the file as a *CFile* object, and another overload of *Load* will be called to complete the load process. Let's look at that one next:

```
BOOL CDIBPal::Load(CFile* fp)

{

    return Load(fp->m_hFile);

}
```

I always feel I'm cheating when I write code like this! I seem to be passing the buck to yet another function, but in this case, it just turns out to be very convenient to convert the open *CFile* object to a Windows file handle and call yet another *Load* function:

```
BOOL CDIBPal::Load(UINT hFile)
{
    HMMIO hmmio;
    MMIOINFO info;
    memset(&info, 0, sizeof(info));
    info.adwInfo[0] = hFile;
    hmmio = mmioOpen(NULL,
                    &info,
                    MMIO_READ | MMIO_ALLOCBUF);
    if (!hmmio) {
        TRACE("mmioOpen failed");
        return FALSE;
    }
    BOOL bResult = Load(hmmio);
    mmioClose(hmmio, MMIO_FHOPEN);
    return bResult;
}
```

This one's a bit more interesting. We still haven't managed to get to the actual file yet, but we're closer. The Windows file handle is used to create an open HMMIO file handle, and the call is passed on to the final *Load* function. The

HMMIO handle simply allows us to use the *mmio* file functions. In many ways, an HMMIO handle is very similar to a regular Windows file handle.

Here's the function that takes the HMMIO handle and actually reads the file. I've cut out some of the comments and error handling here to improve clarity.

```
BOOL CDIBPal::Load(HMMIO hmmio)
{
    // Check whether it's a RIFF PAL file.
    MMCKINFO ckFile;
    ckFile.fccType = mmioFOURCC('P','A','L',' ');
    if (mmioDescend(hmmio,
                    &ckFile,
                    NULL,
                    MMIO_FINDRIFF) != 0) {
        return FALSE;
    }
    // Find the 'data' chunk.
    MMCKINFO ckChunk;
    ckChunk.ckid = mmioFOURCC('d','a','t','a');
    if (mmioDescend(hmmio,
                    &ckChunk,
                    &ckFile,
                    MMIO_FINDCHUNK) != 0) {
        return FALSE;
    }
    // Allocate some memory for the 'data' chunk.
    int iSize = ckChunk.cksize;
    void* pdata = malloc(iSize);
    if (!pdata) {
        return FALSE;
    }
    // Read the 'data' chunk.
    if (mmioRead(hmmio,
                 (char*)pdata,
                 iSize) != iSize) {
        free(pdata);
        return FALSE;
    }
    return CreatePalette((LOGPALETTE*)pdata);
}
```

The file is first tested to make sure that it's a RIFF file and that it has a "PAL " tag identifying it as a palette file. A search is made to find a "data" chunk. If the "data" chunk is found, a block of memory the same size as the "data" chunk is allocated and the chunk is read into the memory block. The memory chunk is known to be a LOGPALETTE structure for a palette file, so all that's left to do is a call to *CreatePalette* that passes the address of the

LOGPALETTE structure. Remember that *CreatePalette* is a member of *CPalette*, from which *CDIBPal* is derived.

That completes the *Load* functions. Let's look now at what's required to create a palette file in its RIFF form from a *CDIBPal* object. We'll create a set of *Save* functions to achieve this goal. We'll start with a pair of functions to save the *CDIBPal* object to an open *CFile* object and to an open Windows file handle:

```
BOOL CDIBPal::Save(CFile* fp)
{
    return Save(fp->m_hFile);
}


BOOL CDIBPal::Save(UINT hFile)
{
    HMMIO hmmio;
    MMIOINFO info;
    memset(&info, 0, sizeof(info));
    info.adwInfo[0] = hFile;
    hmmio = mmioOpen(NULL,
                     &info,
                     MMIO_WRITE | MMIO_CREATE | MMIO_ALLOCBUF);
    if (!hmmio) {
        return FALSE;
    }
    BOOL bResult = Save(hmmio);
    mmioClose(hmmio, MMIO_FHOPEN);
    return bResult;
}
```

As you can see, the *CDIBPal* save code is very similar to the *CDIBPal* load code. The real work is done by the function that writes to the open HMMIO handle:

```
BOOL CDIBPal::Save(HMMIO hmmio)
{
    // Create a RIFF chunk for a PAL file.
    MMCKINFO ckFile;
    ckFile.cksize = 0; // Corrected later
    ckFile.fccType = mmioFOURCC('P','A','L',' ');
    if (mmioCreateChunk(hmmio,
                        &ckFile,
                        MMIO_CREATERIFF) != 0) {
        TRACE("Failed to create RIFF-PAL chunk");
        return FALSE;
    }
    // Create the LOGPALETTE data, which will become
    // the data chunk.
    int iColors = GetNumColors();
    ASSERT(iColors > 0);
```

```
int iSize = sizeof(LOGPALETTE) +
            (iColors-1) * sizeof(PALETTEENTRY);
LOGPALETTE* plp = (LOGPALETTE*) malloc(iSize);
ASSERT(plp);
plp->palVersion = 0x300;
plp->palNumEntries = iColors;
GetPaletteEntries(0, iColors, plp->palPalEntry);
// Create the data chunk.
MMCKINFO ckData;
ckData.cksize = iSize;
ckData.ckid = mmioFOURCC('d','a','t','a');
if (mmioCreateChunk(hmmio,
                    &ckData,
                    0) != 0) {
    TRACE("Failed to create data chunk");
    return FALSE;
}
// Write the data chunk.
if (mmioWrite(hmmio,
              (char*)plp,
              iSize) != iSize) {
    TRACE("Failed to write data chunk");
    free(plp);
    return FALSE;
}
free(plp);
// Ascend from the data chunk, which will correct the length.
mmioAscend(hmmio, &ckData, 0);
// Ascend from the RIFF-PAL chunk.
mmioAscend(hmmio, &ckFile, 0);

return TRUE;
}
```

A new "RIFF" chunk is created with the special "PAL " tag. There is no need to compute the final file size because this will be filled in automatically later as we complete writing all the chunks to the file. Once the header has been written, a LOGPALETTE structure big enough for all the colors in the palette is allocated in memory. Data is copied to the structure from the *CDIBPal* object, and the LOGPALETTE structure is written out as a "data" chunk to the file. When the data has been written, a call is made to *mmioAscend* to exit from the "data" chunk. In this case, the length of the "data" chunk is correctly recorded in the file. A second call to *mmioAscend* writes out the length of the file to the header.

Although this code's use of the *mmio* functions may seem reasonably simple, the *mmio* functions offer a lot of possibilities not used here. If you are interested in what they have to offer you, refer to volume 2 of the *Microsoft Win32 Programmer's Reference* for more details.

A Simple Palette Editor

\anim32\palette

I thought I'd round out all this talk of file input/output with a sample application that reads, writes, and edits palettes. The Palette application can be used to create a new palette, edit the palette's colors, and save the palette to a .PAL file. The view class (in PALVW.CPP) uses the *CDIBPal::Draw* function to draw the palette colors and to detect whether the mouse has double-clicked on a color. If a double click on a color is detected, the user can edit the color in the Select Color dialog box. Double-clicking in the view area outside the current color set allows the creation of a new color in the palette. Clicking the Delete button in the Select Color dialog box deletes a color from the palette. Much of the code is trivial, making use of functions we have already looked at, so we'll focus on only two things here: the mouse handling code in the view and the way the Select Color dialog box works.

Here's the code that handles mouse button double clicks in the view window:

```
void CPaletteView::OnLButtonDblClk(UINT nFlags, CPoint point)
{
    CPaletteDoc* pDoc = GetDocument();
    ASSERT(pDoc);
    CDIBPal* pPal = pDoc->GetPalette();
    if (!pPal) return;
    // Compute the palette index.
    CRect rc;
    GetClientRect(&rc);
    int i = point.x * 16 / rc.right;
    int j = point.y * 16 / rc.bottom;
    int index = j * 16 + i;
    // If the index is greater than the number of colors,
    // expand the number of colors by one and alter the
    // index to the new color slot.
    int iColors = pPal->GetNumColors();
    if (index >= iColors) {
        ASSERT(index < 256);
        pPal->ResizePalette(iColors+1);
        index = iColors;
        iColors++;
        pDoc->SetModifiedFlag(TRUE);
    }

    // Get the color.
    PALETTEENTRY pe;
    pPal->GetPaletteEntries(index, 1, &pe);
    // Show the color chooser dialog.
    CColorDlg dlg;
    dlg.m_red = pe.peRed;
    dlg.m_green = pe.peGreen;
    dlg.m_blue = pe.peBlue;
```

```
    int iResult = dlg.DoModal();
    // Update the color (or restore the old one).
    pe.peRed = dlg.m_red;
    pe.peGreen = dlg.m_green;
    pe.peBlue = dlg.m_blue;
    pPal->SetPaletteEntries(index, 1, &pe);
    if (iResult == IDOK) {
        pDoc->SetModifiedFlag(TRUE);
    }
    // See if we need to delete it.
    if (iResult == IDC_DELETE) {
        // Get all the entries from the
        // current index onwards.
        PALETTEENTRY pe[256];
        pPal->GetPaletteEntries(index,
                                iColors-index,
                                pe);
        // Move each entry down one slot, replacing the
        // current one.
        if (iColors-index > 1) {
            pPal->SetPaletteEntries(index,
                                    iColors-index,
                                    &pe[1]);
        }
        // Resize the palette.
        iColors--;
        pPal->ResizePalette(iColors);
        pDoc->SetModifiedFlag(TRUE);
    }
    // Repaint the affected area.
    Invalidate();

}
```

This code relies on the fact that the *CDIBPal::Draw* function always draws the palette colors in a 16-by-16 grid. It's a little cheesy in that respect, but it's easy to follow and does what we need for now. The mouse coordinates are used to compute which color in the palette was selected. If the selection falls outside the current range of colors, the palette is expanded to include a new color, and the new color is the one that was effectively selected.

The red, green, and blue elements of the selected color are extracted, and the Select Color dialog box is set up with them. Calling its *DoModal* function makes the dialog box visible. Once the dialog box returns, the palette is updated with the new color. If the Delete button was pressed, the entry selected in the palette is removed by a copying of all the entries above it down one position and by a reduction in the size of the palette by one.

Nothing too wonderful going on here, so let's look at the Select Color dialog box, which is a bit more interesting.

The Select Color Dialog Box

I'd like to make two disclaimers here before we look closely at the Select Color dialog box. First, my idea of a user interface design is usually driven by the motive to do the least amount of work possible, and second, I was trying to show a little technology here, not a nice piece of artwork. Having covered myself, I can now show you, in *Figure 12-3*, a screen shot of the dialog box and expect you not to greet it with great hoots of laughter.

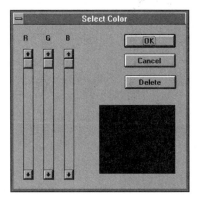

Figure 12-3 *The Select Color dialog box.*

OK, so I was wrong. You're laughing. The dialog box has three scroll bars that allow the user to select the amounts of red, green, and blue for the color. The rectangle at the bottom-right corner shows the current color. In addition to the usual OK and Cancel buttons, the dialog box has a Delete button to allow the user to remove the current color from the palette.

At first sight, such a dialog box doesn't look as if it will be too hard to implement. Two things, however, require a bit of thought. First, how will we create the current color? (Remember, we need a palette entry for any color we want to display.) Second, how will we display that color?

Creating the Color

In order to be able to show a color, we must first create a palette entry for it, so the dialog box needs a palette to work with. Since we need to display only one color, the palette we create needs to have only a single color entry. The dialog box needs a palette as one of its member variables, and since we have gone to so much trouble to develop the *CDIBPal* class, we might as well use a *CDIBPal* object here. Here's a cut-down version of the header file COLORDLG.H showing the variables we are going to use:

```
class CColorDlg : public CDialog
{
    :
    :
```

```
public:
    int m_red;
    int m_green;
    int m_blue;

private:
    CScrollBar* m_psbRed;
    CScrollBar* m_psbGreen;
    CScrollBar* m_psbBlue;
    CDIBPal* m_pPal;
    :
    :
};
```

The public members—*m_red*, *m_green*, and *m_blue*—are used to pass the initial color to the dialog box and to return the final chosen color to the calling code. The *m_psbRed*, *m_psbGreen*, and *m_psbBlue* variables are used as pointers to the scroll bars for convenience in the code. Finally, the *m_pPal* member is a pointer to the *CDIBPal* object, which will hold the color being created.

The constructor and destructor for the dialog box look like this:

```
CColorDlg::CColorDlg(CWnd* pParent /*=NULL*/)
    : CDialog(CColorDlg::IDD, pParent)
{
    //{{AFX_DATA_INIT(CColorDlg)
        // NOTE: ClassWizard will add member initialization here.
    //}}AFX_DATA_INIT
    m_red = 128;
    m_green - 128;
    m_blue = 128;
    m_pPal = NULL;
}

CColorDlg::~CColorDlg()
{
    if (m_pPal) {
        delete m_pPal;
    }
}
```

Note that the *m_pPal* member is set to NULL in the constructor. In the destructor, any palette object is deleted.

Now that we have the variables defined, let's have a look at what happens when the dialog box is created. Remember that the *m_red*, *m_green*, and *m_blue* data values are set by the calling code before the dialog box *DoModal* function is called, so they are defined, as shown on the next page, before the *OnInitDialog* code is executed.

```
BOOL CColorDlg::OnInitDialog()
{
    CDialog::OnInitDialog();

    m_psbRed = (CScrollBar*)GetDlgItem(IDC_RED);
    m_psbGreen = (CScrollBar*)GetDlgItem(IDC_GREEN);
    m_psbBlue = (CScrollBar*)GetDlgItem(IDC_BLUE);
    m_psbRed->SetScrollRange(0, 255, FALSE);
    m_psbGreen->SetScrollRange(0, 255, FALSE);
    m_psbBlue->SetScrollRange(0, 255, FALSE);
    m_psbRed->SetScrollPos(m_red, TRUE);
    m_psbGreen->SetScrollPos(m_green, TRUE);
    m_psbBlue->SetScrollPos(m_blue, TRUE);

    // Create a palette with one color we can animate.
    m_pPal = new CDIBPal;
    LOGPALETTE lp;
    lp.palVersion = 0x300;
    lp.palNumEntries = 1;
    lp.palPalEntry[0].peRed = m_red;
    lp.palPalEntry[0].peGreen = m_green;
    lp.palPalEntry[0].peBlue = m_blue;
    lp.palPalEntry[0].peFlags = PC_RESERVED;
    m_pPal->CreatePalette(&lp);

    return TRUE;
}
```

Pointers to the three scroll bar controls are obtained and saved. Unfortunately, the App Studio feature that allows us to assign variables to controls does not include the ability to assign variables for scroll bars, so we have to do it ourselves here. The range of the controls is set, and the initial positions are set to reflect the initial color settings.

Now the palette is created. A new *CDIBPal* object is created with a single entry. Note that the definition of the LOGPALETTE structure includes one color, so we didn't need to use *malloc* to assign the memory for the structure as we have before. The members of the LOGPALETTE structure are set to the initial color settings, which should all look familiar to you now. The only new item here is the use of the PC_RESERVED flag. Setting this flag tells the Palette Manager that we will be altering the colors of this entry while we are using it and would like to reserve it for our own exclusive use. The Palette Manager will then not map any other application's colors to this entry. If we didn't set this flag, not only would the color in our dialog box display change as we altered the color with the scroll bar controls in the dialog box, but possibly some part of an image in another application that had been mapped to this palette entry would change.

Displaying the Color

Now that we have created a palette with a color to use, we can see how the color is painted to the display rectangle in the dialog box. The first stage is to add a handler to the dialog box for WM_PAINT messages:

```
void CColorDlg::OnPaint()
{
    CDialog::OnPaint();
    PaintColor();
}
```

OnPaint simply calls a helper routine to paint the display rectangle:

```
VOID CColorDlg::PaintColor()
{
    // Select the palette into our sample window DC.
    CDC* pDC = GetDC();
    CPalette* pOldPal = pDC->SelectPalette(m_pPal, FALSE);
    pDC->RealizePalette();
    // Create a brush to use.
    CBrush br (PALETTEINDEX(0));
    // Paint the rectangle in the sample window.
    CRect rc (150,135,280,250);
    pDC->FillRect(&rc, &br);
    // Done with DC, brush, and palette.
    pDC->SelectPalette(pOldPal, FALSE);
    ReleaseDC(pDC);
}
```

The palette is selected into the device context (DC), and a brush is created from the color in the first slot in the palette (the one we are using). *FillRect* is then called to paint the area of the dialog window with the current color. "Whoa, there. What's with the fixed coordinates, Mr. Thompson?" There was no hope of escaping your eagle eyes, was there? Yes, this is a hack. In the ideal world, I would have used App Studio to create a static control where I wanted to paint the color rectangle, and then I would have subclassed that window so that I could do the painting. That would have generated lots of lines of code and required lots of explanation—all to get one colored rectangle to appear in the dialog box. I wanted to keep this simple, so I cheated.

If you were to compile and test the code at this point, the dialog box would appear and the color rectangle would paint. Now we need to make the scroll bars work so that we can change the color. This is the most interesting bit. The first stage is to add a handler to the dialog box for WM_VSCROLL messages, as shown on the next page.

```
void CColorDlg::OnVScroll(UINT nSBCode, UINT nPos, CScrollBar* pScrollBar)
{
    int iPos = pScrollBar->GetScrollPos();
    switch (nSBCode) {
    case SB_TOP:
        iPos = 0;
        break;
    case SB_LINEDOWN:
        iPos++;
        break;
    case SB_PAGEDOWN:
        iPos += 10;
        break;
    case SB_BOTTOM:
        iPos = 255;
        break;
    case SB_LINEUP:
        iPos--;
        break;
    case SB_PAGEUP:
        iPos -= 10;
        break;
    case SB_THUMBTRACK:
    case SB_THUMBPOSITION:
        iPos = nPos;
        break;
    default:
        break;
    }
    if (iPos < 0) iPos = 0;
    if (iPos > 255) iPos = 255;
    pScrollBar->SetScrollPos(iPos, TRUE);

    PALETTEENTRY pe;
    pe.peRed = m_psbRed->GetScrollPos();
    pe.peGreen = m_psbGreen->GetScrollPos();
    pe.peBlue = m_psbBlue->GetScrollPos();
    pe.peFlags = PC_RESERVED;
    CDC* pDC = GetDC();
    CPalette* pOldPal = pDC->SelectPalette(m_pPal, FALSE);
    m_pPal->AnimatePalette(0, 1, &pe);
    pDC->RealizePalette();
    pDC->SelectPalette(pOldPal, FALSE);
    ReleaseDC(pDC);
}
```

The new scroll bar position is calculated and verified to be inside the 0 through 255 range of values we want. The position of the scroll bar is then updated. Now we want to alter the color in the display rectangle so that we can see it. We could destroy the existing palette and create a new one with the new color and then paint the rectangle again. That would work, but a side effect would be that, when we realized the palette, all other applications would get palette messages telling them of the new palette, and they might repaint. As we moved the scroll bar controls, there would be a lot of flickering on the screen. So instead of creating a new palette, we *animate* the current one. We simply tell the Palette Manager that we want to set a new combination of red, green, and blue into the existing color entry of the palette we already have. Remember that we used the PC_RESERVED flag when we created this entry so that we could alter the color components later.

To update the color, we select the palette into the window DC. We make a call to *AnimatePalette*, passing it a PALETTEENTRY array containing the new colors (one in this case), and then we call *RealizePalette* to make the change effective. This simple technique allows us to alter the palette color in real time with no side effects on other applications or any need to repaint anything. We don't need to paint the new color into the display rectangle because, when we change the logical palette entry color, the Palette Manager changes the physical palette entry for that color, which consequently changes what is seen on the screen wherever that palette entry was used.

Palette animation can be used as an animation technique all of its own and is often used to create wave effects, for example, by varying the colors used in the waves. You get the effect of motion without having to paint anything.

Although my Select Color dialog box isn't very pretty to look at, it does what we need and shows you how you might use the *CDIBPal* class to do color animation.

CHAPTER

Sprites That Change Shape

Phased Images

The *CPhasedSprite* Class

A Sample Application to
Show Off Phased Sprites

Moving On from Here

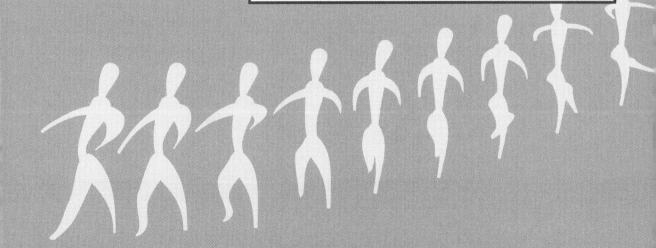

o far, the behavior of the sprites we've created has been a bit flat and boring. In this chapter, we'll look at what's involved in creating sprites that can change shape. By changing the shape and position of a sprite, we can make a character "walk," seeming to move toward or away from the viewer. To accomplish this illusion of movement, we will create a new class, *CPhasedSprite*, based on *CSprite*.

Phased Images

I call a sprite that can change its image a "phased sprite." The name comes from my (now distant) electronics background, where the word "phase" describes the current position of a waveform in the cycle. When I worked on creating character sprites that would appear to walk as they moved, I thought of the various images that would constitute a "walk" cycle as the phases the image would go through. Thinking of the phases of the moon is another approach. The important thing about all of this is that, in order to give a direction to any movement, we must have at least three image phases. With only a single phase, the image is always the same and appears static. With only two image phases, the image seems to be flickering between two states. With three or more phases, the image can be seen to progress through a sequence in a fixed direction. *Figure 13-1* shows an image that has only two phases.

Figure 13-1 *An image switching between two phases.*

Figure 13-2 shows an image with four phases.

Figure 13-2   *An image moving through four phases.*

We can create a sprite with multiple image phases in either of two ways: by attaching an array of images to the sprite (as in **Figure 13-3**) or by dividing up a single image into a grid of subimages (as in **Figure 13-4**). Since our *CSprite* class is derived from *CDIB*, which has only a single image, it is simpler to create a phased-image sprite by dividing up the one existing image in the sprite than it would be to try to find a way to have multiple DIBs attached to a single sprite. This isn't a big point. We could, of course, create a class that had an array of *CDIB* objects—one for each image phase. It's just that the *CSprite* class already has a mechanism for dealing with a single image, and it turns out to require less code to divide up one image into phases than to add additional images to the sprite.

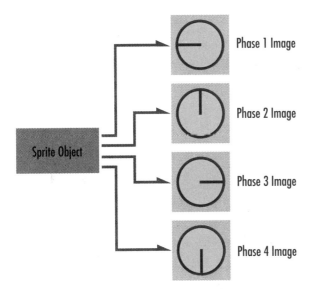

Figure 13-3   *A sprite object with pointers to its phased images.*

Since character animation commonly requires that characters change shape as they walk and size as they move forward and backward in the scene, it is convenient to create a two-dimensional grid of the images in a

Figure 13-4 *A sprite object containing a single compound image of all its phases.*

scene, using one axis for the shapes and the other for the sizes. ***Figure 13-5*** shows an image that was constructed for an object that has three different shapes and three different sizes. The grid lines show the bounds of each cell and would be removed in the final image. Each row of the image contains a different shape, and each column contains a different size. To change the shape of the image, we select a different row from the grid, and to change its size, we select a different column. The *CPhasedSprite* class is designed around these two-dimensional cell image structures.

Figure 13-5 *A compound image of an object with three shapes and three sizes.*

The *CPhasedSprite* Class

The *CPhasedSprite* class was derived from *CSprite*. *CPhasedSprite* divides its image into a number of rows and columns with the constructor setting the number of rows and the number of columns to 1, so the initial behavior is the same as for *CSprite*. Let's begin by looking at the header for the *CPhasedSprite* class in PHSPRITE.H:

```
class CPhasedSprite : public CSprite
{
    DECLARE_SERIAL(CPhasedSprite)
public:
    CPhasedSprite();
    ~CPhasedSprite();

    // New in this class
    virtual int GetNumCellRows() {return m_iNumCellRows;}
    virtual int GetNumCellColumns() {return m_iNumCellColumns;}
    virtual int GetCellRow() {return m_iCellRow;}
    virtual int GetCellColumn() {return m_iCellColumn;}

    virtual BOOL SetNumCellRows(int iNumRows);
    virtual BOOL SetNumCellColumns(int iNumColumns);
    virtual BOOL SetCellRow(int iRow);
    virtual BOOL SetCellColumn(int iColumn);

    // From base classes
    virtual int GetHeight() {return m_iCellHeight;}
    virtual int GetWidth() {return m_iCellWidth;}
    virtual void GetRect(CRect* pRect);
    virtual BOOL HitTest(CPoint point);
    virtual void Render(CDIB* pDIB, CRect* pClipRect = NULL);
    virtual void Serialize(CArchive& ar);

protected:
    int m_iNumCellRows;      // Number of rows in the image grid
    int m_iNumCellColumns;   // Number of columns in the image grid
    int m_iCellRow;          // Current cell row
    int m_iCellColumn;       // Current cell column
    int m_iCellHeight;       // Height of a row
    int m_iCellWidth;        // Width of a column
};
```

As you can see, member variables hold the number of rows and columns, the current row and column, and the height and width of a cell. It isn't really necessary to keep the cell height and width because they can always be computed from the image size and the number of rows or columns, but it simplifies the code to keep them because these values are used a lot.

Member functions support getting and setting the number of rows and columns and also the current row and column. A number of virtual functions from the *CSprite* base class are overloaded here. Any function that deals with the image size (such as *GetWidth*) needs to be overloaded in the *CPhasedSprite* class so that the width returned will be the width of a cell and not the width of the entire image, which is what the base class member function would return. By using virtual functions in this way, the code can use a generic *CSprite* pointer to access both *CSprite* and *CPhasedSprite* objects. When a call is made to the *GetWidth* member, the correct information will be returned. For a *CSprite* object, *GetWidth* will return the width of the DIB image. For a *CPhasedSprite* object, *GetWidth* will return the width of a single cell.

The *CPhasedSprite* constructor and destructor are quite simple:

```
CPhasedSprite::CPhasedSprite()
{
    m_iNumCellRows = 1;
    m_iNumCellColumns = 1;
    m_iCellRow = 0;
    m_iCellColumn = 0;
    m_iCellHeight = CSprite::GetHeight();
    m_iCellWidth =  CSprite::GetWidth();
}


CPhasedSprite::~CPhasedSprite()
{
}
```

The constructor sets the initial state for a 1-by-1 grid of images and sets the cell height and width to be the height and width of the image. Notice that we explicitly call the *CSprite* (base class) versions of *GetHeight* and *GetWidth*.

We'll need to be able to save and load *CPhasedSprite* objects, so we'll need to have the *Serialize* function keep track of the number of rows and columns and what the current state should be:

```
void CPhasedSprite::Serialize(CArchive& ar)
{
    CSprite::Serialize(ar);
    if (ar.IsStoring())
    {
        ar << (DWORD) m_iNumCellRows;
        ar << (DWORD) m_iNumCellColumns;
        ar << (DWORD) m_iCellRow;
        ar << (DWORD) m_iCellColumn;
    }
```

```
    else
    {
        DWORD dw;
        ar >> dw;
        SetNumCellRows(dw);
        ar >> dw;
        SetNumCellColumns(dw);
        ar >> dw;
        SetCellRow(dw);
        ar >> dw;
        SetCellColumn(dw);
    }
}
```

Saving the state is trivial. The base class is serialized first, and then the member variables are written out to the archive as DWORD values. Loading the object back from the archive is a bit more involved. Each value is recovered from the archive, and one of the member functions is called to set the object state.

Let's look at what's required to set the number of rows and the current row. (Because the code for setting the number of columns and the current column is similar to that for setting the number of rows and the current row, we'll look at just the rows code.)

```
BOOL CPhasedSprite::SetNumCellRows(int iRows)
{
    if (iRows < 1) {
        TRACE("Invalid number of rows");
        return FALSE;
    }
    // Compute the height of each row.
    int iCellHeight = CSprite::GetHeight() / iRows;
    if (iCellHeight < 1) {
        TRACE("Can't make them that small");
        return FALSE;
    }
    // Set the new height and row count.
    m_iNumCellRows = iRows;
    m_iCellRow = 0;
    m_iCellHeight = iCellHeight;
    return TRUE;
}
```

The number of rows is validated as a sensible number, and then the variable *m_iNumCellRows* is updated. The current row is reset to 0, and the cell height is updated to reflect the new cell size.

```
BOOL CPhasedSprite::SetCellRow(int iRow)
{
    if ((iRow >= m_iNumCellRows)
```

(continued)

```
    || (iRow < 0)) {
        TRACE("Invalid row");
        return FALSE;
    }
    if (iRow == m_iCellRow) return FALSE; // Nothing to do
    m_iCellRow = iRow;
    // Send a notification to redraw.
    if (m_pNotifyObj) {
        CRect rcPos;
        GetRect(&rcPos);
        m_pNotifyObj->Change(this,
                             CSpriteNotifyObj::IMAGE,
                             &rcPos);
    }
    return TRUE;
}
```

Whether the row is in range is to be tested, and if it is in range, the *m_iCellRow* variable is updated. Since changing the current row means that the image needs to be redrawn, a call is made to the notification object (if present), informing it that the image needs to be redrawn.

Hit Testing and Rendering *CPhasedSprite* Objects

Now let's see how the phased image affects the *HitTest* and *Render* functions. In testing a mouse click to see whether it hits the image, we must take into consideration the fact that the image changes with the phases of the sprite. We could do the test and take account of the sprite's phases in either of two ways: we could alter the *GetPixel* function defined in the *CDIB* class so that it retrieved a pixel from the *x* and *y* coordinates of the current cell rather than the *x* and *y* coordinates of the whole image, or we could overload the *CSprite::HitTest* function to make it work with cell coordinates rather than image coordinates. If we were to alter *GetPixel*, the *HitTest* function defined in the *CSprite* class would work; however, I felt that the functions that manipulated the image itself should remain intact and decided to overload the *HitTest* function to do what I wanted. After all, that was the feature the change was required to support in the first place.

```
BOOL CPhasedSprite::HitTest(CPoint point)
{
    // Test if the point is inside the sprite rectangle.
    if ((point.x > m_x)
    && (point.x < m_x + GetWidth())
    && (point.y > m_y)
    && (point.y < m_y + GetHeight())) {
        // Hit is in sprite rectangle.
        // See if this point is transparent by testing to see if
        // the pixel value is the same as the top-left corner value.
        // Note that top-left of the image is bottom-left in the DIB.
```

```
// Get the address of the top-left pixel
// of the cell, not the DIB. Note that the
// GetPixelAddress function refers to addresses
// in the image DIB, not the cell.
int x, y;
x = point.x - m_x +
    m_iCellColumn * m_iCellWidth;
y = point.y - m_y +
    m_iCellRow * m_iCellHeight;
BYTE* p = (BYTE*)GetPixelAddress(x, y);
ASSERT(p);
if (*p != m_bTransIndex) {
    return TRUE;
}
    }
    return FALSE;
}
```

The only change from the *CSprite::HitTest* version that's required is to offset the *x* and *y* coordinates to the top-left corner of the current cell.

The final routine to look at in *CPhasedSprite* is the *Render* function:

```
void CPhasedSprite::Render(CDIB* pDIB, CRect* pClipRect)
{
    ASSERT(pDIB);
    ASSERT(pClipRect);
    // Get the sprite rectangle and see if it's visible.
    CRect rcDraw;
    GetRect(&rcDraw);
    if (!rcDraw.IntersectRect(pClipRect, &rcDraw)) {
        return; // Not visible
    }
    // Modify the source x and y values for the current phase of
    // the sprite.
    int xs = rcDraw.left - m_x + m_iCellColumn * m_iCellWidth;
    int ys = rcDraw.top - m_y + m_iCellRow * m_iCellHeight;
    ASSERT(xs >= 0 && xs < CSprite::GetWidth());
    ASSERT(ys >= 0 && ys < CSprite::GetHeight());
    CopyBits(pDIB,                            // Destination DIB
            rcDraw.left,                      // Destination x
            rcDraw.top,                       // Destination y
            rcDraw.right - rcDraw.left,       // Width
            rcDraw.bottom - rcDraw.top,       // Height
            xs,                               // Source x
            ys,                               // Source y
            PALETTEINDEX(m_bTransIndex));     // Transparent color index
}
```

There isn't much here that's different from *CSprite::Render*. The only change is that the rectangle describing the image is offset from its normal origin in a *CSprite* image to the origin of the cell we want to render, and the width and height of the image rectangle are the width and height of a single cell rather than of the whole image.

A Sample Application to Show Off Phased Sprites

\anim32\phases

The sample code in the Phases directory was based on the FileIO sample. The first change was to alter the *OnFileLoadSprite* function to create a *CPhasedSprite* object rather than a *CSprite* object:

```
void CAnimDoc::OnFileLoadSprite()
{
    // Create a sprite to hold the image.
    CPhasedSprite* pSprite = new CPhasedSprite;
    // Show the File Open dialog for a sprite.
    if (!pSprite->Load()) {
        delete pSprite;
        return;
    }
    // Add the sprite to the sprite list.
    m_SpriteList.Insert(pSprite);
    SetModifiedFlag(TRUE);
    // Tell the view about the new sprite.
    GetAnimView()->NewSprite(pSprite);
}
```

At this point the application could be built, and if all was well with the typing, we would get an application that ran in exactly the same way as the FileIO sample ran, with the phased sprite behaving exactly as a sprite from its base class does.

Having gotten this to work, I added some more items to the sprite's Property menu, which comes up in response to a right mouse click on the sprite. The new menu items allowed the number of rows and columns in the phased image to be set. I chose to limit the maximum number of phases to four, just to keep the menu small. You could just as easily create a dialog box to allow the user to enter the information. The code to handle these menu items is trivial, but here's some of it to give you an idea of what's involved:

```
void CAnimView::SetSpriteRows(int i)
{
    m_pMenuSprite->SetNumCellRows(i);
    // Render and draw the lot since the sprite has
    // effectively changed size.
    Render();
    Draw();
}
```

```
void CAnimView::OnRows1() {SetSpriteRows(1);}
void CAnimView::OnRows2() {SetSpriteRows(2);}
void CAnimView::OnRows3() {SetSpriteRows(3);}
void CAnimView::OnRows4() {SetSpriteRows(4);}
```

At this point it's possible to load a sprite and set the number of rows and columns that the sprite image was built from and then see the sprite change size and show the first cell correctly. Note that changing the sprite's number of rows or columns requires a repaint in order to see the changes, and rather than try to compute the smallest rectangle that would contain both the old image and the new image, I simply chose to repaint the entire scene.

In order to see the other cell images, I decided to add a little code that would change the current row and column according to where the sprite was on the screen when it was dragged by the mouse. I modified the mouse movement handler in the view to select the different cells:

```
void CAnimView::OnMouseMove(UINT nFlags, CPoint point)
{
    if (m_bMouseCaptured) {
        ASSERT(m_pCapturedSprite);
        m_pCapturedSprite->SetPosition(point.x - m_ptOffset.x,
                                       point.y - m_ptOffset.y);
        // Change the phase of the image.
        CAnimDoc* pDoc = GetDocument();
        CRect rc;
        pDoc->GetSceneRect(&rc);

        // Set the column number according to the y position.
        int iCols = m_pCapturedSprite->GetNumCellColumns();
        int iPos = m_pCapturedSprite->GetY();
        int iCol = iPos * iCols / rc.bottom;
        iCol = iCols - 1 - iCol;
        if (iCol < 0) iCol = 0;
        if (iCol >= iCols) iCol = iCols - 1;
        m_pCapturedSprite->SetCellColumn(iCol);

        // Set the row number according to the x position.
        int iRows = m_pCapturedSprite->GetNumCellRows();
        iPos = m_pCapturedSprite->GetX();
        int iRow = (iPos / 10) % iRows;
        m_pCapturedSprite->SetCellRow(iRow);

        // Render and draw the changes.
        RenderAndDrawDirtyList();
        pDoc->SetModifiedFlag(TRUE);
    }
}
```

The size of the image is determined by which column of the image grid we use. The column chosen is based on the sprite's y axis value, so that, as the sprite moves up, the image gets smaller, which creates the effect of moving into the distance. The shape of the image (the current row in the grid) is designed to cycle as the sprite moves in the x direction. I take the current x position of the sprite, divide it by 10 (so that it changes shape every tenth pixel), and then use the modulus operator to choose the cell row to show.

Some redundant repainting goes on here: the call to *SetCellColumn* forces a repaint, and so does the call to *SetCellRow*. If these functions were going to be called together often, I would be tempted to create a new function that would set both the row and the column and then do a single repaint.

Moving On from Here

At this point you could quite easily take the Phases sample code and create some interesting applications. If you are going to do this, there is one step (omitted here) that will make life simpler for you. Instead of directly using the *CPhasedSprite* class in the document, derive your own class from *CPhasedSprite* and use that instead. In that way, you'll inherit all that *CPhasedSprite* has to offer and make it very simple to add your own routines to control the behavior of the sprites. Adding code to the mouse-move handler to show the sprite phases was easy but not very practical. It would be better to have a routine called by a timer that moved all the sprites according to where you wanted them and then repainted all the dirty areas of the scene in one go. There are lots of possibilities—limited only by your imagination.

Remember too that *CPhasedSprite* is only *one* way of having a sprite that changes shape. You may decide that having a sprite with an array of separate DIBs—one for each possible shape—is better. Or you may decide to use a single image for each distinct shape and write code to stretch or shrink the image in order to change its size. Or you may do away with fixed images altogether and create a sprite that draws itself into its DIB. The solution you choose depends on what you want to achieve and how much work you are prepared to do.

To make life a little more interesting, the next chapter will deal with adding some sound to the animation.

CHAPTER

Sounds

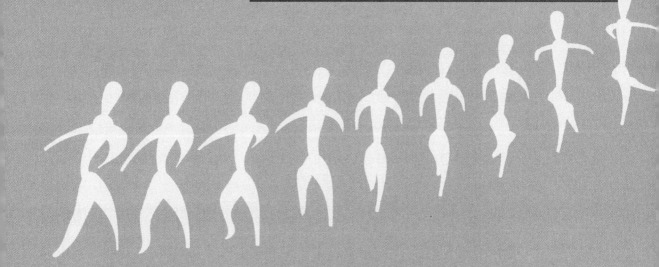

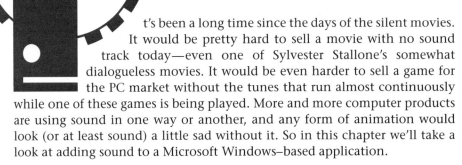

t's been a long time since the days of the silent movies. It would be pretty hard to sell a movie with no sound track today—even one of Sylvester Stallone's somewhat dialogueless movies. It would be even harder to sell a game for the PC market without the tunes that run almost continuously while one of these games is being played. More and more computer products are using sound in one way or another, and any form of animation would look (or at least sound) a little sad without it. So in this chapter we'll take a look at adding sound to a Microsoft Windows–based application.

Doing justice to the subject of sound programming for Windows could take up a whole book of its own, so in order to get going in just one chapter, we'll cut some corners and leave out some of the details. If you want more detailed information on how sound works under Microsoft Windows, refer to one of the Development Library compact discs or volume 2 of the *Microsoft Win32 Programmer's Reference.*

The code in this chapter doesn't add anything to the ANIM.EXE sample we've been developing. Instead, this chapter contains several samples of its own that show some different techniques for playing sounds. If you're not interested in sounds, you might want to skip this chapter.

Sound Types

Given the appropriate hardware on the target machine, we can easily use three types of sounds: CD Audio, MIDI music, and recorded waveforms (speech and other sampled sounds). Each of these sound types has its merits and its drawbacks, both of which are worth noting before we get started on an implementation.

CD Audio

CD Audio is sometimes also referred to as Redbook audio because the book published by Philips that specifies the format of audio CDs is red. Somewhat obviously, your authoring an application to use CD Audio means that your end users will need CD-ROM drives on their machines and copies of your CD to play. This is an expensive and very specific solution if you simply want a few random sounds or a little incidental music—of stunningly high quality. Several of today's multimedia applications use CD Audio. One uses CD Audio to instruct the user in the music of various classical composers (Microsoft's *Multimedia Beethoven: The Ninth Symphony*), and another I can think of offhand uses CD Audio for great music in a children's game (*TuneLand*).

If your music and data are on the same CD and you plan to use CD Audio, you must consider the logistics: you can't be playing the music while you access the data. If you need to change scenes, for example, you'll have to play some MIDI or waveform music to cover the time it takes you to read the data for the next scene before you can return to playing the CD Audio track.

MIDI Music

The good news about MIDI (Musical Instrument Digital Interface) music is that it takes very little memory space, so it can be useful for providing background sound for a scene. The bad news is that most sound cards support only a somewhat primitive set of synthesized sounds, and the result—particularly with the common FM synthesizers—is rather like the music from a set of tubular bells.

MIDI can be implemented on a PC in two ways. In the simpler way, the sound driver does all the work of timing the notes, and the hardware simply plays them. This is how the synthesizer on a Sound Blaster 1.5 card works, for example. This method requires a considerable amount of CPU overhead that you might not want to give away on a low-end machine. The second method of MIDI implementation is to have the sound hardware store the MIDI information and play it, relieving the PC of the critical timing overhead. This method is more expensive to produce (the hardware cost), so it isn't used very often.

MIDI music is available all over the place. It's reasonably easy to produce and makes for great background sounds, but watch that CPU overhead on low-end machines.

Sampled Sounds (Waveforms)

Given the right hardware, sampled audio can do everything that CD Audio can do, and most of what you can do with MIDI music, with very little CPU overhead. The big problem with sampled sounds is that they need huge amounts of storage. Consider 5 minutes of audio from a CD. There are two tracks (left and right), each recorded with 16 bits of data at a sample rate of 44.1 kHz. That's a total of 52,920,000 bytes of data. And, of course, most low-cost sound cards can't handle that sample rate, the 16-bit format, or stereo anyway.

More realistically, sampled sounds are great for speech, sound effects, and very short bits of music. All multimedia PCs can play 8-bit mono sounds at 11.025 kHz or 22.050 kHz. The 11.025 kHz rate is OK for short bits of speech or sound effects, in which the quality doesn't need to be wonderful. For longer sections of speech, 22.050 kHz is a better sampling rate to use. For music, 22.050 kHz is acceptable—certainly to most game players' ears.

Playing Sounds—The Easy Way

There are quite a few different ways to play sounds under Windows—particularly waveforms. These ways range from extremely simple, but limited, methods to extremely complex techniques that offer full control. Ideally, we would like our technique to be simple to use and to offer full control, but that's not how PC sound life is, so we need to choose a solution that fits our needs for a given situation. I thought it would be best to show you several possibilities and let you choose the one most appropriate for what you want to do. We'll begin with what is certainly the simplest and most limited technique and work our way through to a hideously complex technique for a finale.

Using *sndPlaySound*

I'm tempted to simply say, "Here's the code":

```
sndPlaySound("file.wav", SND_ASYNC | SND_NODEFAULT);
```

and leave it up to you to figure out how this would work in an application written using the Microsoft Foundation Class Library (MFC), version 2.0. Two things stop me: my conscience (really!) and fears of what my editor would do to me. I've concluded that a little explanation—and a better piece of sample code—might be in order.

The *sndPlaySound* function was first developed in Multimedia Extensions for Windows so that the *MessageBeep* function could be made to play sounds other than a speaker beep. Not only did *sndPlaySound* work for implementing *MessageBeep*, but it was also widely used in applications for playing sounds. The *sndPlaySound* function is limited to playing sampled sounds (waveforms in .WAV files), so you can't use it to play CD Audio or MIDI music. Nonetheless, for simple sounds, it is adequate. You can use it in two ways: either simply name the file to be played as in the code fragment above (or use an alias name from the sounds section of the WIN.INI file), or load the file image into memory and play it from there. Letting the system load the file and play it means that you get a delay before the sound starts, as the file loads, which is generally not acceptable in an animation, so we'll look at using *sndPlaySound* to play sounds that are already in memory.

I created the Sound sample to show this simple technique. The sample uses a simple class called *CBasicSound* to hold the sound and allows the sound to be played multiple times. Let's look at the code for the class and see how it works. Here's the header file BSOUND.H:

\anim32\sound

```
class CBasicSound : public CObject
{
    DECLARE_SERIAL(CBasicSound)
public:
    CBasicSound();
    ~CBasicSound();
    BOOL Load(CFile* fp);
    BOOL Play();

// Implementation
private:
    char* m_pSoundImage;

protected:
    virtual void Serialize(CArchive& ar);    // Overridden for document I/O

};
```

As you can see, the *CBasicSound* class is very simple. The class is derived from *CObject* and has a member function to load the sound file and another function to play it. A single member variable holds a pointer to the sound image in memory. Here's the *Load* function that creates a memory image from a .WAV file:

```
BOOL CBasicSound::Load(CFile* fp)
{
    // Load the whole file into memory.
    // Free any existing memory.
    if (m_pSoundImage) free(m_pSoundImage);
    // Allocate a new block big enough for the entire file.
    int iLength = fp->GetLength();
    m_pSoundImage = (char*) malloc(iLength);
    ASSERT(m_pSoundImage);
    // Read the entire file into memory.
    int iBytes = fp->Read(m_pSoundImage, iLength);
    ASSERT(iBytes == iLength);
    return TRUE;
}
```

Any existing sound image is freed, and memory for the new image is allocated according to the size of the file. The entire file is then read into the allocated memory block. Let's see the *Play* function next:

```
BOOL CBasicSound::Play()
{
    if (!m_pSoundImage) return FALSE; // Nothing to play.
    return ::sndPlaySound(m_pSoundImage,
                        SND_MEMORY | SND_ASYNC | SND_NODEFAULT);
}
```

If no memory image is present, nothing happens. If an image is present, *sndPlaySound* is called to play it. Note that the sound is played asynchronously, and that if something goes wrong, no default sound is to be played. It's also worth noting here that since the sound is played asynchronously, it could still be playing after the *CBasicSound* object has been deleted, which would cause a memory access violation. You can stop all sounds from being played by calling *sndPlaySound* with a NULL file name.

The remainder of the Sound sample is very simple, so I'll leave it to you to look at the rest of it if you're interested in how it was built.

Using the Media Control Interface (MCI)

The Media Control Interface (MCI) was first developed as a means of controlling devices such as videodisc players. The idea was to have a simple interface that used string commands so that it could be called from languages such as Visual Basic. During the development of MCI, it became clear that the same simple interface could control many different devices, such as video overlay cards, and could also be used for playing sounds—CD Audio, MIDI, and waveforms.

MCI has two levels of interface—string-level and message-level. The string-level interface is the "higher" level and is implemented through the message-level interface. I'm not going to show you the string interface because it's very simple, and if you have an understanding of the message interface (which is a little more versatile), you can certainly understand the string interface. The string interface allows you to construct a command as a string of characters such as "open cdaudio" and send it to the MCI system, which parses the command string and builds an appropriate low-level (message) command. Using the string interface from Visual Basic is very simple because the language has a rich set of string functions.

The message interface is much more like the Windows API we know and love <grin>: you call a function, passing a number of arguments.

The basic idea of MCI revolves around opening a device such as a CD player and sending it commands. For some data types, such as waveform audio data, the file can be opened and automatically associated with a suitable device to play it. MCI uses the file extension to make the association. So we can open an audio .WAV or MIDI file and send it commands similar to those we could send the CD player. Of course, not all devices or data types can support the same commands—it doesn't make sense to ask a video overlay card to perform a seek request, for example—but many commands, such as Open, Play, and Close, are supported by most devices. Because of this widespread support for a base command set, we can design an MCI object that is capable of playing CD Audio, MIDI music, and .WAV files. This MCI object can also play other things, such as video for Windows animations, so it's fairly comprehensive.

The MCI command set is much more expansive than the set we need simply to play some sounds in an animation, so the object we'll create to support MCI will be rather simplistic. Once you've seen how it's built, you should have no trouble expanding it to support other commands as you find you need them.

\anim32\mci

The class is called *CMCIObject* and supports the *Open, Close, Play, Stop,* and *GetPosition* functions. Because there is some difference between opening a device (such as a CD player) and opening a file (such as a waveform file), I have created separate Open functions for these two cases, as you will see. Let's begin with a look at the header file MCIOBJ.H:

```
class CMCIObject : public CObject
{
    DECLARE_SERIAL(CMCIObject)
public:
    CMCIObject();
    ~CMCIObject();
    BOOL OpenFile(const char* pszFileName);
    BOOL OpenDevice(const char* pszDevName);
    void Close();
    void Play();
    void Stop();
    DWORD GetPosition();

// Implementation
protected:
    virtual void Serialize(CArchive& ar);    // Overridden for document I/O

private:
    void MCIError(DWORD dwErr);

    MCI_OPEN_PARMS m_OpenParams;
};
```

As you can see, there are two Open functions: *OpenFile* and *OpenDevice*. A single member variable, *m_OpenParams*, keeps track of the object state. The *MCIError* function is an internal helper function that reports errors to the user via a message box. Let's begin with a look at the constructor and destructor for the object:

```
CMCIObject::CMCIObject()
{
    m_OpenParams.dwCallback = 0;
    m_OpenParams.wDeviceID = 0;
    m_OpenParams.lpstrDeviceType = NULL;
    m_OpenParams.lpstrElementName = NULL;
    m_OpenParams.lpstrAlias = NULL;
}
```

(continued)

```
CMCIObject::~CMCIObject()
{
    // Make sure the object is not in use.
    if (m_OpenParams.wDeviceID != 0) {
        Close();
    }
    ASSERT(m_OpenParams.wDeviceID == 0);
}
```

NOTE

MCI_OPEN_PARMS
is documented in
volume 2 of the
*Microsoft Win32
Programmer's Refer-
ence*, so I won't go
into the details of it
here, but I will com-
ment on some of the
fields as we use them
in other commands.

The constructor sets the initial state of the MCI_OPEN_PARMS structure to reflect the fact that no device or file is currently open. The destructor code ensures that any open file or device is closed before the object is deleted. The device is considered to be closed if *m_OpenParams.wDeviceID* is zero.

Having created a new *CMCIObject*, we must next associate it with a device or a file by using one of the Open functions. Let's start by looking at opening a file as an MCI object:

```
BOOL CMCIObject::OpenFile(const char* pszFileName)
{
    DWORD dwResult;

    if (m_OpenParams.wDeviceID != 0) {
        Close();
    }
    ASSERT(m_OpenParams.wDeviceID == 0);
    m_OpenParams.lpstrDeviceType = NULL;
    m_OpenParams.lpstrElementName = pszFileName;
    dwResult = mciSendCommand(0,
                        MCI_OPEN,
                        MCI_WAIT | MCI_OPEN_ELEMENT,
                        (DWORD)(LPVOID)&m_OpenParams);
    if (dwResult != 0) {
        MCIError(dwResult);
        return FALSE;
    }

    // Set the time format to milliseconds.
    MCI_SET_PARMS set;
    set.dwTimeFormat = MCI_FORMAT_MILLISECONDS;
    dwResult = mciSendCommand(m_OpenParams.wDeviceID,
                        MCI_SET,
                        MCI_WAIT | MCI_SET_TIME_FORMAT,
                        (DWORD)(LPVOID)&set);
    if (dwResult != 0) {
        MCIError(dwResult);
        return FALSE;
    }
    return TRUE;
}
```

Since I like my objects to be as reusable as possible, I try to allow you to call functions such as *OpenFile* more than once for the same object. To support this, the *OpenFile* function first checks to see if the object is already open, and if it is, closes it. The name of the file is copied to the *lpstrElementName* field of the *m_OpenParams* structure. MCI calls files "elements" in this context. The idea is that a "device" may support different elements. So a sound card may have a waveform device driver, and the elements it supports would be wave files. By setting the *lpstrDeviceType* field to NULL, we request MCI to associate the element with the correct device based on the file extension. A call is made to *mciSendCommand* to try to open the file and the associated device. If the call succeeds, all that remains is to set the format for the way we want position information to be returned. I chose to use milliseconds because all devices support this format, and in this simple implementation, I wanted to use one format for all devices.

Let's look now at how a device such as a CD player is opened:

```
BOOL CMCIObject::OpenDevice(const char* pszDevName)
{
    DWORD dwResult;

    if (m_OpenParams.wDeviceID != 0) {
        Close();
    }
    ASSERT(m_OpenParams.wDeviceID == 0);
    m_OpenParams.lpstrDeviceType = pszDevName;
    dwResult = mciSendCommand(0,
                        MCI_OPEN,
                        MCI_WAIT | MCI_OPEN_SHAREABLE |
                         MCI_OPEN_TYPE,
                        (DWORD)(LPVOID)&m_OpenParams);
    if (dwResult != 0) {
        MCIError(dwResult);
        return FALSE;
    }

    // Set the time format to milliseconds.
    MCI_SET_PARMS set;
    set.dwTimeFormat = MCI_FORMAT_MILLISECONDS;
    dwResult = mciSendCommand(m_OpenParams.wDeviceID,
                        MCI_SET,
                        MCI_WAIT | MCI_SET_TIME_FORMAT,
                        (DWORD)(LPVOID)&set);
    if (dwResult != 0) {
        MCIError(dwResult);
        return FALSE;
    }
    return TRUE;
}
```

As you can see, opening a device is very similar to opening a file, except that we now specify the name of the device to open in the *lpstrDeviceType* field. The device is opened with the MCI_OPEN_SHAREABLE flag set. This makes sense for many devices, and it allows multiple applications to control or monitor the same device. The time format is set to milliseconds for consistency with the *OpenFile* function. In general, using TMSF (track, minutes, seconds, frames) with CD Audio might be more useful because it relates better to the way we normally play CDs. But if you are using a chunk of your CD for data and another chunk for Redbook audio, using milliseconds to specify the piece of music to play can work well because this data is often contained in a single track.

Closing an open device is simple:

```
void CMCIObject::Close()
{
    MCI_GENERIC_PARMS gp;
    DWORD dwResult;

    if (m_OpenParams.wDeviceID == 0) return; // Already closed
    Stop(); // Just in case
    dwResult = mciSendCommand(m_OpenParams.wDeviceID,
                        MCI_CLOSE,
                        MCI_WAIT,
                        (DWORD)(LPVOID)&gp);
    if (dwResult != 0) {
        MCIError(dwResult);
    }
    m_OpenParams.wDeviceID = 0;
}
```

MCI uses the device ID to identify what needs to be closed. The *m_Open-Params.wDeviceID* variable is set to 0 to indicate that the object has no open device or file.

Now let's see how the *Play* and *Stop* functions work:

```
void CMCIObject::Play()
{
    MCI_PLAY_PARMS play;
    DWORD dwResult;

    mciSendCommand(m_OpenParams.wDeviceID,
                MCI_SEEK,
                MCI_WAIT | MCI_SEEK_TO_START,
                0);
    dwResult = mciSendCommand(m_OpenParams.wDeviceID,
                        MCI_PLAY,
                        NULL,
                        (DWORD)(LPVOID)&play);
```

```
    if (dwResult != 0) {
        MCIError(dwResult);
    }
}
```

In this very simple implementation, I chose to make the Play command play from the start of the medium each time, so the implementation does a seek to the start of the medium and then begins playback. Without the seek command, calling MCI to begin playback would start play from wherever it last stopped. Note that the *play* structure isn't used in this case. It can be used in conjunction with other flags to specify a start position, a stop position, or a callback function. Because our goal here is to play simple sounds in an animation, we will generally want to play the entire sound from its start, so that's how I coded the function.

The *Stop* function is very simple:

```
void CMCIObject::Stop()
{
    DWORD dwResult;

    dwResult = mciSendCommand(m_OpenParams.wDeviceID,
                              MCI_STOP,
                              MCI_WAIT,
                              (DWORD)(LPVOID)NULL);
    if (dwResult != 0) {
        MCIError(dwResult);
    }
}
```

When long sounds are playing, it's often useful to keep track of where they have gotten to, so I implemented the *GetPosition* function to return the position expressed as the number of milliseconds to the current position from the start of the medium:

```
DWORD CMCIObject::GetPosition()
{
    MCI_STATUS_PARMS status;
    status.dwItem = MCI_STATUS_POSITION;
    if (mciSendCommand(m_OpenParams.wDeviceID,
                       MCI_STATUS,
                       MCI_WAIT | MCI_STATUS_ITEM,
                       (DWORD)(LPVOID)&status) != 0) {
        return 0; // Some error
    }
    return status.dwReturn;
}
```

Note that nothing in the call specifies milliseconds as the format. That was done when we opened the device or file.

\anim32\waves

The MCI sample application uses the *CMCIObject* class to let you open and play a variety of sound files. It also allows you to open and play CD Audio discs. Again, there is nothing too stunning about the code in the rest of the example, so I'll leave it up to you to look at it if you want to.

There is a lot more to using MCI than I have shown here, but what's here covers the basics of playing sounds, and I'm sure that you can easily modify this code for your own needs.

Playing Sounds—The Hard Way

The discussion in this section applies only to playing waveform sounds, so if you're interested only in CD Audio or MIDI, you can stop reading now and save yourself a headache.

Using *sndPlaySound* or the Media Control Interface to play waveform sounds is very simple, and often it's all that's needed, but there is a small category of programmers who demand total control of their environment and want to code right down to the wire. This is your section, folks! What we are going to look at here is using the low-level audio services to play chunks of waveform data. This involves creating two C++ objects—one for the wave data and another for the wave output device itself. Because of the way the low-level audio services work—in particular, the way the callback notifications work—there is some code in my implementation that you might consider to be just a little hacky. So this is a "how *I* did it" section and not necessarily a "how *you* should do it" section. Now that I've frightened off the less dedicated, let's have a look at what playing waveforms the hard way is all about.

How the Low-Level Sound Services Play Waveforms

If a waveform is to be played via the low-level sound services, the waveform must first be read into memory in one or more blocks. The blocks can be any size (say, 8K), and the entire waveform need not be resident in memory when playback starts—the remainder of the blocks will be loaded just before they are needed. For each block of data, a header data structure is allocated and filled out with details of the waveform data to be sent to the device driver. The device driver is opened, and the first block is sent. Subsequent blocks are sent until all are gone. As the device driver finishes playing each block of data, it sends a message to the application to notify it that the particular block is finished and can now be freed. When the last block is finished, the application can close the device driver. In practice, the application doesn't deal directly with the device driver but instead works through a set of functions in the multimedia support DLL (WINMM.DLL).

There is nothing very complex involved in dealing with the sound devices except to note that since the entire process is asynchronous to the execution of the application, we must be sure to write code that isn't going to do silly things like deleting a block of data while it's still in use by the device driver. We also need to be careful to close down a device we are not using so that another application can use it. Sound devices typically support playing only one sound at a time, so if all you want to do is play a few incidental noises, it's a bit rude to stop other applications from making alert sounds and so on.

In trying to create a simple C++ class to play waveforms through this low-level interface, the only awkward part is handling the notification messages that are sent by the device driver as each block is finished. We could have these messages sent to the application, which would then have to have some way to determine which sound object was finished (or at least needed to be freed). Having pointers to the application in the sound objects didn't seem like a very clean solution to me. Ideally, I'd have a self-contained object that could simply be told to play, and it would deal with the mysteries of the implementation without making them visible to me as a user of the object. I also wanted to try to create an object for waveforms that wasn't too tied to the way in which sounds had to be sent to the output device driver when they were played.

The result of much tinkering led me to a solution that has essentially two main object classes: one class handles the waveform objects, and the other handles the output devices on which waveform objects can be played. A third class is used to create a window object to which notification messages can be sent. When a wave output device object is opened, it creates a callback window object to receive any notification messages. *Figure 14-1* shows the relationship between the various objects and data blocks.

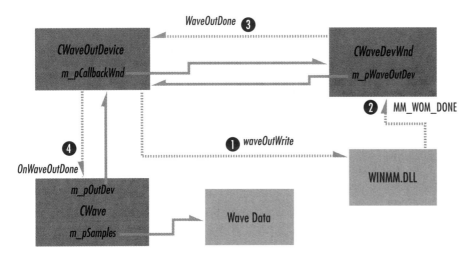

Figure 14-1   *The relationship between the various sound objects and the system.*

The solid arrow lines represent data pointers. The dotted arrow lines represent calls made to various functions or messages sent to an object. Figure 14-1 shows roughly what happens when *waveOutWrite* (1) is used to send a data block to the output device for playing. The system responds when the block is finished playing by sending an MM_WOM_DONE message (2) to the notification window object. The notification object calls *WaveOutDone* (3) in the *CWaveOutDev* object, which in turn calls *OnWaveOutDone* (4) in the *CWave* object.

There are a lot of pointers, function calls, and messages here, and if the whole thing looks unreasonably complex to you, perhaps MCI might seem more attractive now! This scheme does, however, give you plenty of flexibility in how you manage your sound data. Let's look at the classes in a little more detail. We won't look at all the code in each class, only at the main functions.

The *CWave* Class

The *CWave* class is designed to contain the data bits of the waveform itself, provide some simple member functions to load the data from a WAVE file, and play the data on an output device. Functions are also provided to set and get samples from the data. All samples are treated as 16-bit, signed quantities, no matter whether the file actually has 16-bit or 8-bit samples internally. I chose to treat all samples as if they were 16-bit quantities so that an application can manipulate the data without having to know if the original is 8-bit or 16-bit. This makes the application code a lot simpler.

Waveform files in Windows conform to the Resource Interchange File Format (RIFF) architecture, which I briefly described in Chapter 12, "Saving and Loading Scenes." The Load functions for the *CWave* class work in a way very similar to the way the Load functions I described in Chapter 12 for the *CDIBPal* class work, so I won't go into them here. For more information on the waveform file format, see volume 2 of the *Microsoft Win32 Programmer's Reference* or the *Multimedia Programmer's Reference* on the Development Library CD.

Let's look at the *Play* function from WAVE.CPP and see how that works:

```
BOOL CWave::Play(CWaveOutDevice* pWaveDevice)
{
    if (pWaveDevice != NULL) {
        m_pOutDev = pWaveDevice;
        return pWaveDevice->Play(this);
    } else {
        m_pOutDev = &theDefaultWaveOutDevice;
        return theDefaultWaveOutDevice.Play(this);
    }
}
```

The *Play* function has an optional parameter that points to the wave output device on which the sound should be played. The *CWaveOutDevice* class provides a global device that is used by default if no specific device is requested. This is very convenient because most machines have only one output device. If the *pWaveDevice* parameter is left NULL (or simply omitted), the waveform is played on the first device that can support the format.

A similar *Stop* function halts playback:

```
void CWave::Stop()
{
    if (!m_bBusy) return;

    ASSERT(m_pOutDev);
    m_pOutDev->Stop();
}
```

Whatever wave device was selected when the *Play* function was called is called again to stop the playback.

There are quite a few other functions in the *CWave* class, but let's move on to look at how the output device handles playing a waveform.

The *CWaveOutDevice* Class

The *CWaveOutDevice* class provides an *Open* function to select a wave output device capable of handling a particular format. The *CWaveOutDevice* class also provides *Play* and *Stop* functions to control the playback of specific *CWave* objects. Because the *CWaveOutDevice* object needs to monitor the MM_WOM_DONE messages from the device driver, the object makes use of a *CWaveDevWnd* object to receive those messages. Let's begin by looking at how an output device is opened. This code is from the WAVEODEV.CPP file:

```
BOOL CWaveOutDevice::Open(WAVEFORMAT* pFormat)
{
    MMRESULT mmr;

    // Make sure we have a callback window.
    if (!m_pCallbackWnd) {
        m_pCallbackWnd = new CWaveDevWnd;
        ASSERT(m_pCallbackWnd);
        if (!m_pCallbackWnd->Create(this)) {
            TRACE("Failed to create callback window");
            delete m_pCallbackWnd;
            m_pCallbackWnd = NULL;
            return FALSE;
        }
    }
    // See if already open for this format.
    if (IsOpen()) {
```

(continued)

```
            // See if it can handle this format.
            if (CanDoFormat(pFormat)) {
                return TRUE;
            } else {
                TRACE("Open for different format");
                return FALSE;
            }
        }
        // See if we can open for this format.
        mmr = waveOutOpen(&m_hOutDev,
                          WAVE_MAPPER,
                          pFormat,
                          (DWORD)(m_pCallbackWnd->GetSafeHwnd()),
                          0,
                          CALLBACK_WINDOW);
        if (mmr != 0) {
            MMERR(mmr);
            return FALSE;
        }
        return TRUE;
    }
```

The *Open* function first checks to see whether a callback window handler has been installed and, if such a handler hasn't been, installs one by creating a *CWaveDevWnd* object, calling the object's *Create* function, and storing a pointer to the object in the *m_pCallbackWnd* variable. If a wave output device is already open, a test is made to see if the device can handle the requested format. If it can't, the request to open the device fails. If one is not already open, a device is opened for the requested format. Note that the open request includes the window handle of the callback window object. This is where notification messages from the device driver will be sent.

Next let's see the *Play* function that plays *CWave* objects:

```
BOOL CWaveOutDevice::Play(CWave* pWave)
{
    if (!Open(pWave->GetFormat())) {
        return FALSE;
    }

    // Allocate a header.
    WAVEHDR* phdr = (WAVEHDR*)malloc(sizeof(WAVEHDR));
    ASSERT(phdr);
    // Fill out the wave header.
    memset(phdr, 0, sizeof(WAVEHDR));
    phdr->lpData = (char*) pWave->GetSamples();
    phdr->dwBufferLength = pWave->GetSize();
    phdr->dwUser = (DWORD)(void*)pWave;     // So that we can find the
                                            // object.
```

```
    // Prepare the header.
    MMRESULT mmr = waveOutPrepareHeader(m_hOutDev,
                                        phdr,
                                        sizeof(WAVEHDR));
    if (mmr) {
        MMERR(mmr);
        return FALSE;
    }
    // Mark the wave as busy.
    pWave->SetBusy(TRUE);

    // Start the wave playing.
    mmr = waveOutWrite(m_hOutDev,
                       phdr,
                       sizeof(WAVEHDR));
    if (mmr) {
        MMERR(mmr);
        return FALSE;
    }

    // Add one to the block count.
    m_iBlockCount++;

    return TRUE;
}
```

To play a chunk of wave data, we must create a header that contains information about the format and length of the data to be played. The *Play* function first allocates a WAVEHDR structure and fills it out with data extracted from the *CWave* object. A call is made to *waveOutPrepareHeader*, which gives the device driver an opportunity to lock the header and data memory to guarantee that they will be present at interrupt time and thus avoid the delay possible if the memory otherwise might need to be paged in. Note too that the *dwUser* field has a pointer to the *CWave* object placed in it so that when a notification message that this block is finished comes back from the driver, we can identify which *CWave* object the block belongs to.

The *CWave* object is marked as busy (in use), and *waveOutWrite* is called to begin playback. Note that if you modified the *CWave* class to use multiple data chunks for a single waveform, each chunk will need its own header, and each header-data pair must be sent separately to the device driver by means of a call to *waveOutWrite* made once for each pair. For each block sent to the driver, the *m_iBlockCount* variable is incremented so that we can keep track of when all the blocks are finished and close the driver when it's no longer in use.

When the device driver has finished playing the block, it sends an MM_WOM_DONE message to the callback window. Let's see what happens there next.

The *CWaveDevWnd* Class

The *CWaveDevWnd* class is a simple window class that handles the MM-_WOM_DONE messages from the device driver and (in effect) forwards them to the appropriate wave output device and wave objects. Here's the handler function from the WAVEDEVWN.CPP file:

```
LRESULT CWaveDevWnd::OnWomDone(WPARAM w, LPARAM 1)
{
    ASSERT(1);
    WAVEHDR* phdr = (WAVEHDR*) 1;
    CWave* pWave = (CWave*)(phdr->dwUser);
    ASSERT(pWave->IsKindOf(RUNTIME_CLASS(CWave)));
    CWaveOutDevice* pOutDev = pWave->GetOutDevice();
    ASSERT(pOutDev);
    pOutDev->WaveOutDone(pWave, phdr);
    return 0;
}
```

The *LPARAM* parameter of the message is a pointer to the WAVEHDR structure that was sent to the device driver in a call to *waveOutWrite*. Remember that we're using the *dwUser* parameter to hold a pointer to the *CWave* object and that each *CWave* object contains a pointer to its associated *CWaveOutDevice* object. So, having extracted all these pointers, we can tell the *CWaveOutDevice* object that the current wave block is finished. Let's return to the *CWaveOut-Device* class to see what happens next.

The Voyage Home

Here's the *CWaveOutDevice::WaveOutDone* function, which processes the MM-_WOM_DONE events:

```
void CWaveOutDevice::WaveOutDone(CWave* pWave, WAVEHDR* pHdr)
{
    // Unprepare the header.
    MMRESULT mmr = waveOutUnprepareHeader(m_hOutDev,
                                          pHdr,
                                          sizeof(WAVEHDR));
    if (mmr) {
        MMERR(mmr);
    }
    // Free the header.
    free(pHdr);

    // Decrement the block count.
    ASSERT(m_iBlockCount > 0);
    m_iBlockCount--;
    if (m_iBlockCount == 0) {
```

```
        // Close the device.
        Close();
    }

    // Notify the object it is done.
    pWave->SetBusy(FALSE);
    pWave->OnWaveOutDone();
}
```

A call is made to *waveOutUnprepareHeader* to allow the driver to unlock the header and data memory if it originally locked them. The header is then freed, the block count is decremented, and if no blocks remain to be returned from the device driver, the output device is closed so that other applications can use it.

The *CWave* object that was associated with the header is notified that the output device is no longer busy (in use), and its *OnWaveOutDone* handler is called in case it wants to perform some tidy-up function. The current implementation of *CWave::OnWaveOutDone* does nothing:

```
void CWave::OnWaveOutDone()
{

}
```

As you can see, the round trip for a single waveform data block is quite complicated and, in the implementation shown here, really doesn't do much more than you can achieve by using MCI functions in a much simpler way.

The Right Way

Sounds can be played in several ways. The right way is the way that works best for you in your application. For simply playing a little MIDI music or for a few sound effects, the *CMCIObject* class provides an easy starting point from which you can develop your own extensions, and that's what we'll use in some of the examples that follow in later chapters.

The code here shows only one possible way of skinning this particular cat. If you plan to use the low-level interfaces, one variation on my design you might like to try is creating the *CWaveOutDevice* class from *CWnd* and having it receive the notification messages directly. This would obviate having to create the *CWaveDevWnd* class at all.

CHAPTER

Moving and Colliding

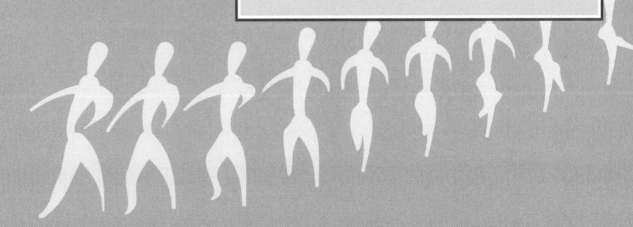

nough technology—time for some fun. You've read the book; now see the movie. In this chapter, we'll look at using the existing sprite and view classes to create a more interesting application. We'll have the sprites move around on their own, and we'll implement a simple collision-detection scheme so that the sprites can interact with each other.

The Collide sample shows a simulation of balls colliding on a flat, frictionless surface. In creating this sample, I was tempted to go much further. Although there are many interesting, fun things you can add to this code (and I wanted to add them all), this book is primarily about helping you write animated applications of your own design, not a showcase for what I could do. I have left the enhancements to you. A few bugs remain in the "physics," too—that is, the algorithm isn't quite correct. The code in Collide certainly doesn't produce a real world simulation, but it's fun to watch, and maybe you can improve the physics if you're so inclined. Enjoy!

The Collide Application Classes

The Collide sample was built primarily from the Phases sample in Chapter 13, but because I wanted to show how you could use the sprite class in your own applications, I did some things somewhat differently. In particular, I created a new sprite class called *CMySprite*, which is derived from *CPhasedSprite* as an example of how you might create your own sprite class with its own behavior. The view class (*CAnimView*) contains the *NewBackground*, *NewSprite*, and *Render* functions that have been with us for many of the other samples, but it also contains new code for moving the sprite positions and changing the animation speed. Because the *NewBackground*, *NewSprite*, and *Render* functions seem to be a fixed part of the view class, I could have created a view class to contain them and then derived a new view class from that for this application. That might have been tidier, but it would have been a little pointless. Simply hiding the implementation of a few routines isn't my idea of creating reusable code. In any case, there are plenty of reasons why you might want to alter the way these functions work in your own application, so my putting them right under your nose is a good way (in my opinion) of reminding you that they are there when you're working on the view class code. *Figure 15-1* shows the main classes used in the Collide sample.

\anim32\collide

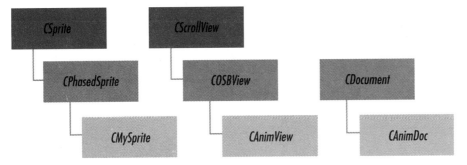

Figure 15-1 *The main classes of the Collide application.*

We'll return to the details of these classes a little later.

Making Sprites Move

Since we have already implemented code that allows you to drag a sprite around with the mouse, we won't have much problem moving the sprites. The interesting job will be getting the sprites to appear to be moving around by themselves. Of the several approaches we might take to achieve this effect, I'd like to look at three in particular.

Using Multiple Threads

We could give each sprite its own thread of execution and thus make each truly autonomous. Each sprite could have some data that controlled the path it was to take and could move itself along the path while using notification calls to the sprite list object to send data on which areas of the scene needed to be repainted. Another thread could do the repaint job. If this sort of design gets you all hot and sweaty with excitement, read no further—go forth and code.

I gave a lot of consideration to using one thread per sprite since it looks like such a clean solution. There are, however, a lot of issues involved in multithreaded systems that you need to consider in order to avoid deadlock conditions. What this means in practice is that you have to write more code. Writing more code means more complexity, more potential for bugs, and sometimes a reduction in performance. None of this fallout appeals to me, so I rejected the multithreaded solution. If you're still keen to try it, by all means do so. You might also want to read some of the excellent articles by Ruediger Asche, Nancy Cluts, and Kyle Marsh in the Microsoft Development Library for more information about deadlock detection in multithreaded systems and writing multithreaded Microsoft Windows–based applications in general.

Using Timer Messages

During our early days of learning to program for Windows, most of us used a timer when we wanted to create some sort of continuous activity in a Windows-based application. The simplest use of a timer involves having it send a WM_TIMER message to one of the application's windows at fixed intervals. The application performs some chunk of processing in response to the message and goes back to sleep until the next message arrives. This works very nicely in many applications but is a bit limited for use in an animation engine because of the maximum frequency at which the WM_TIMER messages can be sent. In the Collide sample, I have used timer messages for the slow- and medium-speed options so that you can see how timer messages might be used. I used a different mechanism to achieve the top speed, and we'll look at that shortly.

Getting WM_TIMER messages sent to the view window is simply a matter of calling *CWnd::SetTimer*, specifying the interval for sending the messages. We could, for example, use ClassWizard to add a WM_CREATE handler to the *CAnimView* class and have it create a timer this way:

```
int CAnimView::OnCreate(LPCREATESTRUCT lpCreateStruct)
{
    if (COSBView::OnCreate(lpCreateStruct) == -1)
        return -1;

    m_uiTimer = SetTimer(1, 100, NULL);
    return 0;
}
```

The *m_uiTimer* variable is used to keep the timer ID returned by the call to *SetTimer*. The example code here shows a timer being set up to send messages every 100 milliseconds.

We use ClassWizard to add a handler for WM_TIMER messages to *CAnimView*, and that might look something like this:

```
void CAnimView::OnTimer(UINT nIDEvent)
{
    ...
    // Do something useful.
    ...
}
```

"Something useful" might be to move each sprite to a new position and redraw the changes. We'll see exactly what the Collide sample does a little later.

If we do use a timer, we must be sure to close it down when the view window is destroyed. Again, we can use ClassWizard to add a handler for WM_DESTROY and put the cleanup code in that function:

```
void CAnimView::OnDestroy()
{
    if (m_uiTimer) {
        KillTimer(1);
        m_uiTimer = 0;
    }
    COSBView::OnDestroy();
}
```

Using timer messages has the very nice side effect of providing a well-defined speed for the animation's movement (so long as what we try to do each cycle takes less time than the message interval). But what if we want to go at the fastest speed possible? We can use a different technique for that.

Using an Idle Time Handler

If we want the application to go absolutely flat out while we still keep the user interface functional (which is rather nice for the user), we can create a function that is called whenever the application is idle—that is, whenever it's not processing a message. The Microsoft Foundation Class Library (MFC), version 2.0, architecture provides a very convenient mechanism for this. The library's *CWinApp* class includes an *OnIdle* function that is called when an application would otherwise simply be waiting for a message to process. You can include code in your own *OnIdle* function to perform a cycle of the animation. In order to use the *OnIdle* function, you must include a definition in the application's header file. Here's the code from ANIM.H in the Collide sample:

```
class CAnimApp : public CWinApp
{
public:
    .
    .
    .
// Overrides
    virtual BOOL OnIdle(LONG lCount);
    .
    .
    .
};
```

The function itself can then be included in the application code:

```
BOOL CAnimApp::OnIdle(LONG lCount)
{
    if (!m_pIdleView) return FALSE;
    m_pIdleView->Tick();
    return TRUE; // Need more cycles.
}
```

In the example here, you can see that I included an *m_pIdleView* member variable in the application's main class to keep track of which window I want to process the idle event. If the pointer to the window is not null, a call is made to a routine to process the idle event. In this case, a function I created called *Tick* does the work.

Let's go back and look at the view class for Collide in more detail and see how it uses timers or idle time to create a moving animation.

The View Class

The view class for the Collide sample handles all the user interface functions and the timer or idle time events required to make the sprites move. The user interface is very simple. A set of menu commands controls the overall speed of the animation, which may be set to stop, slow, medium, or fast. At any time, the user can use the mouse to drag a sprite to a new position. If the animation is set to the stopped mode and the user drags a sprite, the sprite's velocity is set to 0, and it will remain in the position at which the user has dropped it when the animation is restarted. If the animation is in motion when the user captures a sprite and drags it with the mouse, the vector from the capture point to the release point is used to determine the sprite's new velocity vector. In this way the user can "throw" one of the sprites with the mouse, and it will continue to move in the direction in which the user threw it.

The menu items and buttons that control the speed simply call a helper function to actually set the speed and determine how the update events will be generated. Here, for example, is the handler function for the slow-speed menu item:

```
void CAnimView::OnActionSlow()
{
    SetSpeed(200);
}
```

In this case, the speed is set to an arbitrary value of 200 units.

Let's look at the *SetSpeed* helper function to see what happens next:

```
void CAnimView::SetSpeed(int iSpeed)
{
    // Stop the current timer.
    if (m_uiTimer) {
        KillTimer(1);
        m_uiTimer = 0;
    }
    // Stop the idle loop mode.
    CAnimApp* pApp = (CAnimApp*) AfxGetApp();
    pApp->SetIdleEvent(NULL);
    m_iSpeed = iSpeed;
    if (iSpeed == 0) return;
    if (iSpeed > 0) {
        m_uiTimer = SetTimer(1, iSpeed, NULL);
        return;
    }
```

```
// Set up the idle loop mode.
pApp->SetIdleEvent(this);
}
```

If a timer is currently being used for the slow or medium speed, the timer
is stopped and the *m_uiTimer* variable set to 0 so that we know that no timer is
running. A call is made to another helper function to reset the idle time event
mode in case that was set. This is done by calling *SetIdleEvent*, another helper
function in the application's main class, which is implemented in ANIM.H:

```
void SetIdleEvent(CAnimView* pView)
        {m_pIdleView = pView;}
```

Passing NULL as a parameter effectively turns off the idle event mode
since the *OnIdle* handler simply returns if no view has been defined:

```
BOOL CAnimApp::OnIdle(LONG lCount)
{
    if (!m_pIdleView) return FALSE;
    m_pIdleView->Tick();
    return TRUE; // Need more cycles.
}
```

Looking at the *SetSpeed* code again, we see that if the speed is set to 0, no
further action is required. For slow speeds, a timer is started that will send
WM_TIMER messages to the window to be handled by the *OnTimer* function.
For the high-speed case, a call is made to the *CAnimApp::SetIdleEvent* function,
passing a pointer to the view class as a parameter. This will cause the *Tick*
function in the view class to be called when the application is idle. I implemented *Tick* as a macro in ANIMVIEW.H:

```
void Tick() {OnTimer(1);}
```

Why not call *OnTimer* directly? Only because the way in which ClassWizard
creates handler function tables results in protected rather than public functions. Creating a simple public macro overcomes this cleanly.

Let's look now at the *OnTimer* function and see how it moves the sprites:

```
void CAnimView::OnTimer(UINT nIDEvent)
{
    int i = 0;
    POSITION pos;
    CMySprite* pSprite;
    CAnimDoc* pDoc = GetDocument();
    CSpriteList* pspList = pDoc->GetSpriteList();
    if (pspList->IsEmpty()) return; // No sprites
    // Update the position of each sprite.
    for (pos = pspList->GetHeadPosition(); pos != NULL;) {
        pSprite = (CMySprite*)pspList->GetNext(pos);
        ASSERT(pSprite->IsKindOf(RUNTIME_CLASS(CMySprite)));
        i += pSprite->UpdatePosition(pDoc);
```

(continued)

```
            // See if the sprite collided with any other sprite
            // below it in the list.
            for (POSITION pos2 = pos; pos2 != NULL;) {
                CMySprite* pSprite2 = (CMySprite*)pspList->GetNext(pos2);
                if (pSprite2 != pSprite) { // Can't collide with itself!
                    // Test for collision.
                    if(pSprite->CollideTest(pSprite2)) {
                        // Sort out what needs to change.
                        i += pSprite->OnCollide(pSprite2, pDoc);
                        // Make a silly noise.
                        pDoc->SoundClick();
                    }
                }
            }
        }
        if (i) {
            // Draw the changes.
            RenderAndDrawDirtyList();
        }
    }
```

The *UpdatePosition* function of each sprite in the list is called to give the sprite a chance to compute a new position. Once the sprite has had a chance to move, a test is made to see if it is now in collision with any of the other sprites. If a collision is detected, the *OnCollide* function for the sprite is called and the collision sound is played.

Tests for collision are made only with sprites further down the list. This avoids the redundant testing of both sprites in each possible pair. When a collision is encountered, the *OnCollide* function needs to be called for only one sprite of the colliding pair because the way the *CMySprite* class is designed, both sprites involved in the collision are updated. This isn't, perhaps, quite the perfect object-oriented solution, but I found it very convenient as I worked out the physics.

Once the entire sprite list has been walked, a test is made to see if any change occurred. If there's been a change, a render and draw sequence updates the screen with the changes.

Let's look now at how the collision detection is done, and we'll follow that with a look at the *CMySprite::OnCollide* function.

Collision Detection in the *CMySprite* Class

Ideally, collision detection would be based solely on the shape of the two objects involved. Since we already have a *HitTest* function for the *CSprite* class, we could test both sprites to see if any of their visible—that is, their hit-testable—pixels overlap. For large sprites, that means calling the *HitTest* function a lot of times, which is going to make things pretty slow. We could perhaps generate a monochrome bitmap image of the nontransparent areas of each sprite and perform an AND operation to see if any pixels overlap, but again, this would be quite time consuming if it were done often.

A better approach is to create a two-part test. The first part simply sees if the sprites overlap at all by testing for the intersection of their bounding rectangles. If the rectangles overlap, a collision is possible, and it's worth doing a more refined test. The second part, perhaps a better test, could be a pixel-by-pixel analysis. For the Collide example, I decided to simplify the problem a little more by assuming that all the images were circles that barely touched the edges of their bounding rectangles. By making this assumption, I was able to use the radius of the circles to determine whether a collision had occurred. *Figures 15-2* through *15-4* show the possible states the code detects.

Figure 15-2   *The sprite bounding rectangles don't intersect—no collision.*

Figure 15-3   *The sprite bounding rectangles intersect, but the visible parts of the sprites don't—no collision.*

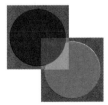

Figure 15-4   *The visible parts of the sprites overlap—collision.*

Obviously, this won't work for noncircular objects, but then neither will the physics I've used in the example. If you want irregularly shaped objects to behave realistically, you'll need to implement a better collision-detection scheme and also some much better physics.

Now that we've qualified it, let's look at the collision-detection function:

```
int CMySprite::CollideTest(CMySprite* pSprite)
{
    // Do the simple rectangle overlap test first.
    CRect rcThis, rcOther;
    GetRect(&rcThis);
    pSprite->GetRect(&rcOther);
    if (!rcThis.IntersectRect(&rcThis, &rcOther)) {
        // The rectangles don't overlap.
        return 0;
    }

    // The rectangles overlap.
    // Compute the coordinates of the centers of the circular sprites.
    CRect rc1, rc2;
    GetRect(&rc1);
    pSprite->GetRect(&rc2);
    int x1 = rc1.left + (rc1.right - rc1.left) / 2;
    int y1 = rc1.top + (rc1.bottom - rc1.top) / 2;
    int x2 = rc2.left + (rc2.right - rc2.left) / 2;
    int y2 = rc2.top + (rc2.bottom - rc2.top) / 2;

    // Compute the distance between the centers of the circular sprites.
    int dx = x1 - x2;
    int dy = y1 - y2;
    double d = sqrt(dx * dx + dy * dy);

    // See if the circular sprites overlap.
    if (d < (rc1.right - rc1.left) / 2 + (rc2.right - rc2.left) / 2) {
        return 1;
    }

    return 0;
}
```

Now that we can test whether one sprite is in collision with another, we need a way to alter the velocity vectors of the two colliding sprites and get them moving on their new paths. An awkward problem arises here because of the way we quantize time in this simulation. By the time we detect a collision, the objects already overlap by at least one pixel. If we simply modify the velocity vectors of the sprites and continue the program, on the next cycle there is a good chance that the sprites will still be in an overlapping position (having not yet rebounded far enough), and we will have to do the collision calculation again. This can result in an oscillation in which the balls never come apart, which is not quite realistic. The solution I chose was simply to move the balls on their new post-collision paths until they were no longer in collision. This movement is done in a small program loop and consequently appears much faster than the normal movement of the objects in the simulation. Most of the time you won't notice this shift in speed, but occasionally you'll see one of the balls seem to jump a bit after a collision.

This is not a physics text, so I don't propose to explain the algorithm used to compute the velocities of the balls after a collision. If you're interested in understanding the algorithm, you might consult a high school physics textbook. (Some cover this question better than others.) The important principle here is that for a perfectly elastic collision, both momentum and energy are conserved. Here's the code:

```
int CMySprite::OnCollide(CMySprite* pSprite, CAnimDoc* pDoc)
{
    // Do some physics.
    if ((m_vx == 0) && (m_vy == 0)
    && (pSprite->GetX() == 0) && (pSprite->GetY() == 0)) {
        return 0;
    }

    // Compute the coordinates of the centers of the objects.
    CRect rc1, rc2;
    GetRect(&rc1);
    pSprite->GetRect(&rc2);
    int x1 = rc1.left + (rc1.right - rc1.left) / 2;
    int y1 = rc1.top + (rc1.bottom - rc1.top) / 2;
    int x2 = rc2.left + (rc2.right - rc2.left) / 2;
    int y2 = rc2.top + (rc2.bottom - rc2.top) / 2;

    // Compute the angle of the line joining the centers.
    double a = atan2(y2 - y1, x2 - x1);
    double cos_a = cos(a);
    double sin_a = sin(a);

    // Compute the velocities normal and perpendicular
    // to the center line.
    double vn1 = m_vx * cos_a + m_vy * sin_a;
    double vp1 = m_vy * cos_a - m_vx * sin_a;
    int vx2, vy2;
    pSprite->GetVelocity(&vx2, &vy2);
    double vn2 = vx2 * cos_a + vy2 * sin_a;
    double vp2 = vy2 * cos_a - vx2 * sin_a;
```

(continued)

```
// Compute the momentum along the center line.
double m1 = m_mass;
double m2 = pSprite->GetMass();
double k = m1 * vn1 + m2 * vn2;

// Compute the energy.
double e = 0.5 * m1 * vn1 * vn1 + 0.5 * m2 * vn2 * vn2;

// There are two possible solutions to the equations.
// Compute both and choose.
double temp1 = sqrt(k*k - ((m1/m2)+1)*(-2*e*m1 + k*k));
double vn2p1 = (k + temp1) / (m1+m2);
double vn2p2 = (k - temp1) / (m1+m2);

// Choose the solution that is not the current state.
if (vn2p1 == vn2) {
    vn2 = vn2p2;
} else {
    vn2 = vn2p1;
}

// Compute the new vn1 value.
vn1 = (k - m2*vn2) / m1;


// Compute the new x and y velocities.
int vx1 = (int)(vn1 * cos_a - vp1 * sin_a);
int vy1 = (int)(vn1 * sin_a + vp1 * cos_a);
vx2 = (int)(vn2 * cos_a - vp2 * sin_a);
vy2 = (int)(vn2 * sin_a + vp2 * cos_a);

m_vx = vx1;
m_vy = vy1;
pSprite->SetVelocity(vx2, vy2);

// Move the sprites until they are no longer in collision.
if ((m_vx != 0) || (m_vy != 0) || (vx2 != 0) || (vy2 != 0)) {
    while(CollideTest(pSprite)) {
        UpdatePosition(pDoc);
        pSprite->UpdatePosition(pDoc);
    }
}

return 1; // Say something changed.
}
```

The only tricky part to the whole thing is choosing which of the two solutions to the quadratic equation is the correct one. You can see here that I have used an equality test between two floating-point values, which is very dangerous because the small errors in most floating-point packages will contrive to make this test fail on occasion. Once again, I leave it up to you to improve the code if you see fit.

One other modification you may care to make in determining whether the sprites are in collision is to use their z-order. Using this information makes it possible for you to have one sprite glide behind another yet still collide with a third that shares its z-order level.

But What About...?

So, you've noticed that this is the last chapter. You've just flipped through the last pages of the book, looking briefly at the appendixes, and now you're wondering why I didn't show you how to make an elephant fly (or whatever your favorite animation task is). Well, I'm sorry, but that's up to you.

As I created the sample applications, I was often tempted to embellish them with neat features or to try to create a real application that did a bit more than simply illustrate the text. I believe that complex examples simply show you what the writer can do as a programmer and not necessarily what you, the reader, can do with the code. It's a learning thing with me. I want *you* to learn so that you'll be able to create great applications. I can't write them for you—you'll have to do that yourself. I hope I've given you some insight into how you might go about doing it for yourself. Good luck!

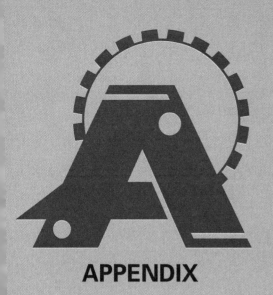

APPENDIX

Using the
WinG Library

ince the early chapters of this book were written, Microsoft has released a graphics helper library called WinG (pronounced win-gee). WinG provides a device- and platform-independent way of getting absolutely the best possible graphics performance from Microsoft Windows. WinG was developed to help MS-DOS games developers port their applications to Windows and consequently was originally coded for the 16-bit Windows 3.1 platform. WinG is also available for 32-bit platforms, where it generally uses the *CreateDIBSection* application programming interface (API) in much the same way I have in the *COSBView* class in the samples for this book.

If you like the idea of using the latest and greatest technology, you might want to experiment with WinG. If you are writing code for both 16- and 32-bit platforms, WinG will certainly help you with some of the portability issues because it gives you a single interface for updating the screen and yet allows you great flexibility.

As a demonstration of how WinG can be used, I ported the *COSBView* class in the Collide sample. The results are in the WinGColl directory. The only differences in the source code are in OSBVIEW.H and OSBVIEW.CPP. I also altered the make file to add the WING32.LIB library to the linker input list.

If you compare the *COSBView* classes in the Collide and WinGColl samples, you'll notice how similar using WinG is to using *CreateDIBSection*. That was intentional in the design of WinG's API set. It was designed to essentially give the functionality of *CreateDIBSection* to applications written for the 16-bit Windows 3.1 environment.

Here are the new member variables required to support WinG:

```
class COSBView : public CScrollView
{
    :
    :
```

```
private:
    HDC m_hdcWinG;                  // Handle to WinG DC
    HBITMAP m_hbmOld;               // Handle to old bitmap in DC
    HBITMAP m_hbmWinG;              // Handle to WinG bitmap
    :
    :
};
```

The essential parts are (1) a handle to a WinG device context (DC) that will be created when the view is created and used throughout the life of the view and (2) a handle to a bitmap that WinG will create and that we will be using as the off-screen buffer. Notice that this is a handle to a device-dependent bitmap (DDB), not a device-independent bitmap (DIB). WinG works some magic on 16-bit Windows so that you still have direct access to the bitmap bits. On a 32-bit platform, WinG uses *CreateDIB-Section*, which as we've already seen allows you direct access to the bits *and* returns you a DDB handle.

\anim32\wingcoll

The constructor is responsible for creating the WinG DC:

```
COSBView::COSBView()
{
    m_pDIB = NULL;
    m_pPal = NULL;
    m_hbmWinG = NULL;
    m_hbmOld = NULL;
    m_hdcWinG = WinGCreateDC();
    ASSERT(m_hdcWinG);
}
```

Notice the call to *WinGCreateDC*.

The main changes to the code are in the *Create* and *Draw* functions. Here's the new version of *COSBView::Create*:

```
BOOL COSBView::Create(CDIB* pDIB)
{
    // Create a palette from the DIB that we can use to do screen drawing.
    if (m_pPal) delete m_pPal;
    m_pPal = new CDIBPal;
    ASSERT(m_pPal);
    if (!m_pPal->Create(pDIB)) {
        TRACE("Failed to create palette");
        delete m_pPal;
        m_pPal = NULL;
        return FALSE;
    } else {
        // Map the colors so that we get an identity palette.
        m_pPal->SetSysPalColors();
    }
```

(continued)

```
    // Delete any existing DIB and create a new one.
    if (m_pDIB) delete m_pDIB;
    m_pDIB = new CDIB;
    BOOL bResult = FALSE;
    if (m_hbmWinG) ::DeleteObject(m_hbmWinG);
    ASSERT(m_hdcWinG);
    // Note: WinG DCs are nonpalettized, so don't sel/rel palette.
    BYTE* pBits = NULL;
    m_hbmWinG = WinGCreateBitmap(m_hdcWinG,
                                 pDIB->GetBitmapInfoAddress(),
                                 (VOID**) &pBits);
    ASSERT(m_hbmWinG);
    ASSERT(pBits);
    // Create the CDIB object from the buffer.
    bResult = m_pDIB->Create(pDIB->GetBitmapInfoAddress(), pBits);
    m_hbmOld = (HBITMAP)::SelectObject(m_hdcWinG, m_hbmWinG);

    // Set the colors from the table in the DIB.
    m_pDIB->MapColorsToPalette(m_pPal);
    ::WinGSetDIBColorTable(m_hdcWinG,
                           0,
                           256,
                           m_pDIB->GetClrTabAddress());

    if (!bResult) {
        TRACE("Failed to create off-screen DIB");
        delete m_pDIB;
        m_pDIB = NULL;
        return FALSE;
    }

    CSize sizeTotal;
    sizeTotal.cx = m_pDIB->GetWidth();
    sizeTotal.cy = m_pDIB->GetHeight();
    SetScrollSizes(MM_TEXT, sizeTotal);


    return TRUE;
}
```

As before, we create a palette and map it to the system colors to make it into
an identity palette. A new *CDIB* object is created for the off-screen buffer,
and *WinGCreateBitmap* is called to create the actual buffer. The handle to the
WinG buffer is selected into the WinG DC created by the constructor. The
CDIB object is then wrapped around the WinG buffer using the pointer to
the bits obtained from calling *WinGCreateBitmap*.

We need to tell WinG about the color set we want to use, and the simplest way to do this is to map the colors of the off-screen DIB to the palette and then tell WinG to use the color table in the DIB by calling *WinGSetDIB-ColorTable*.

Now we have a buffer and also a DC (*m_hdcWinG*) that we could perform graphics device interface (GDI) operations on. We could add a function to retrieve the DC to OSBVIEW.H:

```
HDC GetBufferDC() {return m_hdcWinG;}
```

We could also return a DC to the buffer if we always used *CreateDIBSection*—this doesn't apply just to using WinG.

Let's look at the *Draw* function now:

```
void COSBView::Draw(Rect* pRect)
{
    CClientDC dc(this);
    CRect rcDraw;

    // Make sure we have what we need to do a paint.
    if (!m_pDIB) {
        TRACE("No DIB to paint from");
        return;
    }

    // See if a clip rect was supplied, and use the client area if one
    // wasn't.
    if (pRect) {
        rcDraw = *pRect;
    } else {
        GetClientRect(rcDraw);
    }

    // Get the clip box.
    CRect rcClip;
    pdc->GetClipBox(rcClip);

    //  Create a rectangle for the DIB.
    CRect rcDIB;
    rcDIB.left = rcDIB.top = 0;
    rcDIB.right = m_pDIB->GetWidth() - 1;
    rcDIB.bottom = m_pDIB->GetHeight() - 1;

    // Find a rectangle that describes the intersection of the draw
    // rect, clip rect, and DIB rect.
    CRect rcBlt = rcDraw & rcClip & rcDIB;
```

(continued)

```
// Copy the update rectangle from the off-screen DC to the
// window DC. Note that the DIB origin is the bottom-left corner.
int w, h, xs, xd, yd, ys;
w = rcBlt.right - rcBlt.left;
h = rcBlt.bottom - rcBlt.top;
xs = xd = rcBlt.left;
yd = rcBlt.top;
ys = rcBlt.top;

HDC hdc = pdc->GetSafeHdc();
HPALETTE hpalOld = ::SelectPalette(hdc,
                                   (HPALETTE)(m_pPal->m_hObject),
                                   FALSE);

::RealizePalette(hdc);
::WinGBitBlt(hdc,
             xd, yd,
             w, h,
             m_hdcWinG,
             xs, ys);

// Select old palette if we altered it.
if(hpalOld) ::SelectPalette(hdc, hpalOld, FALSE);
}
```

The clipping code should look familiar—it's unchanged. The interesting part is the call to *WinGBitBlt*, which replaces the call to *BitBlt* that we used when the code was using *CreateDIBSection*.

As you can see, using WinG is quite simple—much the same as using *CreateDIBSection*. Whether it's better for you to use WinG, only you can decide.

APPENDIX

A Static-Link Library

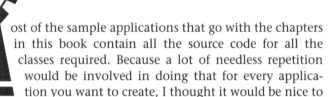

ost of the sample applications that go with the chapters in this book contain all the source code for all the classes required. Because a lot of needless repetition would be involved in doing that for every application you want to create, I thought it would be nice to build a single static-link library that includes all the classes. The result of this work is in the Library directory.

A single header file ANIMATE.H includes all the other headers required. You can put ANIMATE.H in STDAFX.H so that it gets compiled only once. I made the make file for the library generate either a debug build (ANIMATED.LIB) or a retail build (ANIMATER.LIB). You need to add the appropriate library to the linker input line for your project.

All the source code is in the library\src directory together with the make file for building it. The library\help directory contains a Help file and its source text as both a Microsoft Word for Windows 6.0 file and an .RTF file.

Some of the code in the library classes differs from that in the chapter samples. In some cases I have added functionality; in others I've simply fixed bugs or tidied up the code. If you're uncertain which version of a particular piece of code to use, the library version will be the best choice.

The *CWaveOutDevice* class has been changed so that it no longer requires a separate window object for callback messages. *CWaveOutDevice* is now derived from *CWnd* instead of from *CObject*, so it can get the callback messages itself.

I added a *CSound* class simply to be able to put .WAV files into an application as resources and be able to play them. Media Control Interface (MCI) has no way to play a memory resident .WAV file, so the *CSound* class is very convenient if you want to add a few fixed sounds to an application. The *CSound* class is used in the RunDog sample.

The Help file for the library was made with the Windows Help Project Editor (WHPE), Word for Windows 6.0, and the Windows Help Authoring Template for Word for Windows 6.0 (WHAT6.DOT). (The WHPE.EXE and WHAT6.DOT files are both available in the July 1994 Microsoft Development Library.) The library\help directory contains all the source and instructions for rebuilding the Help file, if you should want to enhance it.

INDEX

Nigel Thompson

Nigel Thompson was born in England on October 11, 1955, which makes him pretty old for a Microsoft developer.

At Weymouth Grammar school in 1970, he learned to write computer programs in EGTRAN, a variant of FORTRAN IV, for an English Electric Leo-Marconi KDF9 computer. Nigel attended Southampton University in England, where he graduated in 1977 with an honors degree in electronics, specializing in semiconductor physics.

Nigel began his professional career as a diffusion engineer, working for the Mullard company in England manufacturing UHF bipolar transistors. He learned all about the Zilog Z80 one weekend while house-sitting a friend's cat. Armed with this experience, he got his first job as a microprocessor engineer for Sarasota Engineering, using RCA's 1802 to create traffic data collection systems. While working for Sarasota, Nigel wrote an 1802 assembler in BASIC, which he later ported to PL/Z, Zilog's high-level language for the Z80.

Many similar jobs later, Nigel founded his own company, Redwood Electronics. Redwood's first project was the building of a machine to convert data from 8-inch IBM diskettes to half-inch magnetic tape files using an 8088-based PC clone and some custom-designed interfaces.

Nigel worked as a part-time contractor for QA Training in England, teaching Windows 1.0 and later Windows 2.0 programming courses.

Nigel joined Microsoft in 1989 as a software design engineer in the Multimedia section of the Windows group. He went on to create the first Windows sound driver as a skunk-works project and later led the development of the system components of the Level I Multimedia Extensions to Windows. He spent a year porting the Multimedia Extensions to Windows NT before joining the Developer Network group, where he currently writes technical articles for the Windows-challenged.

The manuscript for this book was prepared and submitted to Microsoft Press in electronic form. Text files were prepared using Microsoft Word 2.0 for Windows. Pages were composed by Microsoft Press using Aldus PageMaker 5.0 for Windows, with text in Stone Serif and display type in Stone Serif Semi Bold. Composed pages were delivered to the printer as electronic prepress files.

Cover Graphic Designer
Rebecca Geisler

Interior Graphic Designer
Kim Eggleston

Calligraphy Artist
Dia Calhoun

Illustrator
David Holter

Principal Typographer
Barb Runyan

Principal Editorial Compositor
John Sugg

Principal Proofreader/Copy Editor
Shawn Peck

Indexer
Hugh Maddocks

Follow the Windows™ 95 Story!

For up to the minute changes in information on Windows 95, visit the WIN_NEWS forum, which you can find at the following locations:

On Marvel: *\\categories\computers and software \software/microsoft\windows95\winnews*

On CompuServe: *GO WINNEWS*

On the Internet: *ftp://ftp.microsoft.com/PerOpSys/ Win_News/Chicago http://www.microsoft.com*

On AOL: keyword *WINNEWS*

On Prodigy: jumpword *WINNEWS*

On Genie: *WINNEWS* file area on Windows RTC

You can also subscribe to Microsoft's electronic newsletter *WinNews*. To subscribe, send Internet e-mail to *enews@microsoft.nwnet.com* and put the words *SUBSCRIBE WINNEWS* in the text of the e-mail.

When Windows 95 is released, be sure to head to your bookstore for complete accounts of developing for and using Windows 95.

An insider's perspective
on the hows and whys
of programming in
Microsoft's
groundbreaking
new development
environment

ISBN 1-55615-661-8
512 pages, with one CD-ROM
$39.95 ($53.95 Canada)

The Microsoft® Visual
C++™ development
system offers an
exciting new way to
create Windows™-based applications.
Now you can combine the power of object-
oriented programming with the efficiency of the C
language. The application framework approach in Visual C++ version
1.5—centering on the Microsoft Foundation Class Library version
2.5—enables programmers to simplify and streamline the process of creating
robust, professional applications for Windows.

INSIDE VISUAL C++ takes you one step at a time through the process of
creating real-world applications for Windows—the Visual C++ way. Using
ample source code examples, this book explores MFC 2.5, App Studio, and
the product's nifty "wizards"—AppWizard and ClassWizard—in action. The
book also provides a good explanation of application framework theory,
along with tips for exploiting hidden features of the MFC library.

Whether you are relatively new to programming for Windows or you are an
old dog ready for new tricks, Kruglinski's insider expertise makes INSIDE
VISUAL C++ the fastest route to mastering this powerful development system.

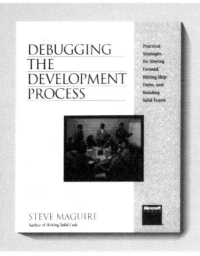

Fine-tune the development process with techniques and strategies your team can use to become consistently successful.

ISBN 1-55615-650-2
216 pages, $24.95 ($32.95 Canada)

In this eagerly awaited companion to the award winning, bestselling *Writing Solid Code*, Steve Maguire describes the sometimes controversial but always effective practices that enabled his software teams at Microsoft to develop high-quality software—on schedule.

With the refereshing candor reviewers admired in *Writing Solid Code*, Maguire talks about what did and what didn't work at Microsoft and tells you:

☞ How to energize software teams to work effectively

☞ How to deliver on schedule and without overwork

☞ How to pull twice the value out of everything you do

☞ How to get your team going on a creative roll

If you're part of a development team, this book is for you. Once you've read it, you'll want to give it to your manager, your peers, and your friends.

More Ways to Smooth Software Development
with the *Programming Practices Series*
from Microsoft Press

Code Complete	**Writing Solid Code**
Steve McConnell	*Steve Maguire*
ISBN 1-55615-484-4	ISBN 1-55615-551-4
880 pages, $35.00 ($44.95 Canada)	288 pages, $24.95 ($32.95 Canada)

Microsoft Press® books are available wherever quality books are sold and through CompuServe's Electronic Mall—GO MSP.
Call **1-800-MSPRESS** for more information or to place a credit card order.* Please refer to **BBK** when placing your order. Prices subject to change.
*In Canada, contact Macmillan Canada, Attn: Microsoft Press Dept., 164 Commander Blvd., Agincourt, Ontario, Canada M1S 3C7, or call 1-800-667-1115.
Outside the U.S. and Canada, write to International Coordinator, Microsoft Press, One Microsoft Way, Redmond, WA 98052-6399 or fax +(206) 936-7329

IMPORTANT— READ CAREFULLY BEFORE OPENING SOFTWARE PACKET(S). By opening the sealed packet(s) containing the software, you indicate your acceptance of the following Microsoft License Agreement.

MICROSOFT LICENSE AGREEMENT
(Book Companion Disks)

This is a legal agreement between you (either an individual or an entity) and Microsoft Corporation. By opening the sealed software packet(s) you are agreeing to be bound by the terms of this agreement. If you do not agree to the terms of this agreement, promptly return the unopened software packet(s) and any accompanying written materials to the place you obtained them for a full refund.

MICROSOFT SOFTWARE LICENSE

1. GRANT OF LICENSE. Microsoft grants to you the right to use one copy of the Microsoft software program included with this book (the "SOFTWARE") on a single terminal connected to a single computer. The SOFTWARE is in "use" on a computer when it is loaded into the temporary memory (i.e., RAM) or installed into the permanent memory (e.g., hard disk, CD-ROM, or other storage device) of that computer. You may not network the SOFTWARE or otherwise use it on more than one computer or computer terminal at the same time.

2. COPYRIGHT. The SOFTWARE is owned by Microsoft or its suppliers and is protected by United States copyright laws and international treaty provisions. Therefore, you must treat the SOFTWARE like any other copyrighted material (e.g., a book or musical recording) except that you may either (a) make one copy of the SOFTWARE solely for backup or archival purposes, or (b) transfer the SOFTWARE to a single hard disk provided you keep the original solely for backup or archival purposes. You may not copy the written materials accompanying the SOFTWARE.

3. OTHER RESTRICTIONS. You may not rent or lease the SOFTWARE, but you may transfer the SOFTWARE and accompanying written materials on a permanent basis provided you retain no copies and the recipient agrees to the terms of this Agreement. You may not reverse engineer, decompile, or disassemble the SOFTWARE. If the SOFTWARE is an update or has been updated, any transfer must include the most recent update and all prior versions.

4. DUAL MEDIA SOFTWARE. If the SOFTWARE package contains both 3.5" and 5.25" disks, then you may use only the disks appropriate for your single-user computer. You may not use the other disks on another computer or loan, rent, lease, or transfer them to another user except as part of the permanent transfer (as provided above) of all SOFTWARE and written materials.

5. SAMPLE CODE. If the SOFTWARE includes Sample Code, then Microsoft grants you a royalty-free right to reproduce and distribute the sample code of the SOFTWARE provided that you: (a) distribute the sample code only in conjunction with and as a part of your software product; (b) do not use Microsoft's or its authors' names, logos, or trademarks to market your software product; (c) include the copyright notice that appears on the SOFTWARE on your product label and as a part of the sign-on message for your software product; and (d) agree to indemnify, hold harmless, and defend Microsoft and its authors from and against any claims or lawsuits, including attorneys' fees, that arise or result from the use or distribution of your software product.

DISCLAIMER OF WARRANTY

The SOFTWARE (including instructions for its use) is provided "AS IS" WITHOUT WARRANTY OF ANY KIND. MICROSOFT FURTHER DISCLAIMS ALL IMPLIED WARRANTIES INCLUDING WITHOUT LIMITATION ANY IMPLIED WARRANTIES OF MERCHANTABILITY OR OF FITNESS FOR A PARTICULAR PURPOSE. THE ENTIRE RISK ARISING OUT OF THE USE OR PERFORMANCE OF THE SOFTWARE AND DOCUMENTATION REMAINS WITH YOU.

IN NO EVENT SHALL MICROSOFT, ITS AUTHORS, OR ANYONE ELSE INVOLVED IN THE CREATION, PRODUCTION, OR DELIVERY OF THE SOFTWARE BE LIABLE FOR ANY DAMAGES WHATSOEVER (INCLUDING, WITHOUT LIMITATION, DAMAGES FOR LOSS OF BUSINESS PROFITS, BUSINESS INTERRUPTION, LOSS OF BUSINESS INFORMATION, OR OTHER PECUNIARY LOSS) ARISING OUT OF THE USE OF OR INABILITY TO USE THE SOFTWARE OR DOCUMENTATION, EVEN IF MICROSOFT HAS BEEN ADVISED OF THE POSSIBILITY OF SUCH DAMAGES. BECAUSE SOME STATES/COUNTRIES DO NOT ALLOW THE EXCLUSION OR LIMITATION OF LIABILITY FOR CONSEQUENTIAL OR INCIDENTAL DAMAGES, THE ABOVE LIMITATION MAY NOT APPLY TO YOU.

U.S. GOVERNMENT RESTRICTED RIGHTS

The SOFTWARE and documentation are provided with RESTRICTED RIGHTS. Use, duplication, or disclosure by the Government is subject to restrictions as set forth in subparagraph (c)(1)(ii) of The Rights in Technical Data and Computer Software clause at DFARS 252.227-7013 or subparagraphs (c)(1) and (2) of the Commercial Computer Software — Restricted Rights 48 CFR 52.227-19, as applicable. Manufacturer is Microsoft Corporation, One Microsoft Way, Redmond, WA 98052-6399.

If you acquired this product in the United States, this Agreement is governed by the laws of the State of Washington.

Should you have any questions concerning this Agreement, or if you desire to contact Microsoft Press for any reason, please write: Microsoft Press, One Microsoft Way, Redmond, WA 98052-6399.

Register Today!

Return this
Animation Techniques in Win32®
registration card for:

✔ a Microsoft Press® catalog

✔ exclusive offers on specially
priced books

U.S. and Canada addresses only. Fill in information below and mail postage-free. Please mail only the bottom half of this page.

1-55615-669-3A   *Animation Techniques in Win32—Owner Registration Card*

_____
NAME

_____
INSTITUTION OR COMPANY NAME

_____
ADDRESS

_____
CITY   STATE   ZIP

MicrosoftPress.

Quality Computer Books

**For a free catalog of
Microsoft Press® products, call
1-800-MSPRESS**